Demographic Change and Tourism

srh
Berlin University of Applied Sciences
Ernst-Reuter-Platz 10 | 10587 Berlin
T +49 (0) 30 51 56 50 - 100
www.srh-berlin.de
Träger: SRH Hochschulen Berlin GmbH

Demographic Change and Tourism
ISBN: 978-92-844-1342-3 (UNWTO)
ISBN: 978-92-990058-0-4 (ETC)

Published by the World Tourism Organization and the European Travel Commission
Printed by the World Tourism Organization, Madrid, Spain
First printing 2010

World Tourism Organization
Calle Capitán Haya, 42
28020 Madrid, Spain
Tel.: (+34) 915 678 100
Fax: (+34) 915 713 733
Website: www.unwto.org
Email: omt@unwto.org

European Travel Commission
19A Avenue Marnix (PO Box 25)
1000 Brussels, Belgium
Tel.: (+32) 2 - 548 90 00
Fax: (+32) 2 - 514 18 43
Website: www.etc-corporate.org
Email: info@visiteurope.com

Table of Contents

Acknowledgements

This report was prepared by Trajectory on commission to the European Travel Commission (ETC) and the World Tourism Organization (UNWTO).

The report, which forms part of ETC's ongoing Market Intelligence Programme, was carried out under the supervision of Ms Sandra Carvão from UNWTO's Market Trends, Competitiveness and Trade in Tourism Services Section in collaboration with Ms Lisa Davies (ETC) on behalf of ETC's Market Intelligence Group (MIG).

The members of the ETC Market Intelligence Committee (MIC) who contributed to this exercise were: Mr Leslie Vella (Chairman MIG and Malta Tourism Authority), Ms Lisa Davies (ETC Executive Unit), Mr John Kester and Ms Sandra Carvão (UNWTO), Ms Carla Aguirre (VisitSweden), Ms Gaëlle Berréhouc (Atout France – Agence de Développement Touristique de la France), Mr Christian Ørsted Brandt (VisitDenmark), Mr David Edwards (VisitBritain), Mr Brian Maher (Fáilte Ireland), Mr Vincent Nijs (Toerisme Vlaanderen, Belgium), Mr Arturo Ortiz (Turespaña), Mr Mili Razovi (Split & Dalmatia County Tourist Board, Croatia), Mr Joachim Scholz (German National Tourist Board), Ms Judit Sulyok (Hungarian National Tourist Office), Ms Helena Varona (Turismo de Portugal) and Mr Tom Ylkänen (Finnish Tourist Board). Ms Valeria Croce, from the Department for Tourism and Hospitality Management of the MODUL University Vienna also contributed to this report.

Chapter 1

Background and Objectives

Demography is one of the external factors that shape tourism demand and development. The structure of societies is continuously changing, and for both public and private organizations working in the tourism field it is relevant to study these changes in order to anticipate and react upon them in the most competitive way.

Translated into the marketing area, demographic changes are likely impact on the patterns of travel demand, including frequency, length of stay, products, and consequently on the communication strategies of National Tourism Organizations (NTOs) and private companies alike.

The World Tourism Organization (UNWTO) and ETC wanted to develop a report in this area which should serve as a reference work for its member countries/NTOs, as well as for the industry at large, to achieve a better understanding of current and future demographic changes and their impact on tourism.

The overall objective of the report is to deliver a comprehensive analysis of demographic trends, how these are impacting and will impact on tourism demand in specific generating markets, and how consequently destinations and companies can benefit from and adapt to such trends in order to become increasingly competitive in the market place.

More specifically, the report provides answers to three main questions:

1. What are the main demographic trends worldwide?
2. What are the main demographic trends in major and emerging tourism source markets such as the United States of America, Brazil, Canada, Germany, the United Kingdom, France, Italy, the Netherlands, Spain, the Russian Federation, Japan, China and India?
3. What impact do such trends have on tourism demand and travel behaviour overall and in the aforementioned markets in particular?

The report highlights how destinations and the private sector can make the most out of these trends in terms of product development and marketing. These issues have been analysed in both a retrospective (i.e. what has been changing) and prospective manner (i.e. what are the expected changes in the medium to long term (i.e. within the next ten to twenty years).

Within this framework, the report focuses on three major areas and their impact on consumers' lifestyles – and consequently on tourism:

- population growth and ageing;
- household composition and travel parties;
- migration.

Following the Executive Summary, the report is structured as follows:

- Sections 3 and 5 provide an overview of the key demographic changes at global and country level.
- Sections 4 and 7 look into the key areas of demographic change and its impacts on tourism.
- Section 6 provides an overview of lifestyles trends and its implications for tourism.
- Section 8 is a data section that also provides a commentary on demographic change in key current and potential source markets.

Chapter 2

Executive Summary

Demographics will have a dramatic impact upon tourism in the coming decades. It will impact upon the types of tourists that will travel, where they originate from, where they travel to, the types of accommodation they require and the activities they engage in while away.

Growth of the world's population

The total world population is forecast to grow over the period from 6.9 billion to 8.3 billion (between 2009 and 2030). This growth will not be evenly spread across the globe, rather different regions will expand at different rates and some will actively decline as a percentage of the total.

Europe for instance will decline by 1% while the Americas and Asia will increase by 17% and 18% respectively; much of Asia's growth will be driven by India and China, who will amount for just under 20% of the world's population each (China 17.6% and India 17.9%).

The proportional distribution of the global population is not projected to change greatly. However, the slight decline in Europe will make itself felt in the form of an ageing population. There will be a dramatic growth in the European over 50s population, while during the same period the Asian population will remain mostly under 45.

Population growth will generate substantial expansion in overseas travel. In 2000 the rate of international journeys was 11.5 per 100 people. If the rate did not accelerate then population increase alone would see a 20% rise in international travel, however increases in wealth particularly in developing countries are expected to see the rate of journeys grow to 20 per 100.

Other demographic trends

Fertility and life expectancy are two of the biggest factors affecting global demographics. Life expectancy has been increasing year on year for decades in most of the world and this is a trend that is projected to continue (in some African countries suffering from the AIDS epidemic it has fallen dramatically). This trend intersects with declining fertility across much of the world. The United Nations' forecasts assume that fertility rates will all tend to converge at an average of 1.85 children per woman, with some differences across individual countries. These declines in fertility are heavily influenced by many of the developments that have extended life expectancy across the globe. Infrastructural and medical developments that prolong lifespan – especially in developing countries – tend to improve infant mortality rates and this brings down fertility levels.

Other key issues are changes to work patterns and social values that increasingly bring women into the workplace, downplaying social mores that assign a higher value to male children and so on. As these values begin to converge, so do the demographic factors they engender.

The final important factor is Migration. This influences tourism in two ways, through Migration Led Tourism (MLT) and Tourism Led Migration (TLM). TLM is generally migration that takes place to fill vacancies in the tourism industry of a nation or region; for instance young people from eastern and central Europe migrating to western Europe. MLT is tourism generated by migration of any type, often people visiting friends or relatives in their new homes, or migrants returning to their place of birth to do the same.

2.1 Demographic Change and Tourism

It is important to bear in mind that not all demographic changes will necessarily hold repercussions for tourism. A recent report by the German Federal Ministry of Economics and Technology found that demographic alterations are likely to have an impact on tourism only if they 'arise in those groups (e.g. older people, children, the less affluent, single parents etc) which represent a sizeable volume, will be considerably larger or smaller in volume and whose behaviour differs from other groups'.[1] Nonetheless this report identifies several demographic trends in the 13 focal countries that are likely to have significant impact upon future tourism in Europe.

Ageing population

Population ageing is a phenomenon occurring across the globe; however it has taken different forms in different regions. Broadly we have divided these into two models: the 'Three Peaks' model, and the 'Slope' model.

The Three Peaks model is characterised by three successive spikes in population each progressively older than the last. This pattern corresponds to a population in which there is a clear majority of one age group at any one time, and this majority progressively aging, generating a peak on the graph (we took our forecasts at 1990, 2010 and 2030, if we had used 4 years or 5 it would have been the 4 or 5 peaks model). As a rule the Three Peaks model is seen in developed countries like Canada, and Italy.

The Slope model, by contrast, shows an age distribution that is bunched towards the younger years, with a notable tail off in the numbers of older people (hence the slope). It tends to be a feature of developing nations such as India and Brazil.

Due to its history of social engineering and the large scale social and economic changes taking place in China recently, it displays a combination of both of the above models.

Life expectancy increasing and converging across the globe

Across the countries examined life expectancy is increasing and male and female life expectancies are beginning to converge. There are only a few notable exceptions to this pattern. In the Russian Federation life expectancy actively declined in the 1990s and will not grow significantly between 2010 and 2030 going from 66 to 71 years. Meanwhile the difference in male and female life expectancy is not projected to moderate remaining at a stark 10 years. In Japan, life expectancy will increase, but male and female life expectancy is projected to diverge further; by 2030 it will have increased from around six to just under nine.

The next issue when it comes to life expectancy is the issue of healthy life expectancy – that is, not just how long people live, but what level of health they enjoyed while they are alive. The trend across the world has been for morbidity to decline at the same time – though not at the same rate as – life expectancy increases worldwide. A HSBC retirement report found that only 16% of those over 70 said that they had poor or very poor health.[2] Individual countries – particularly developed ones – can display a considerable range on this subject, ranging from Canada with 3% to Germany with 12%.

Therefore, not only is an increase in older tourists expected (because they live longer and are richer) but they will be fitter and younger looking in outlook.

---

1 Federal Ministry of Economics and Technology (2009), *The Impact of Demographic Change on Tourism and Conclusions for Tourism Policy* (abridged), FMET, Berlin.

2 HSBC (2009), *The Future of Retirement – It's Time to Prepare* (Online): http://www.hsbc.com/1/PA_1_1_S5/content/assets/retirement/2009_for_report_en.pdf (28/06/09).

Household composition, family structures and travel parties

One of the main subsidiary effects of the demographic changes will be a change in the household composition in the countries looked at. While there are no clear cut patterns of fertility in the countries considered, broadly it can be seen that fertility declined in developed countries, but that in northern and western Europe it tended to rebound closer to the replacement level (2.1 children per woman). Meanwhile developing countries began the period with significantly above replacement level fertility and have subsequently declined towards replacement level, though different nations have done so at different rates.

The impact of these changes can already be seen in the developed world. We have seen a shift from what Willmott and Young called the Horizontal to the Vertical family. That means that families have tended to shift from being largely flat – with many members of the same generation to being long – with a greater spread across the generations.

This suggests that tourism is going to be required to adapt itself to provide a more varied offer. Travel parties may now be comprised of grandparents taking grandchildren on holiday, or of whole families that potentially contain great grandparents as well, with consequences for the activities on offer, type of accommodation required and staffing levels.

The rise in the developed world of the single traveller has been a significant development. It reflects a growing trend in wider society for young people to spend a period of time living alone or with friends before marrying and starting a family. If this trend is echoed in the developing world this will have a serious impact as places like India and China are set to become some of the world's largest producers of international tourists.

Population location

The population of all the countries looked at (and the world) is set to become increasingly urban over the period. In addition to this factor, the rising importance of the developing world will have a large influence on tourism in the next two decades.

While urban populations are set to increase all over, the rates of increase will differ considerably. Italy's rate of urban growth is projected to accelerate, for instance, while the United States of America will slow somewhat. Cities dwellers tend to have a more cosmopolitan outlook, as a result of living in a more culturally diverse environment. This means they are more likely to travel abroad and this will help drive the rise in tourism that is projected.

Compared to the developing world, the relative decline in importance of the developed West is both noticeable and well known. Europe's proportion of the global population is set to decline to 9% roughly equal with that of the Caribbean and the Americas. Meanwhile northern America (United States of America and Canada) contributes around 6% of the world's population, though only 1% of this is in Canada and the rest is the United States. Asia on the other hand easily dwarfs all these continents, and will continue to do so. In 2030 Asia will account for 60% of the world's population; with India and China each contributing just less than 20%.

A final factor that affects population distribution is migration. As has been discussed migration can affect tourism in two ways; tourism can draw migrants to parts of the world where there is a need for workers. And migration can draw tourists to visit their places of birth, or relatives working abroad. These two processes are clearly interlinked. Worldwide migrants made up 3% of the population between 1990 and 2005, however the global average masks the fact that Europe's migrant population went from 4% in 1960 to 9% today. If this trend continues then the migrant population of Europe could reach 12% by 2030. This would have obvious impacts, particularly for the VFR market in European tourism.

Oceania is the region with the highest proportion of immigrants, though the United States has the largest proportion of any single nation 14% just behind 16% in Oceania. While these trends may not correspond as well to TLM (particularly not the Hispanic population that makes up the majority of migrants to the United States of America) they are liable to generate a large amount of MLT as families travel to visit relatives abroad.

Source market	Key demographic issues
World	Increased life expectancy – women lead men, falling fertility – still above replacement, rising population 5 to 8 billion (from 1990-2030).
Regions	
Europe	Rapidly falling fertility, ageing population high level of migration.
Asia	Rising population particularly India and China, relatively high fertility, large scale urbanisation.
Latin America and the Caribbean	Fertility falling to replacement level, slightly ageing population, extended life expectancy.
Northern America: United States of America and Canada	Ageing population, declining fertility but stark differences between the United States of America and Canada, especially regarding life expectancy. High migration.
Countries	
Brazil	Fertility falls sharply. Life expectancy extends but large gap between male and female, population remains young.
Canada	Historically low fertility improves slightly. Ageing population, closing gap between male and female life expectancy.
China	Fertility levelling out, population ageing and dramatic urbanisation.
France	Fertility dips then rises sharply, reaching 1.85 by 2030. Population ages much in line with rest of Europe.
Germany	Low fertility not forecast to improve dramatically. Life expectancy rises from already high level.
India	Fertility declines but remains above replacement level. Life expectancy increases and population ages but remains mainly under 40.
Italy	Low fertility does not recover very much and population ages.
Japan	Fertility low and projected to decline somewhat. Population ageing and projected largest groups 55-59 and 80-84.
Netherlands	Fertility rises during period in line with Castles' study. Population rises but not as much as some others (see above).
Russian Federation	Large gender disparity 88 men per 100 women projected to decline to 84. Fertility dropped sharply but projected to rise steadily but not above replacement. Population does not age in same way, becomes slightly younger for period, before ageing significantly by 2030.
Spain	Fertility dropped very low – reached 1.18 at one point but will rise though not to replacement level. Population ages considerably and difference between male and female life expectancy remains reasonably large.
United Kingdom	Fertility dipped in 70s and briefly in 90s but has recovered – will be around 1.85 by 2030. Population to age considerably and will be 92% urban by 2030.
United States of America	Fertility peaked at 2.5 between 2005 and 2010 but will drop after, will be 1.85 by 2030. Life expectancy increases but stark national differences with Canada and Europe.

2.2 Lifestyle and Tourism

These trends do not directly relate to strictly demographic matters but they will be hugely important for tourism. As demographic changes take place they are liable to affect the importance or otherwise of these trends.

Increased prosperity and attitudes towards work, leisure and travel

Rising affluence around the globe has implications for attitudes towards work and leisure. As income rises it tends to be accompanied by a shift in values from work to leisure as people are greater able to afford things they want without having to put so much emphasis on employment. This trend is visible in Europe, where there has been a decline in working hours since the 1970s as well as in Latin America and the Caribbean. It is even beginning to appear in the United States of America and East Asia which have traditionally worked considerably longer hours than Europe and much of the developing world. Of course the effect of increased prosperity does not remain simple. Beyond a certain level of prosperity people may cease to feel the full benefits of improvements. People in the developed West have begun to display increasing dissatisfaction with their lifestyles, particularly in the United States where incomes have stagnated while cost of living has risen resulting in a real terms decline in standards of living for many. The economic downturn of 2008/2009 is liable to have only exacerbated this feeling. Economic constraints are liable to impact upon people's holiday choices for several years to come.

Related to this feeling of dissatisfaction is a common feeling that time pressures are becoming excessive and the modern world too complicated despite the fact that the majority of contemporary westerners now have significantly more leisure time than ever before. As a result 'Value for Time' has become and will remain an increasingly important priority in people's decision making processes, leading on to more experience intensive holidays, often of a shorter duration. The recession will only have hardened the cash-poor, time-poor equation in people's minds further promoting the trend in shorter city break style holidays particularly as much of future tourism will originate from Asia. This should provide growth in the budget but also the traditional sightseeing categories.

Values and attitudes

There are four major attitudinal trends that will impact upon tourism in the next two decades. These are: the growth of more internationalist and cosmopolitan attitudes; ethical issues (and related to that environmental concerns, covered separately); and an increasing sense of adventure and willingness to try things.

In the rise of the cosmopolitan internationalist, globalisation of trade and industry, educational networks, social networks, media and civil society have produced a generation that is more international in its outlook than any before. This is demonstrated in membership of international organisations, studying abroad, taking part in human rights campaigns and so on. This trend looks set to continue in two notable forms. Firstly, it will be increasingly dominated by the rise of Global Asia. Data from the World Values Survey shows young Asians are the group with the biggest increase in international concern; as Asia comes to dominate the world market more and more this can only continue. By contrast, the World Values Survey indicates that Global America is in retreat, young Americans are less and less interested in global perspectives and events than their parents or even their grandparents were.

Closely linked to an internationalist outlook is a rise in ethical concerns. Particularly in western Europe the World Values Survey shows a sharp rise in membership of ethical organisations, political campaigns, and support for foreign aid. However, as well as a generational increase, there is an overall increase across all generations implying that developmental benefits from increased tourism are likely to engender more tourism and generate more positive stories about the contributions of tourism to sustainability and development to counter act the negative impression that can be given.

Environmental concerns have been growing year on year since 1995, as measured by membership of Green organisations. The only exception to this pattern has been in the United States of America where there has recently been a slight fall in membership. Importantly there is a distinct generational shift in membership of these organisations, with people growing up in the last decade being the most prominent members. This implies that by 2030 those aged around 50 and below are most likely to be concerned and any attempt to target that market should be aware of this. Environmental concerns have risen sharpest in East Asia, possibly because in this region people are already experiencing the consequences of climate change and other environmental threats.

Tempering the rise in environmental concern is an increasing reluctance to pay extra for green products and options. This is most marked in the United States of America where consumers have suffered from wages that declined in real terms compared to significant rises in the cost of living. In particular it will become increasingly difficult to charge consumers extra for environmental services, options or products which they perceive to engender no further cost to the supplier, or which are undertaken in replacement for a tax or tariff.

There is also a trend towards the greater appreciation of risk and adventure in holiday travel, particularly in the developed world. There is evidence that this is an age rather than a generational trend. It is likely, therefore that as people age their attitude towards risk and adventure will modify, and more traditional holidays will begin to hold greater appeal for them. An ageing population will therefore have considerable impact on the development of this trend.

Technology

Increased access to technology and particularly to the internet has been a major driver of global awareness which has been such a driver of tourism. The internet has been a vital development within the tourism industry itself as consumers use it to research ideas, compare notes, gather information and of course book trips online.

Across the globe, internet access is growing particularly in developing countries. Between 2005 and 2007 penetration (as measured by internet connections per 100 people) nearly doubled in places like China and (albeit from a very small base) India. Already high in Brazil, it increased 65% to 35 connections per 100. Perhaps more important, has been the growth of mobile internet, in many developing countries internet access has become primarily based around this with fixed line connections being by-passed completely.

This is important not just because the internet will become increasingly important as a sales and marketing medium as the numbers with access to it grow but also because of the demographic distribution of usage. Not surprisingly, younger people are much more likely to frequently use a personal computer. As these people take their technology skills with them when they age so online activity will become ever more important for travel and tourism.

The fragmentation of tastes

The trends discussed above can all be viewed as constituent of a larger trend. Once again this is not a demographic trend per se but it is highly influenced by demographics. Rising affluence, greater internationalism, an appetite for risk taking, more sophisticated marketing, the feeling of greater time pressures, and improved access to technology all contribute to a fragmentation of tastes. This is particularly the case in developed countries where a unique experience has become a selling point for a holiday by itself. People increasingly feel that they want a holiday that expresses some element of their individuality and that offers them an experience that is unavailable elsewhere.

There are signs that this is becoming true of the developing world also, but in the main tourism generators: India and China travel tastes appear to be somewhat more conservative. Marketing and communications strategies should therefore be aware that they are unlikely to be selling to a homogenous block, but rather a series of shifting tribes and segments that will need to be catered for.

2.3 Summary and Implications for Tourism

There are major challenges and opportunities for tourism inherent in the demographic changes that lie ahead. Fundamentally, these involve population growth and age structure change driven by differential fertility rates and vastly improved health care. Some of the implications of these for tourism are considered below.

Population and ageing

- Tourists from developing countries are likely to be younger with very distinctive needs from the older tourists from more traditional source markets.
- This could force a stark choice for tourism destinations in their marketing, communications and product development. Do you choose to attract older or younger tourists? Or try to attract both and run the risk of not satisfying either segment?
- For the transport and accommodation, the tension between designing products and services for older and younger tourists may not be so stark. Design that takes into account the needs of older tourists (for example providing greater ease of use) might simply come to be seen as examples of good design for all.
- There may be a radical challenge in current assumptions about the implications of ageing for tourism needs and wants. For example, we may see younger tourists who are still working full time looking for time to relax on holiday, whilst older tourists who generally have more time on their hands go on holiday to try new activities.

Life expectancy

- Increased life expectancy will mean there are larger numbers of older tourists from existing markets in developed countries. The needs of these consumers may be many such as the need for proximity to medical care (this is important given the forecast increase in conditions such as obesity and allergies in future).
- Fortunately, developments in telemedicine should help facilitate travel and tourism for older (and younger) tourists with chronic medical conditions – but access to reliable information and communications technology will be expected by these tourists in future.
- Older tourists will have a 'younger' outlook than previous generations of older tourists and may well be more adventurous wanting to try new things.
- Despite this, greater numbers of these older tourists will have minor disabilities (such as difficulties climbing stairs etc). Both the accommodation and transport sectors of the industry need to take account of this in terms of design and staff training.

Household composition and family structures

- Overall, as households and families become more diverse – more multi-generational, more singles, more 'second' families and so on – the whole of the tourism sector will have to respond to this diversity.
- Marketing and communications will have to address new needs and wants that result from these emerging family and household structures. For example, communications will have to demonstrate an understanding of the diverse needs of those travelling in multi-generation parties.

- Accommodation providers also need to respond to this new demographic diversity through more flexible accommodation (especially adjoining rooms designed for the needs of three generations).
- Accommodation pricing might also seek to tap into (rather than alienate) the growing singles markets. This might involve more attractive pricing for single people or improved childcare and babysitting for single parents in hotels and resorts.

Population location

- The changing distribution of the population across the globe (along with changes in the economic centre of power) will see an increase in the importance of Asian tourists to the European market.
- This requires all elements of the industry to be sensitive to the cultural and religious needs of these tourists.
- Among urban dwellers in developed markets the experience of urban life might create a demand for rural tourism experiences (for a change of scene and a change of pace).
- For these groups we envisage a strong appeal for tourism products that offer a 'back to nature' element (perhaps experiences on farms that put tourists in touch with the realities of food and drink production).

Migration

- In the recent past migration into Europe has increased significantly. This looks set to continue as migration does within parts of Europe.
- This will give a strong boost to the VFR and migration led tourism markets.
- These tourists will have a diverse set of needs depending on their circumstances. Most economic migrants will be relatively poor and dependent on low cost forms of travel such as budget airlines or coach travel.
- However, there will be a significant minority of relatively wealth migrants (and their families) working in the great financial centres of Europe or whose children are located in Europe for their education. These tourists will have very different needs and may use premium travel options and stay in premium accommodation.

Other issues

- The attractions of leisure, tourism and travel remain strong. Tourism and holidays will remain a high priority for consumers in developed markets and will increase as a priority for consumers in emerging markets.
- As will the faster growth of tourism in less affluent and less experienced emerging markets will not only boost budget travel but also more traditional tourism activities (like sightseeing and shopping).
- Given that younger consumers are more concerned about international development issues and global poverty, the tourism industry should do all it can to communicate the development benefits of tourism.
- Finally, all of these factors combined, suggest an increasing fragmentation of tastes and markets in future. This trend is already well established in developed markets, but it will also spread to emerging markets as they become more prosperous. This will make accurate segmentation and accurately targeted marketing and communications even more important (and ever more challenging!).

Chapter 3

The Demographic Challenge

3.1 An Overview

The changing world demography is recognised as a critical issue for the future of tourism as for many other sectors.

The subject has been a cause of continual concern for much of the last decade with the realisation that the 'baby-boomer' generation of the western world was approaching retirement without sufficient working age adults in the population to support them. Indeed, as far back as 1977 Geoffrey Calvert had addressed the issue in his work *Pensions and Survival – The Coming Crisis of Money and Retirement*[1]. More recently the impacts of demographic change were addressed in texts such as the EURAG publication *Europe: A Changing Society*[2] and, rather more pessimistically, in A. J. Scholefield's work *The Death of Europe*[3] and in Richard Ehrman's *The Power of Number's*[4].

In terms of the impact on leisure and tourism specifically, recent years have seen the publication of numerous journals and articles addressing the issue. Particularly pertinent to this report are Glover and Prideaux's *Populations Aging for the Development of Tourism Products and Destinations*[5] which addresses some of the issues touched upon in this report in greater detail. As well as Patterson's work on ageing and leisure activities: *Growing Older*[6] and Linda Nazareth's study of the impact of retirement on the wider economy: *The Leisure Economy*[7].

The general recognition within the industry of the importance of demography was demonstrated in a workshop held in Slovenia in February in 2009, as part of the ETC Research Directors' meeting. Of the ten top trends identified as being most important for the future of tourism, five were demographic related ones.

[Note: workshop participants – after being explained the exact nature of the trends – were asked to rate them on two dimensions. First, how likely they felt each trend was to happen ('certainty') and what impact each would have on the tourism industry in Europe. This 'future mapping' process is a recognised technique for identifying the critical trends to concentrate on – those that are more certain and having the most impact are often the ones to concentrate on (alternative 'scenarios' can be generated by adding the high impact but less certain trends.]

The results of this workshop are plotted below and it can be seen that an ageing population and, in addition, a healthy ageing population were considered the two most important factors. Smaller family sizes and the changing nature of populations and the impact on national cultures (multiculturalism) were also in the top ten, as was the potential growth in numbers of people (and increasingly affluent ones) from emerging markets.

1 Calvert, G. (1977), *Pensions and Survival – The coming Crisis of Money and Retirement*, Maclean-Hunter, London.

2 Experts Committee EURAG, European Federation of the Elderly, and Association of Retired and Persons over 50 (1998), *Europe: A Changing Society, the Effects of Demographic Change in the Next Millennium*, EURAG.

3 Scholefield, A. J. (2000), *The Death of Europe – How Demographic Decline Will Destroy the European Union.*

4 Ehrman, R. (2009), *The Power of Number's – Why Europe needs to get Younger, Policy Exchange, London.*

5 Glover, P. and Prideaux, B. (2009), 'Populations Aging for the Development of Tourism Products and Destinations', *Journal of Vacation Marketing* (Online), vol. 15 (1), pp. 25-37.

6 Patterson, I. (2006), *Growing Older: Tourism and Leisure Behaviour of Older Adults*, CABI, Oxfordshire.

7 Nazareth, L. (2007), *The Leisure Economy: How Changing Demographics, Economics and Generational Attitudes will Reshape our Lives and our Industries*, John Wiley and Sons, New Jersey.

Figure 3.1 A 'map' of trends and their potential impact on tourism

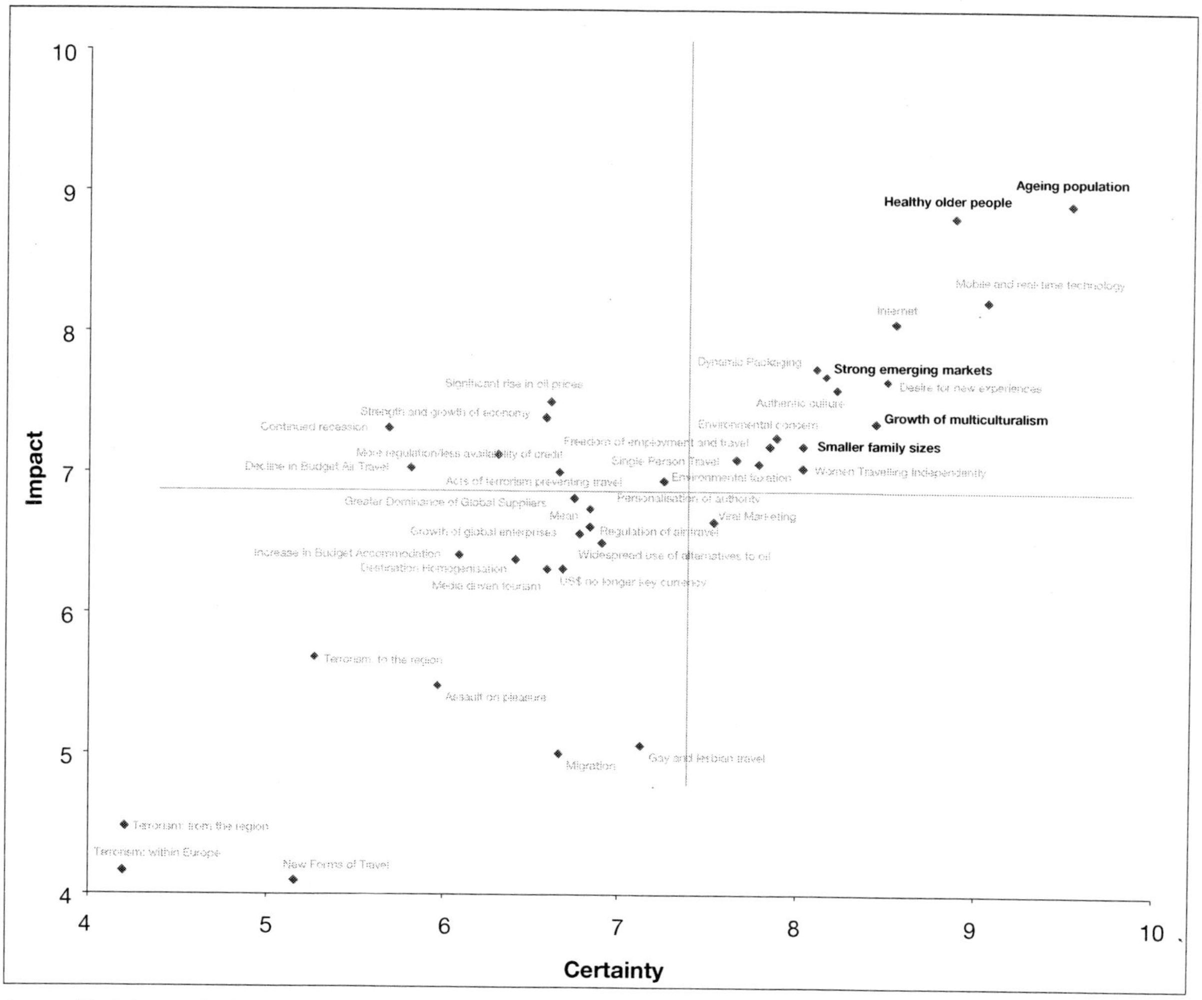

Source: Workshop at the European Travel Commission (ETC) Research Directors' Meeting, Slovenia, February 2009.

3.2 The Growth of the World Population

There are really two major aspects of the importance of demography. First, the growth in the world's population (set to rise from 6.9 billion now to 8.3 billion in 2030 – an increase of more than 20%). While the world population will grow by 1.4 billion people over the next 20 years, Europe's population is expected to decline by 1% and the Americas and Asia to rise by 17% and 18% respectively. The 'other' region is forecast to increase by 47% – with Africa, of course, the biggest component. By 2030, China will have 17.6% of the world's population and India 17.9%.

Figure 3.2 World population, 1990-2030 (× 1000)

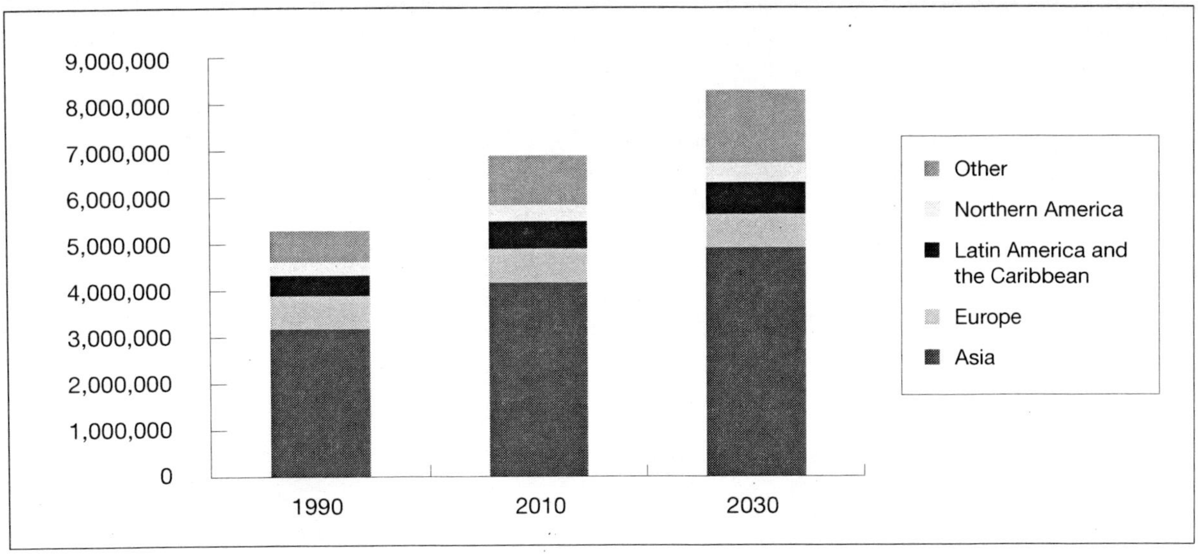

Source: Population Division of the Department of Economic and Social Affairs of the United Nations Secretariat, *World Population Prospects: The 2008 Revision*, 2009.

In terms of the proportional distribution of the global population, there is not too great a change between the regions over time despite the major differences in growth rates in some regions – Europe minus 1% versus plus 47% in Africa. These differential growth rates translate into only these two regions (Europe and Africa) showing a major change in proportionate terms while the others stay relatively constant (Asia accounts for 60% of the world population in 1990 and 2010 and 59% in 2030, for example). The declining importance of Europe in terms of the total number of people is an issue made more relevant for tourism by the growth of the 50-plus population in this region. The growing importance of Africa in population numbers is less relevant to tourism since the continent has not traditionally been significant as a source market. Also, the continuing young profile of the continent (over half the population will be under 25 in 2030) suggests a minority impact on Europe's tourist industry in the next twenty years. Also noteworthy is that while ageing, most of the Asian population will still be relatively young in 20 years time – still 65% will be under the age of 45 by the year 2030 the implications of which we cover later.

Case Study 1 Chinese tourists in Europe

As China increases its share and importance in world economy more and more countries are making efforts to attract the fast growing Chinese outbound market. Many of these attempts including those of Europe have focussed on presenting the destination as a unique cultural experience, and in practical attempts to resolve visa issues, one of the major obstacles to increased inbound from China in Europe.

Chinese tourists have been coming to Europe in ever increasing numbers since October 2003 when the European Union and China secured an agreement which gave many parts of the continent Approved Destination Status (ADS). China has the potential to send up to 100 million tourists abroad by 2020. Demographically many of these will be in the 16-35 age groups from the (relatively) new urban middle class with disposable income and a desire to purchase goods and experiences that they can display back home as tokens of their trips. Visits to German industrial centres (German industry has been highly influential in helping China develop its own economic base) and Swiss ski resorts feature prominently in tour itineraries alongside more traditional attractions such as Paris and Rome.

In terms of regional location, the relative decline in importance of the West in population terms is both noticeable and well known. To summarise, Europe's proportion of the global population is set to decline significantly from 1990-2030 from 14% to around 9%. This figure is the same for Latin America and the Caribbean. The region makes up around 9% of the world's population; at least a third of this is accounted for by Brazil alone, this is set to remain throughout the period 1990-2030. Looking at northern America (United States of America and Canada), the region constitutes about 6% of the global population, a figure that is projected to remain stable until 2030. This figure is largely due to the size of the United States, while Canada's contribution amounts to less than 1%. Asia on the other hand displays a continually high proportion of the global populace; the continent makes up around 60% of the world's population mainly due to the size of India and China each of which amount to around 20% each. It is worth noting that China declines to this level, while India rises to it, indicating that the relative positions of these two nations may even invert in the years after 2030.

Figure 3.3 Distribution of the world population by region (%)

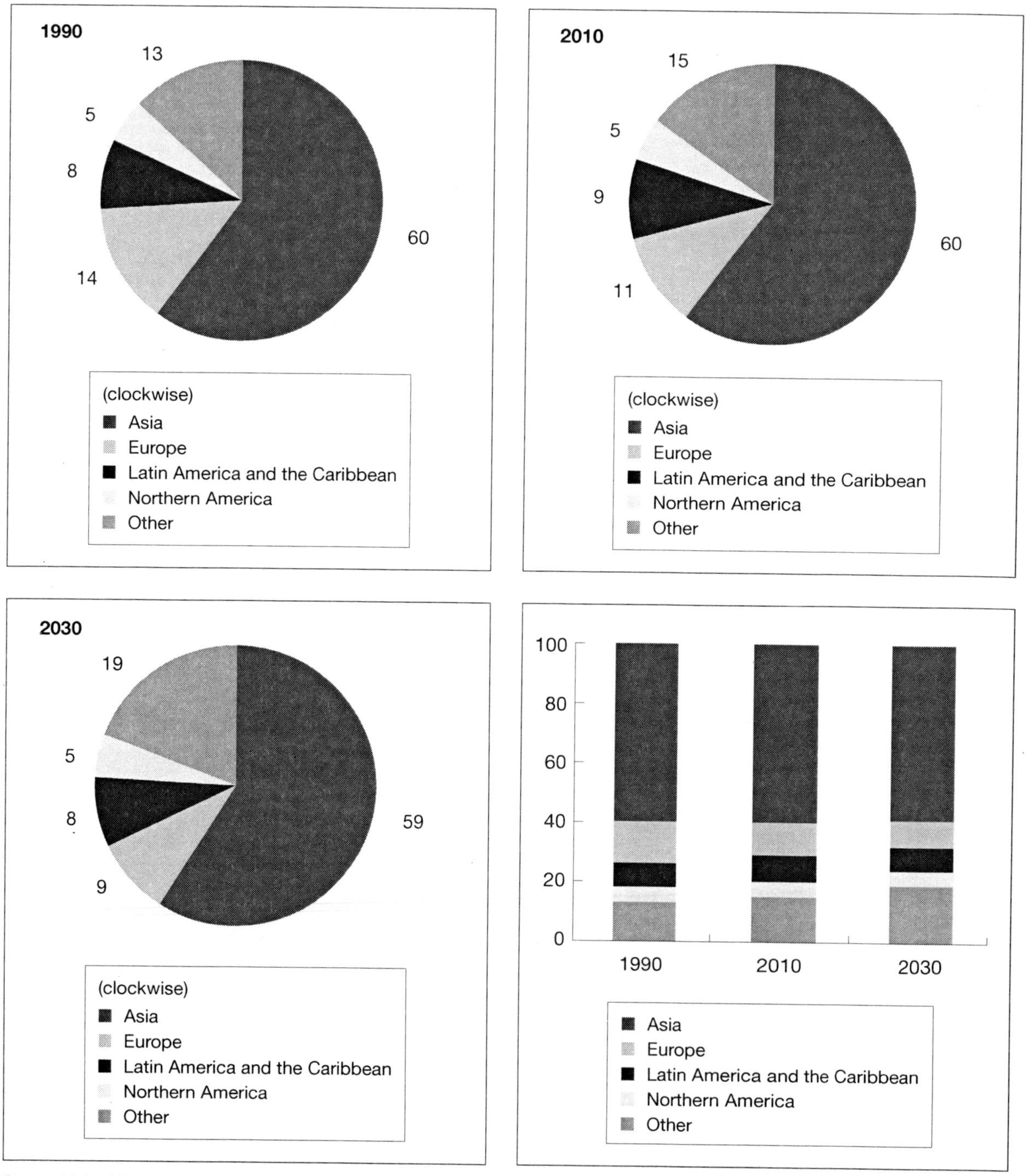

Source: United Nations World Population Forecasts, Trajectory.

This global population increase should boost tourist numbers significantly. And as economies get richer then a higher proportion of their citizens can afford to travel too. The number of international tourist arrivals as a proportion of the world's population has increased from 6.2% in 1980 to 13.7% in 2008. The presumed increases in wealth in future years will allow ever more people (and especially those from the developing world) to engage in international travel. In the year 2000 there were 11.5 international tourist arrivals per 100 people. If this rate of travel were to remain stable, then population growth alone would see an increase in international travel of 20% to 2030.

However, the UNWTO forecasts that the rate of international travel will increase to 20 trips per 100 people by 2020[8]. This is up from 6 in 1980 and 11 in 2000. So, the likely doubling of the rate of international travel, along with a 20% increase in population suggests continued strong growth for international travel in the long term future, with more people travelling more frequently.

Figure 3.4 International tourist arrivals per 100 population

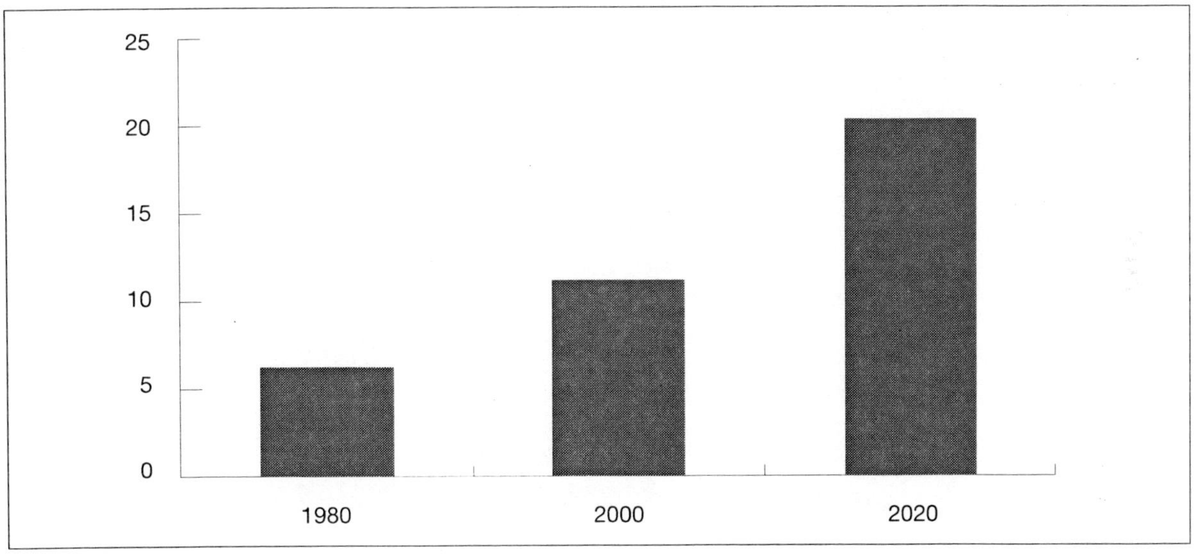

Source: World Tourism Organization (UNWTO), *Tourism 2020 Vision.*

Figure 3.5 Population growth and international tourist arrivals (× 1000)

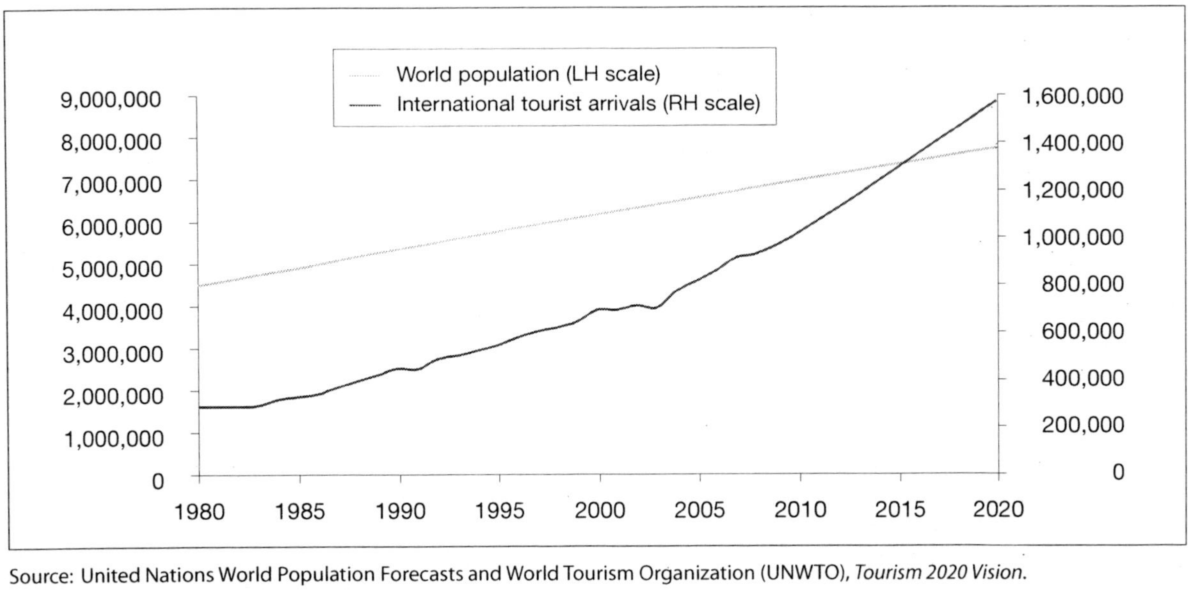

Source: United Nations World Population Forecasts and World Tourism Organization (UNWTO), *Tourism 2020 Vision.*

8 World Tourism Organization, *Tourism 2020 Vision.*

3.3 Changing Age Structures

The second important issue in demographics is the changing age structure of the population and specifically the ageing of it across the world.

This latter point is illustrated in the chart below.

The chart uses the statistical technique of correspondence analysis to summarise the changing age profiles of different countries over time. The axes themselves are meaningless and merely represent the two dimensions that best allow a 2×2 table (in this instance numbers in each age group by country/date) to be presented graphically. The 'map' attempts to place countries nearer to the ages where they are relatively over-represented so, for example India in 1990 had an exceptionally young population relative to other countries (the 0-4 age group was the largest in India at that time) and so is placed to the extreme left of the map. Japan is ageing more quickly than other countries (with the over 80s being far the largest group in 2030) and is so placed on the extreme right. Those countries in the centre of the chart have more balanced population distributions and so are placed specifically because the analysis is trying to place them closer to all the age bands.

Case Study 2 Health tourism in India

An example of a successful effort to benefit from the ageing demographics is provided by the phenomenon of health tourism. Ageing western populations, overburdened health systems and advantageous exchange rates have driven increasingly large numbers of tourists to travel abroad to have (often major) operations performed at a fraction of the cost back home.

India has a huge reserve of highly trained medical professionals, and a history of providing doctors and surgeons in the West. Because of this the country is able to brand itself as a reliable and less expensive alternative for medical operations that would cost tens of thousands in Europe. A heart operation in France may cost the equivalent of GBP 13,000 for example, where as in Bangalore the cost is GBP 4,300.

In 2005, 150,000 tourists visited India for a range of operations and procedures. As Europe's population ages the market for health tourism is set to expand dramatically. Holidays that include heart bypasses, hip operations and cataracts removal are already common. In fact, they are so well integrated into the Indian travel market that specialist tour operators now offer private cars to ferry travellers from airport to hospital bed, and some even incorporate trips to tourist sites such as the Taj Mahal in their itinerary.

Figure 3.6 A 'map' of the changing age structures in the key markets

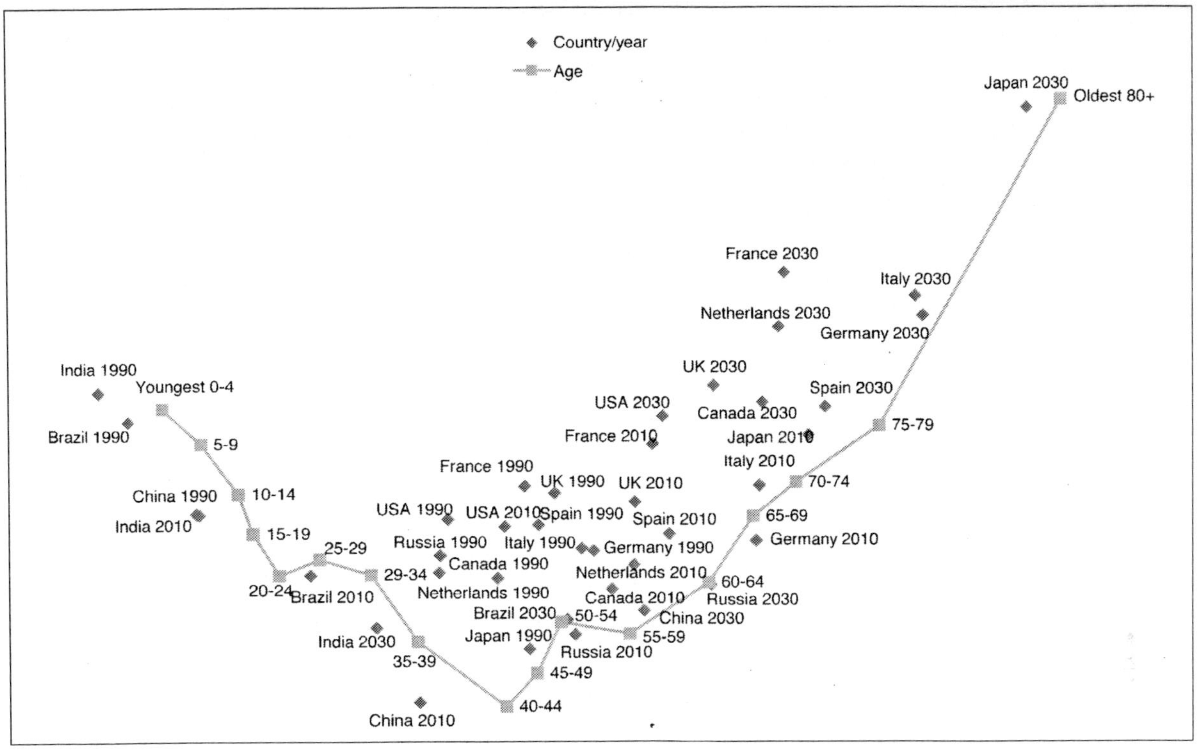

Source: United Nations World Population Forecasts, Trajectory.

It is clear from the map that all countries across the world are ageing. Over the next 20 years, the developing nations are moving towards being younger middle-aged while the developed nations are becoming more characterised by older age groups. (As already noted, Africa will remain a very 'young' region.)

3.4 Other Demographic Trends

Related, and of course responsible for the overall ageing of the world's population are the issues of fertility and longevity (as living standards and health care improve). Longevity (life expectancy) is generally increasing across the world (it is falling dramatically in some African countries suffering from the AIDS virus). The chart shows the long-term course of life expectancy in some developed countries.

Figure 3.7 Life expectancy in selected countries

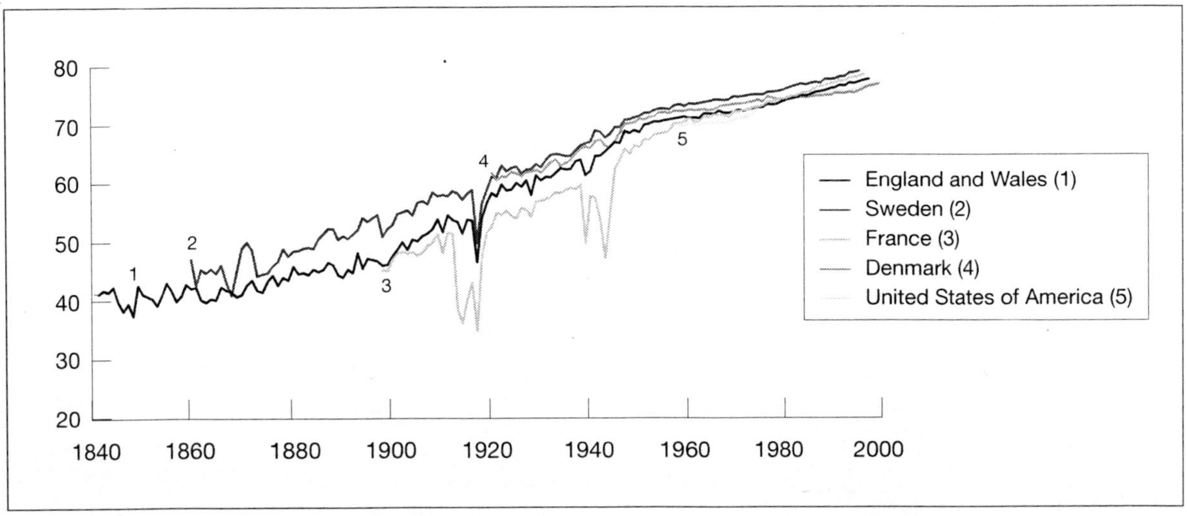

Source: Human Mortality Database.

Forecasts by the United Nations show an expected continued increase in life expectancy across the developed and developing worlds (see chapter 8 for details of individual countries).

Trends in fertility seem to be converging across the globe. Higher fertility rates in the developing world have been falling and are expected to continue to do so. In the developed world they have been falling too with, in some countries, a recent upturn but only to levels still below replacement. The United Nations assumption is that this pattern will continue with all countries moving towards a rate of 1.85 per woman (still below replacement levels).

A bi-product of these changes in fertility (and the ability to control it), longevity and health care (and changes to cultural mores and economic factors which have led to a negative view of female offspring) are changing gender structures. Basically, here too patterns are converging across the globe.

As people live longer and healthier lives, and as incomes increase, so their whole life becomes less dominated by work with a shorter working life and working hours; earlier retirement (possible through better pensions); and increased leisure time.

A final point, and related to the work issue, is the growth of migration. Partly a result of globalisation and the need, and desire, for labour to be mobile round the world. This important issue is covered later in section 4.3.3.

Chapter 4

Demographic Change and Tourism

It is important to remember that though demographic alterations can be significant; this does not necessarily impact upon travel and tourism patterns. A report by the German Federal Ministry of Economics and Technology, *The Impact of Demographic Change on Tourism and Conclusions for Tourism Policy,* argued that demographic alterations are likely to have an impact on tourism only if they "arise in those groups (e.g. older people, children, the less affluent, single parents) which represent a sizeable volume, will be considerably larger or smaller in volume and whose behaviour differs from other groups".[1] For instance the report found that demographic changes would have very little significant impact on short break holidays in the German market when seen against the intrinsic variety within the market anyway. However the report found that demographic shifts would have sizeable impacts upon the holiday (5+nights) market, as well as on supply-side issues such as employment, with the workforce serving in the industry ageing and becoming deskilled. In this section we examine several demographic features that we feel will have a significant impact upon tourism.

4.1 An Ageing Population

There are some great similarities in the changing age profiles of the source countries under analysis not least in the changing age profiles. Full details of individual countries are included in the Appendix and here is summarised the major patterns and differences, suggesting there are two fundamental 'models'.

4.1.1 Age Profile: The Three Peaks Model

This model of age profile is most common among the developed nations of western Europe; countries such as Germany, the United Kingdom, the United States of America, Italy, Spain, Canada and France (though in a more moderate form). It is also visible in Japan in a slightly modified form (Japan's age profile is similar to western Europe's except that it shows a double-peak for each year). In this model, the age profile of the country involved has three prominent peaks at each of the decades under review corresponding to a clear majority of one age group; a group which has significantly aged at each stage. The profile is a product of the tendency of developed nations to have an ageing population following a boom then slump, then subsequent rise in fertility, in addition to increasing life-expectancy meaning that the larger proportion of the populace born just before the slump live longer and so make up an even greater proportion of the populace. The age of this peak group (or groups) depends on when the nation underwent its particular fertility boom and slump. The cohort effect means that this produces a quantifiable bump in the population of a certain age, producing a peak on the chart which moves to the right as the period progresses. France displays this in a more moderate form than the rest of Europe because it has maintained historically higher fertility while much of Europe experienced a post-sixties fertility slump; this means that the rise and fall of the various age cohorts has been less dramatic than say that seen in Germany. The Russian Federation notably also bucks the trend, as its fertility has been considerably more erratic, producing a series of sharper but smaller peaks, at least six in the period under review.

1 Federal Ministry of Economics and Technology (2009), *The Impact of Demographic Change on Tourism and Conclusions for Tourism Policy* (abridged), FMET, Berlin.

Figure 4.1 Example of the 'Three-Peaks' model: Canadian population by age band (%)

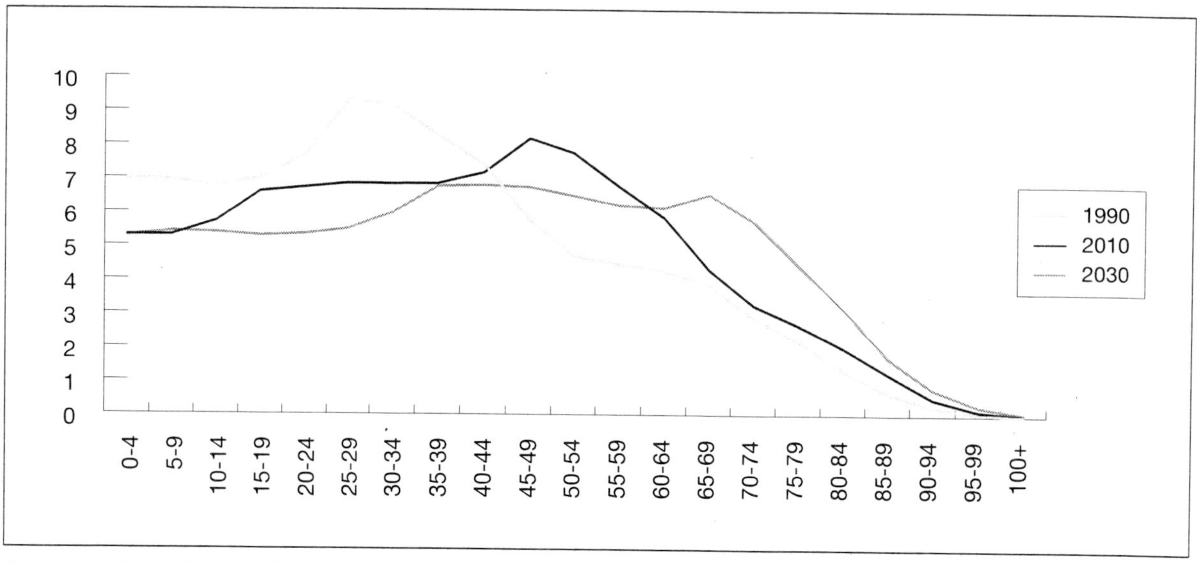

Source: Population Division of the Department of Economic and Social Affairs of the United Nations Secretariat, *World Population Prospects: The 2008 Revision*, 2009.

Figure 4.2 Example of the 'Three-Peaks' model: Italian population by age band (%)

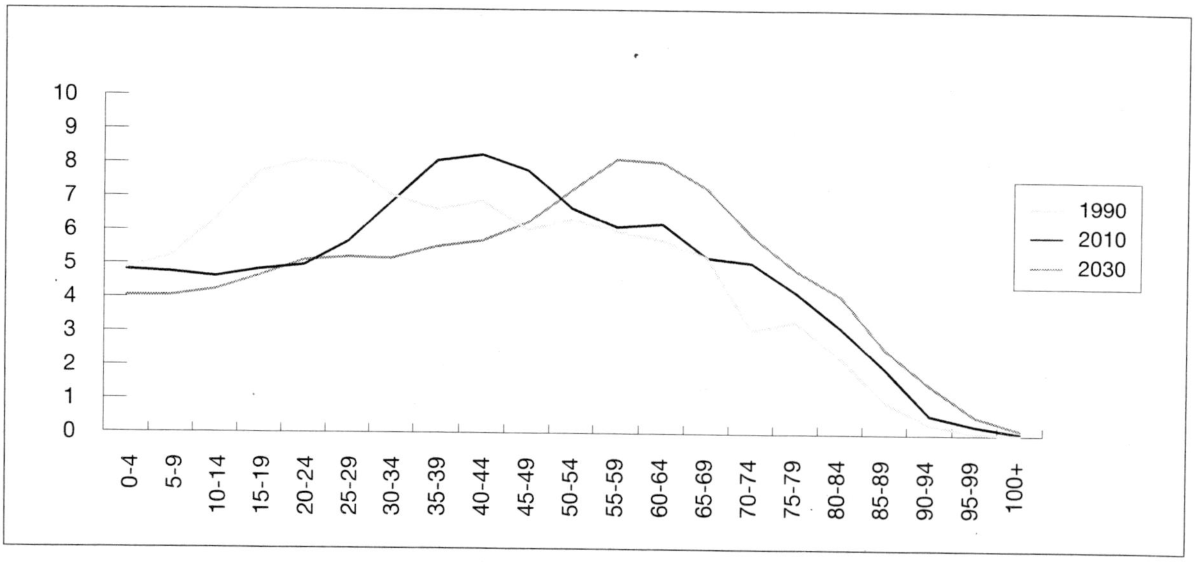

Source: Population Division of the Department of Economic and Social Affairs of the United Nations Secretariat, *World Population Prospects: The 2008 Revision*, 2009.

The age group 80+ is also growing and at a quicker pace than their younger counterpart (60-79). In Italy for example it is expected to grow from 3% to 5%.

4.1.2 Age Profile: Slope Model

Developing nations like India and Brazil display a sloping age profile with the majority of the population bunched to the left of the chart, and a significant slope downwards to the right. This slope tends to moderate somewhat later in the period, a result of the ageing of cohorts combined with an extension of life-expectancy increasing the proportion of the population in older age groups, as well as an increase in the total population; however the majority remains in the younger age brackets throughout the period. In fact, by 2030 the majority of the population is aged to 39 (young market) while the most relevant age classes are in the break 25-49 (young-adult market).

Figure 4.3 Example of the 'Slope' model: Indian population by age band (%)

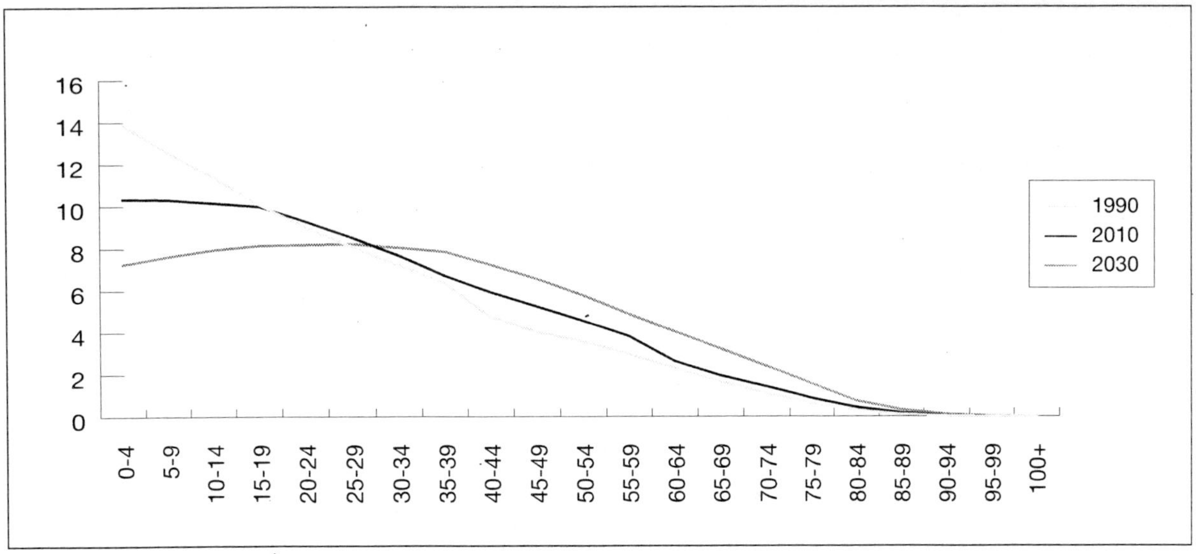

Source: Population Division of the Department of Economic and Social Affairs of the United Nations Secretariat, *World Population Prospects: The 2008 Revision*, 2009.

Figure 4.4 Example of the 'Slope' model: Brazilian population by age band (%)

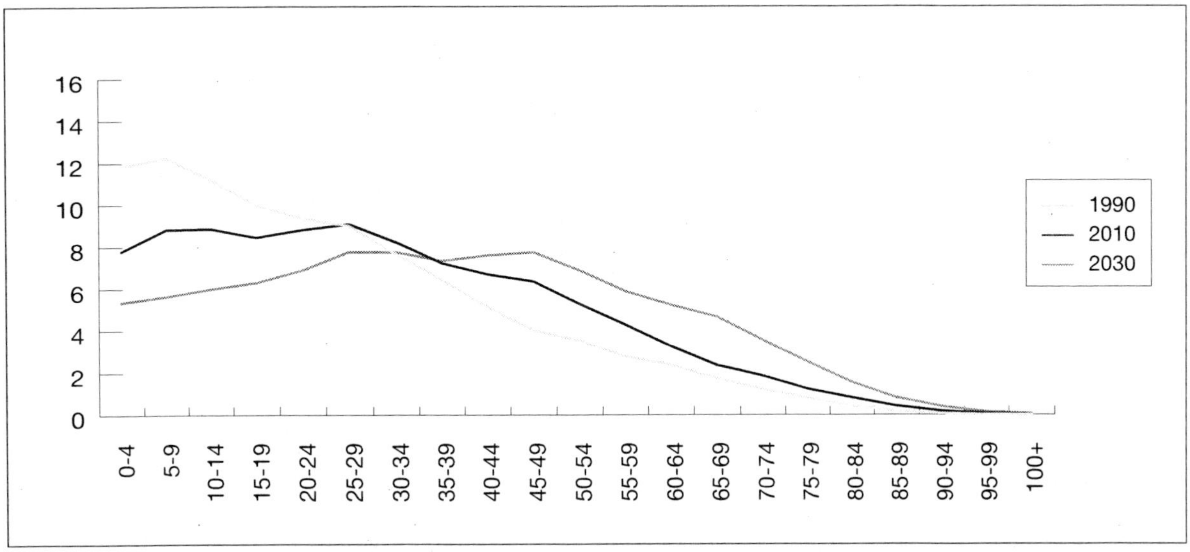

Source: Population Division of the Department of Economic and Social Affairs of the United Nations Secretariat, *World Population Prospects: The 2008 Revision*, 2009.

China notably displays a combination of the two models above, Three Peaks but which display a clear slump to the right. This is a product of China's recent decline in fertility and ageing of population following a prolonged period of very high fertility which only recently came to an end, indicative of the radical social changes that have taken place within China in the past decade. By 2030, China's population keeps a bi-modal distribution, with a larger age group in the class 40-44 and a second relevant segment in the age 60-69 (adult 'younger-olds' market).

Figure 4.5 China – A combined model? Chinese population by age band (%)

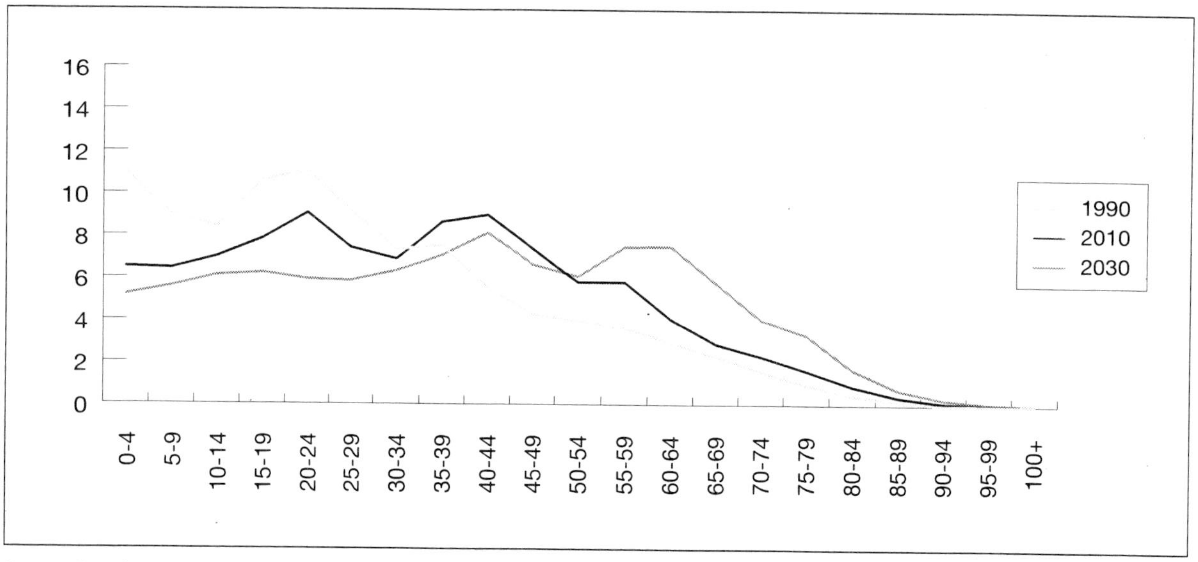

Source: Population Division of the Department of Economic and Social Affairs of the United Nations Secretariat, *World Population Prospects: The 2008 Revision*, 2009.

4.1.3 Life Expectancy: Increasing and Converging across the Globe

In all the countries being looked at, life expectancy is increasing, and in most the difference between male and female life expectancy is reducing. Generally, this has been a constant process; however there are three notable exceptions. Unlike the rest of Europe and much of the rest of the world Russian life expectancy is not predicted to grow very much in the coming decades. Between 1990 and 2010 it dipped significantly from 69 to 66 years. After this it is set to recover but by 2030 the average expectancy will still only be 71.6 years. As usual female life expectancy will lead male life expectancy, but this time the difference will become a stark ten years two decades from now; going from 73.6 versus 63.8 in 1990 to 76.5 versus 66.5 in 2030. In Japan rather than moderating the gender difference it is set to increase over the period from around 6 years to just under 9 years. The same is true in China; in 1990 there were just less than three years difference between male and female life expectancy at 66 and 68.8. However by 2030 this will have extended to four years difference at 74.7 and 78.6.

Case Study 3 One Stop Shop for Accessible Tourism in Europe (OSSATE)

As life expectancy has begun to increase across Europe and the rest of the world a far larger proportion of contemporary travellers are older than previously and consequently more likely to have mobility issues. There is a need and a niche for services which can support these groups, and open up tourism for those who may previously have been excluded.

European travel agencies have already begun to take account of the ageing of the population of Europe with several campaigns designed to target older and disabled travellers as well as campaigns to encourage accommodation of disabled and older tourists' needs. For instance, The European Commission has established the project *One Stop Shop for Accessible Tourism in Europe* (OSSATE) which provides information and resources to older and disabled travellers in order to facilitate their greater engagement in tourism opportunities.

The OSSATE project has two strands. The first is the promotion of better facilities and access for elderly and disabled travellers around Europe; improving wheelchair access and so on as well as a 'disability-friendly service approach' from managers and staff and all other service providers. The second is dispersing information about these services to disabled tourists around Europe.

Figure 4.6 Russian life expectancy (years)

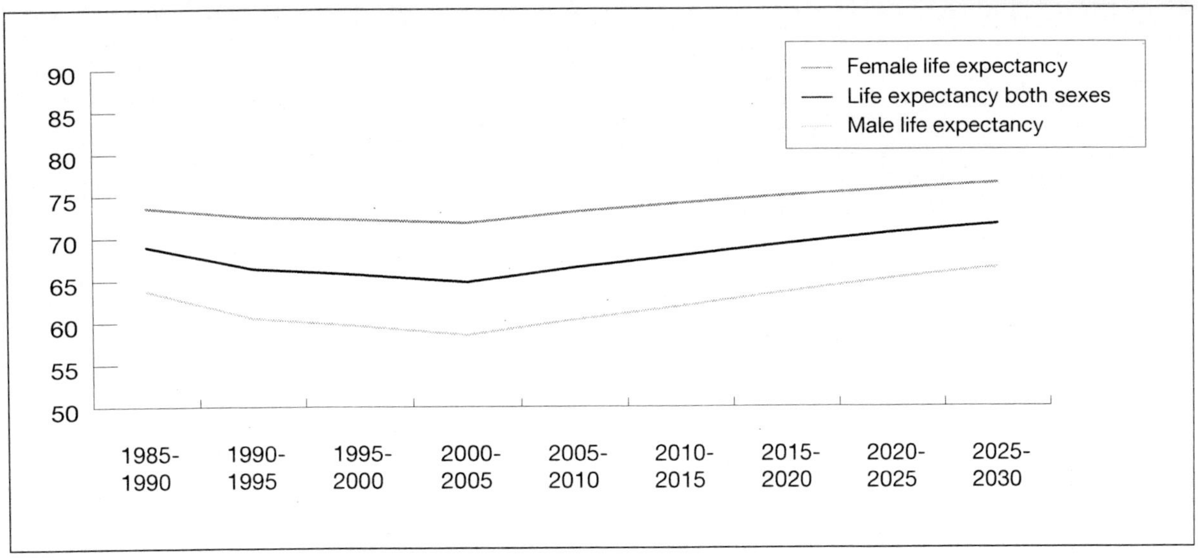

Source: Population Division of the Department of Economic and Social Affairs of the United Nations Secretariat, *World Population Prospects: The 2008 Revision*, 2009.

Figure 4.7 Chinese life expectancy (years)

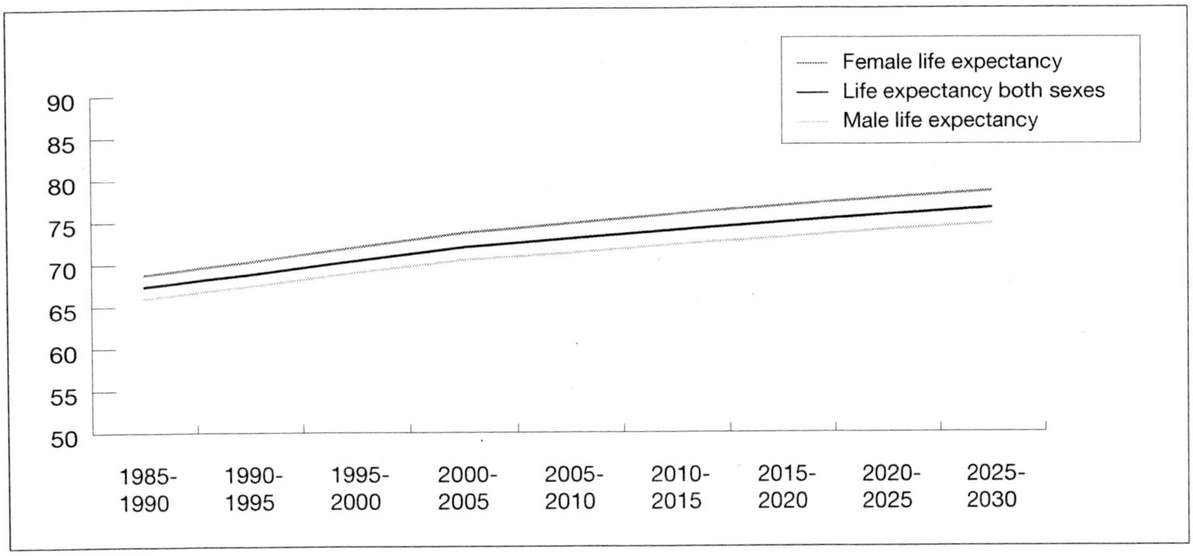

Source: Population Division of the Department of Economic and Social Affairs of the United Nations Secretariat, *World Population Prospects: The 2008 Revision*, 2009.

Figure 4.8 Japanese life expectancy (years)

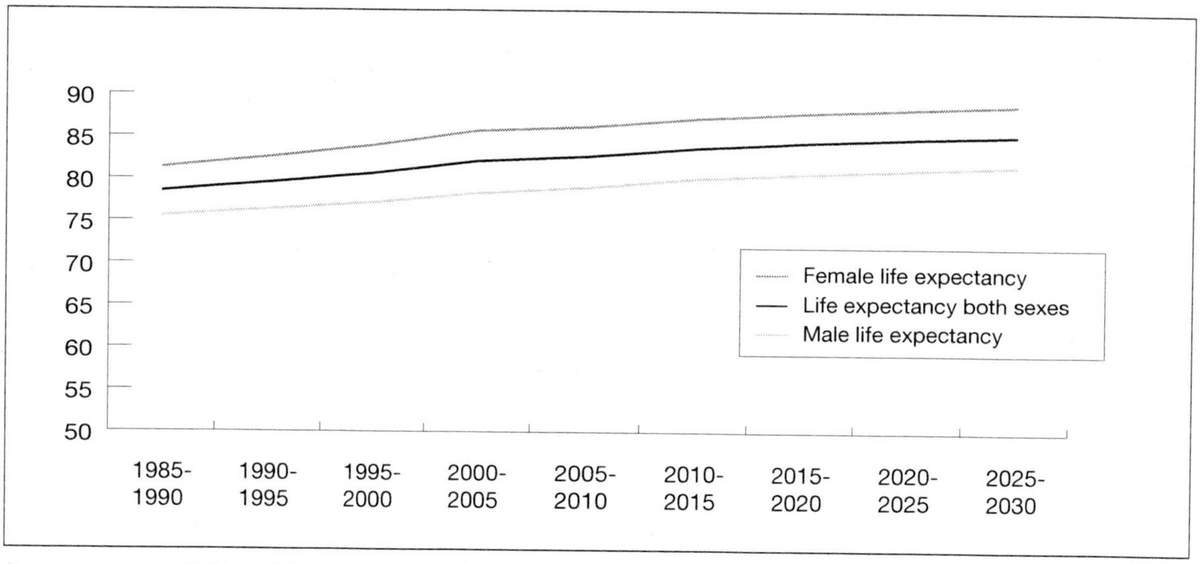

Source: Population Division of the Department of Economic and Social Affairs of the United Nations Secretariat, *World Population Prospects: The 2008 Revision*, 2009.

A critical issue about life expectancy is to what extent it is healthy life expectancy. Are people living longer, healthier lives or are they just having a longer period of morbidity at the end of their lives? The evidence here is mixed but on the whole points to an increased period of longer healthy life as well as total life. Researchers in Sweden argue this to be the case, as does a global analysis around the world by Mathers et al.[2]. Some researchers in Britain, not least its own National Statistics Office had been concerned whether this was true but even here the mood is changing. As the Parliamentary Office of Science and Technology said in a report on this issue 'the general consensus in the academic community is that these trends reflect increased years of mild disability and a decline in severe disability'. People are having longer healthy lives although some may be suffering mild complaints as they get older.

This fact was noted in HSBC's The Future of Retirement report:

> *"[...] globally only 16% of people in their 70s say they feel in poor or very poor health. In the mature economies the percentage is even lower, at about 8% – with individual country results ranging from a remarkable 3% in Canada to 12% in Germany. Individuals in the transitional economies of Latin America and Asia also reported a low level of poor health, with only 10% in Brazil and Mexico and 18% in Asia, (as low as 9% in Singapore and the Philippines). However the figures rise to 32% in South Africa; and to 35% in the transitional economies of Europe, represented by Russia and Turkey. Indeed only 8% of Russians in their 70s felt in good or very good health the lowest in the survey. The growing divide in Europe is thus striking with nearly three-quarters of people in the UK in their 70 stating good or very good health compared with under 10% of Russians of the same age range."*

Clearly, not only is an increase in older tourists expected (because they are healthier – and richer it should be added) but also ones that are fitter and younger looking in outlook. As the HSBC report also said:

> *"[...] People are now able to do things after the age of 60 that were previously reserved for those in their 40s and 50s, such as working, contributing to family life and taking part in active sports."*

2 Mathers et al. (2001), 'Healthy life expectancy in 191 countries, 1999', *The Lancet*, Vol. 357, pp. 685-691.

Summary of key age and life expectancy trends

Age profiles

- Different countries' age profiles are changing in similar ways – there are two basic models.
- The **'Three Peaks Model'** typical of developed countries: here each age profile is characterised by a prominent peak for each of the three decades under review as a 'boomer' generation gradually ages.
- The boom is generally followed by a slump in population further accentuating the peaks.
- The **'Slope Model'** is more typical of developing nations: with population highly concentrated to the left (or younger end) of the profile and sloping to the right (older end).
- The angle of slope tends to moderate towards the end of the period as increased life expectancy increases the number of older people in the demographic.
- However, even by 2030 the majority of the population remains in the younger age groups in these countries.
- China is distinctive, showing a combination of both models.

Life expectancy

- In all countries under review, life expectancy is increasing.
- In most, the gap between male and female life expectancy is narrowing.
- The Russian Federation is an unusual example with lower rates of increase in life expectancy and a widening of the gap between female and male life expectancy.
- On balance, the expert view is that the period of healthy life expectancy is also increasing.
- However, it is useful to draw the distinction between mild disability and severe disability – people are living longer, healthier lives but may suffer more mild disabilities as they get older.
- Currently, there are very large differences between the self-reported health status of older citizens in the countries covered by this report.

4.2 Household Composition, Family Structures and Travel Parties

Family structures are changing too as people live longer and as fertility rates fall. There are no clear-cut patterns of fertility in the countries that were analysed for this report. However, broadly speaking it can be seen that developed countries' fertility has undergone a slump around the beginning of the period (some just before it) but that this has moderated and most of them are forecast by 2030 to be at a level of fertility a little below the 2.1 replacement level. In most of these countries the specifics of their fertility shifts corresponds to Castles' writings – the differences between more or less patriarchal societies of northern and western versus southern, central and eastern Europe. This theory states that in less patriarchal societies women initially chose to have fewer children but the greater level of support in those societies for single and working parents meant they subsequently did not have to make such a stark choice between careers and children. In more patriarchal or traditional societies of the Mediterranean and eastern Europe (Spain, Italy and the Russian Federation in this case) fertility remained higher for longer, however eventually the lack of support for single and working mothers in those societies meant that when women did enter the workforce and were forced to decide between children and careers, they overwhelmingly chose careers and so fertility rates remained low. There are, of course complications to this model, France, for instance, is considered to have a strongly Catholic, family centred society, yet its high levels of social support and countervailing socially progressive cultural forces mean that it has maintained historically higher fertility than much of Europe. Similarly, Germany is part of the European North-west yet has very low fertility indeed.

Case Study 4 Ibiza nanny service

One impact of the changes in family structure and travel parties, along with rising affluence and the extension of various life stages is that parents are now increasingly taking children on holidays which are not specifically catered around them. Instead, more and more parents are demanding that aspects of the holiday be built around their own wants, generally apart from their children and are willing to pay for the luxury. Companies that can offer a service which provides for the varying demands of the individuals in a family group, rather than simply as a family group per se can benefit greatly from these changes.

In Ibiza, there is a prime example of this trend: www.ChildcareIbiza.com provides a nanny service to parents of young children who wish to enjoy the attractions of the island on their own. The service provides childcare for sessions ranging from four to twenty hours and specialises in providing overnight care for parents who wish to enjoy the island's nightlife and then have a lie-in the next morning to recover. The service charges between € 60 and € 450 depending on the number and length of sessions desired and has already attracted positive reviews as well as satisfied customers, some of whom include famous DJs and personalities.

Developing countries like India and China show a quite different pattern; they began the period with far higher than replacement level fertility; as high as 4 children per woman in India and 3 in Brazil, however as the impact of social and economic developments begin to take hold this is expected by the United Nations to decline towards replacement level, for India and China, or even a little below in the case of Brazil.

Figure 4.9 Brazilian fertility

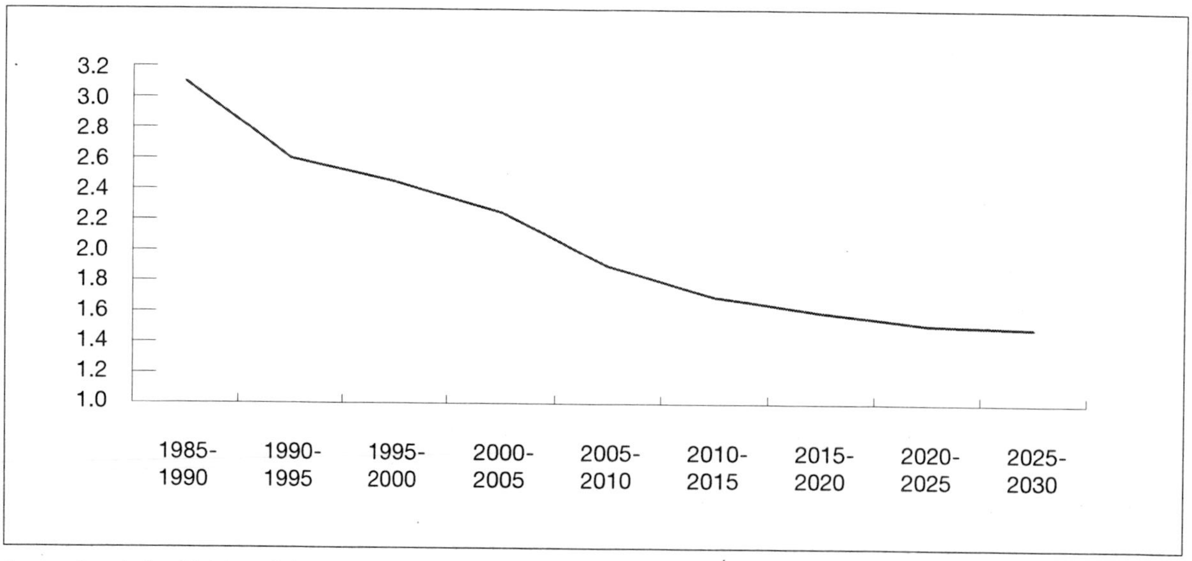

Source: Population Division of the Department of Economic and Social Affairs of the United Nations Secretariat, *World Population Prospects: The 2008 Revision*, 2009.

Figure 4.10 German fertility

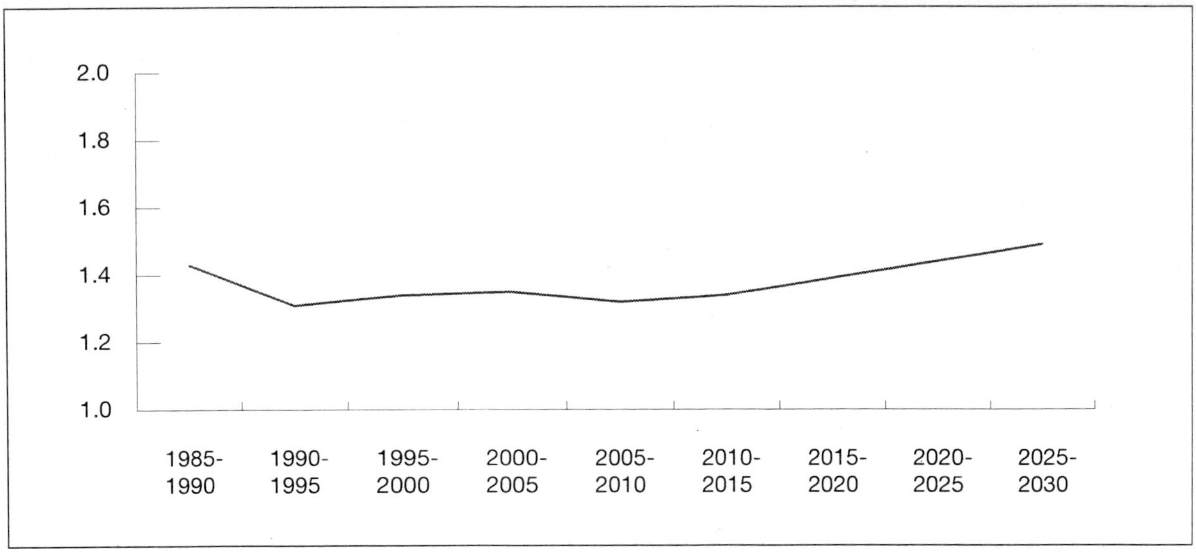

Source: Population Division of the Department of Economic and Social Affairs of the United Nations Secretariat, *World Population Prospects: The 2008 Revision*, 2009.

Figure 4.11 United Kingdom fertility

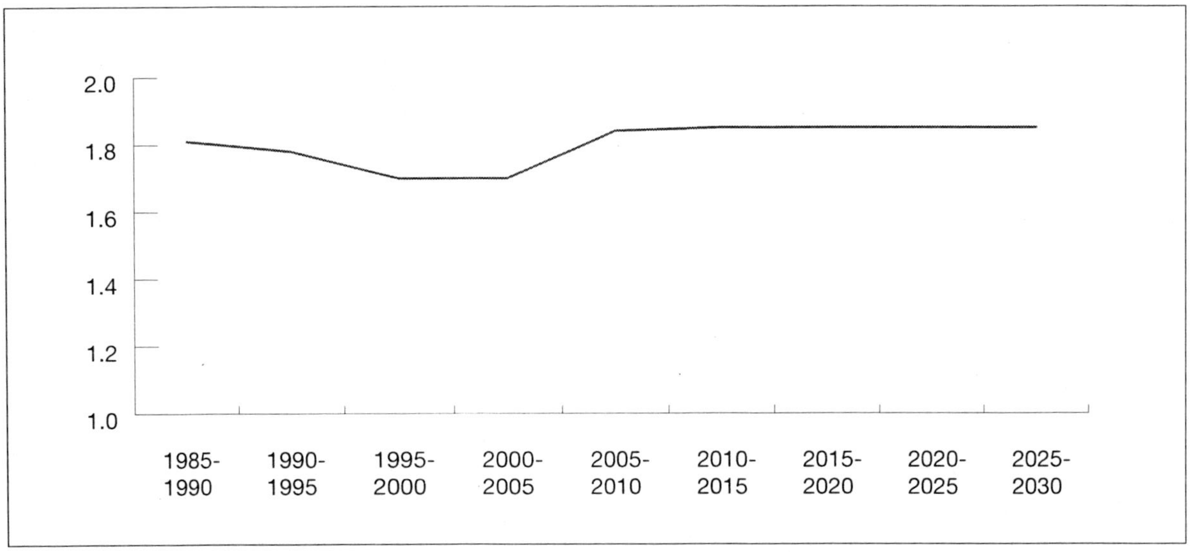

Source: Population Division of the Department of Economic and Social Affairs of the United Nations Secretariat, *World Population Prospects: The 2008 Revision*, 2009.

The impact on the structure of the family is profound. The increased longevity and reduced fertility is leading to what British sociologists Peter Willmott and Michael Young described as the movement from a 'horizontal' family mainly consisting of siblings, cousins and aunts and uncles to one they describe as 'vertical' (subsequently sometimes described by others as the 'beanpole family'. Here there are more grandparents and great-grandparents alive.

Figure 4.12 Changing family structures

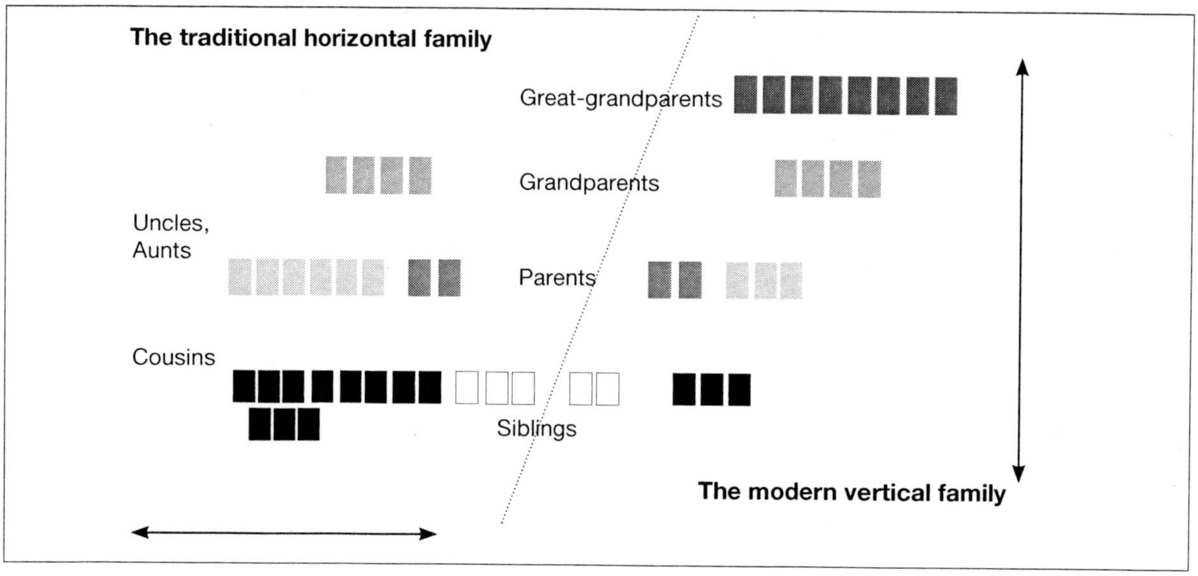

Source: Willmott and Young, *Symmetrical Family.*

This suggests that in terms of the tourism market that grandparents may well become important – either in taking grandchildren away on holiday (suggesting a difficult offer to cater for both young and old) or in part of a multi-generational (three generations) group.

> *"The trend for families to become more important in society will definitely continue as future generations of retirees will be more prepared for later life, both financially and health-wise".*
>
> Nelson Chow, *Professor Chair of Social Work and Social Administration, University of Hong Kong quoted in the HSBC Future of Retirement report.*

Equally in the developed world, there is now an accepted 'new' stage in people's lives – that of 'singleton'. Here there is a recognised period when young people leave their family home and live alone or with friends until they move in with a partner (the exception here is Italy where men still stay at home until their late twenties).

This had led to an increase in the tourists going on singles holiday and if the trend takes off in developing nations could be an important market in the future (especially as the younger age groups are so important in those countries).

Another category important in the West is the 'gap year' student travelling the globe. As more people enter higher education and as incomes increase then this group is likely to grow, again especially if developing markets follow this trend. Although normally low value consumers, this group could be important as there is the opportunity for the destination country or area to charm such people at a young age increasing the opportunity of their return later in life.[3]

Summary of key household composition, family structure and travel party trends

- Family structures are determined by trends in life expectancy (see above) and fertility rates (above).
- Patterns in fertility rates are more diverse by country than for the other trends covered here.
- Generally, fertility rates fell in developed countries in recent decades – in many cases below the 2.1 children per woman replacement level – but this has now moderated in most cases.

3 For more information, see *Youth Travel Matters – Understanding the Global Phenomenon of Youth Travel*, UNWTO, 2008.

- Within Europe there have been big historical differences in fertility rates between north-western Europe and southern, central and eastern Europe.
- Developing countries typically have much higher fertility rates, but as social and economic development takes hold these are forecast to drop towards replacement level.
- These trends result in a transformation of family structures from 'horizontal' families (where most family members were siblings or cousins) to 'vertical' families (where most family members are from different generations).
- The number of single people may well grow with potential implications for tourism.

4.3 Population Location

4.3.1 Urban and Rural Distribution

The most obvious factors in where the tourists of the future might be located are the continued movement of people in to cities and the growing importance of the developing world.

Figure 4.13 Proportion of the world population living in urban areas (%)

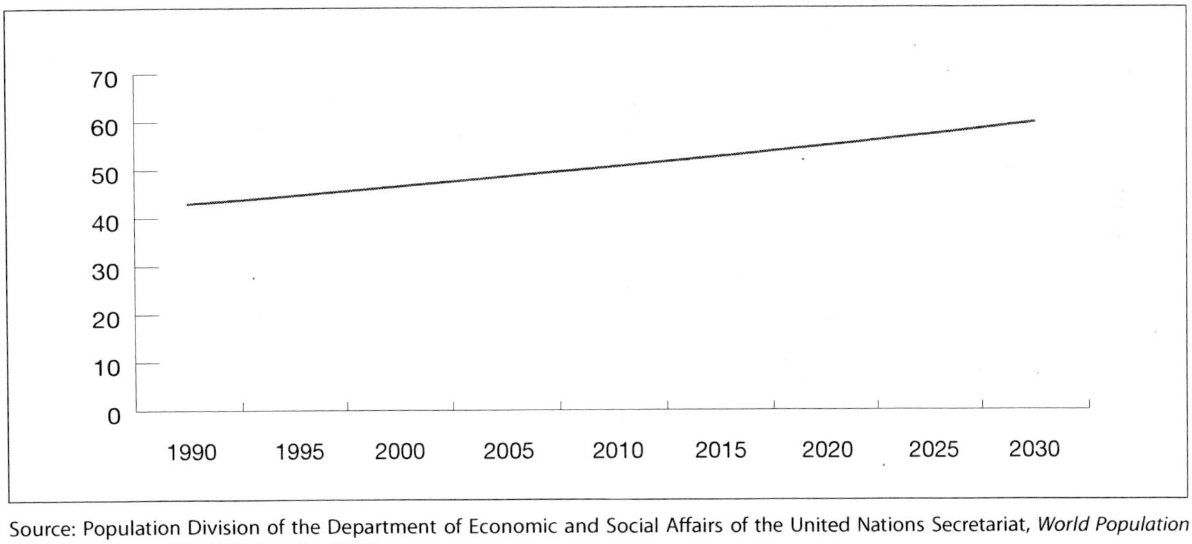

Source: Population Division of the Department of Economic and Social Affairs of the United Nations Secretariat, *World Population Prospects: The 2008 Revision*, 2009.

The proportion of citizens living in urban areas in all of the countries under review (if not the world) is predicted to increase significantly – but to varying degrees – within the 1990-2030 period. For example, Italy's urban population will accelerate while the rate of movement will slow somewhat in the United States (see charts below).

One implication of a growing urban population is that city dwellers are much more likely to travel. In part this is because of increased incomes in urban areas but also because such residents are more exposed to other people and other cultures – they are likely to have a more cosmopolitan outlook.

Figure 4.14 Examples of different urbanisation patterns: Indian urban population (%)

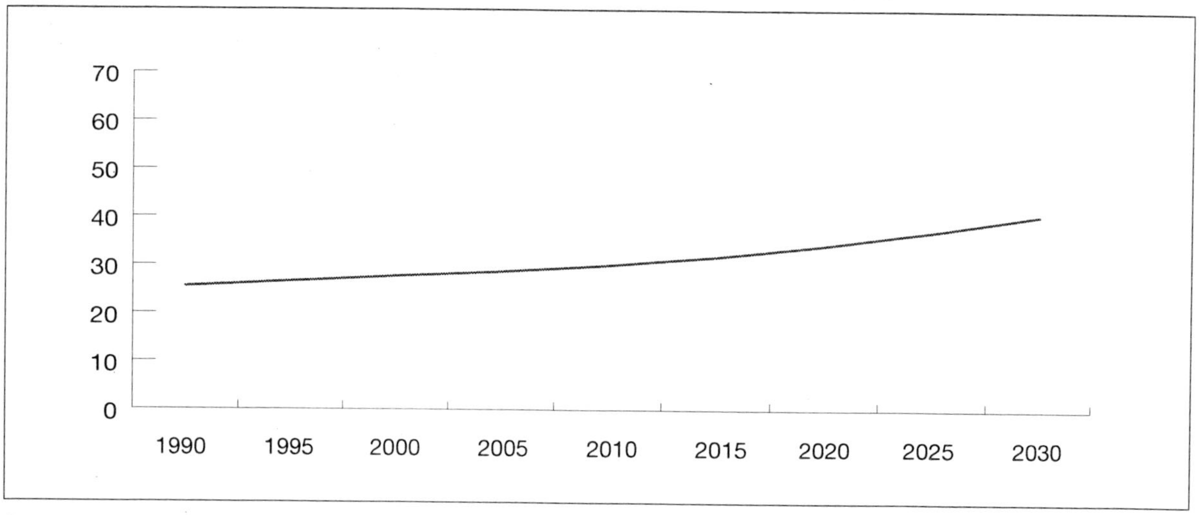

Source: Population Division of the Department of Economic and Social Affairs of the United Nations Secretariat, *World Population Prospects: The 2008 Revision*, 2009.

Figure 4.15 Examples of different urbanisation patterns: Urban population of the United States of America (%)

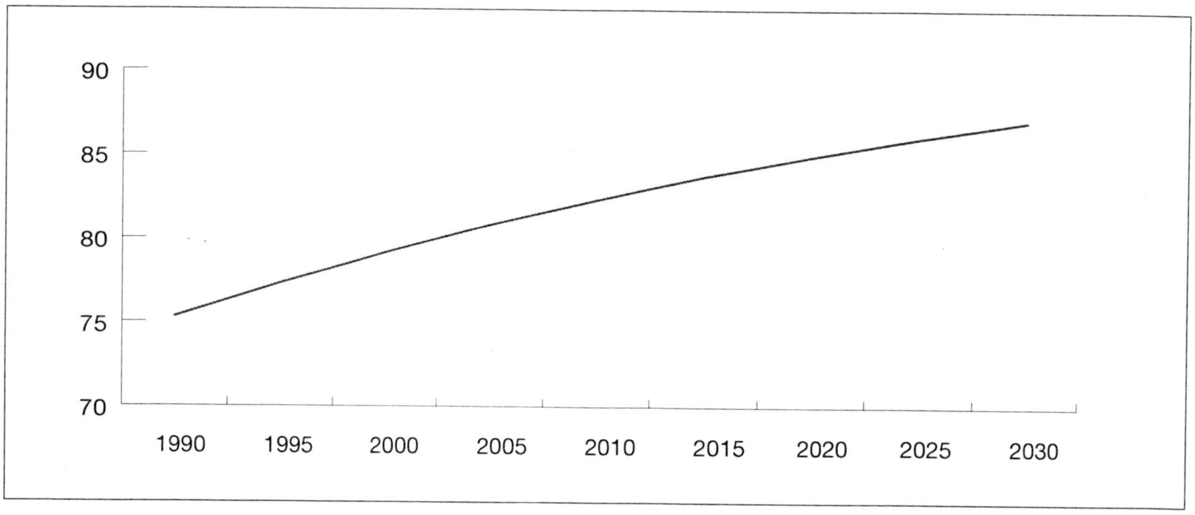

Source: Population Division of the Department of Economic and Social Affairs of the United Nations Secretariat, *World Population Prospects: The 2008 Revision*, 2009.

4.3.2 Migration

A final point related to population location is the growth of migration. This arises because people are lured by the work and opportunities that other locations can offer, thanks in part to the growth of globalisation.

Worldwide, migrants accounted for 3% of the total population in 2005, hardly changed from 1990. However, even if that rate remained for the next 20 years the growth of the world population implies 42 million extra migrants by 2030.

Figure 4.16 Estimated number of migrants, 1990-2005 (millions)

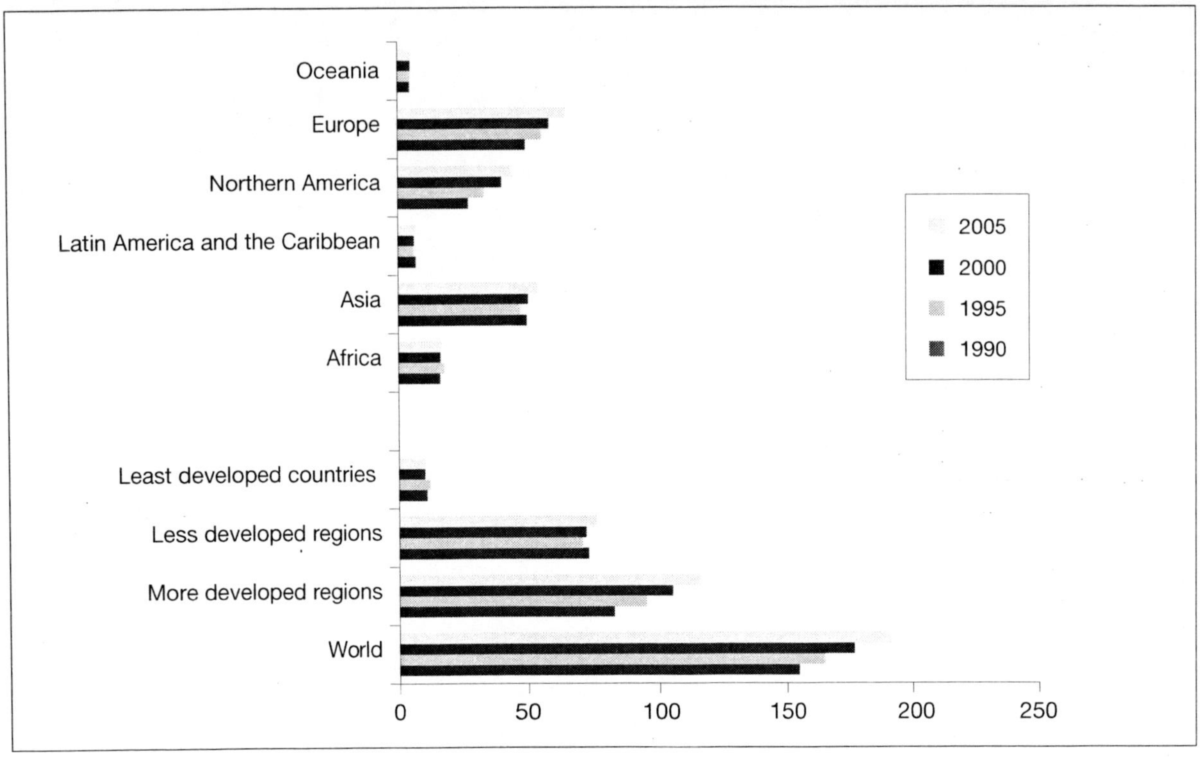

Source: Population Division of the Department of Economic and Social Affairs of the United Nations Secretariat, *Trends in Total Migrant Stock: The 2005 Revision*, 2006.

Migration can have important implications for tourism and in two ways. First is what has been defined as 'tourism-led migration' (TLM) and second is 'migration-led tourism' (MLT)[4]. The former includes the movement of workers to other countries to fill tourism employment gaps (for example, young people from central Europe to western Europe). It also includes pensioner migration in Asia and new residency for owners of 'second homes'. The latter refers to home visits by non-resident migrants (including not only those working in the tourist industry but those in other sectors like non-tourist related construction or health services) or where migrants encourage others to do so. In these cases, the workers travel home to their country of origin or their friends and/or relatives come to visit them in their country of work. Both forms of migration make important social and economic contributions to countries ranging from cultural exchange to providing labour for tourism related industries. They also help to drive in both originating and destination countries a growth in trips involving visiting friends and relatives (VFR).

However, the global picture of immigration rather masks a quite remarkable increase in Europe from under 4% of the population in Europe in 1960 to nearly 9% today as the figure 4.17 shows.

4 World Tourism Organization, *Tourism and Migration – Exploring the Relationship between Two Global Phenomena*, UNWTO, 2009, Madrid.

Figure 4.17 Immigrants as a proportion of the total population (%)

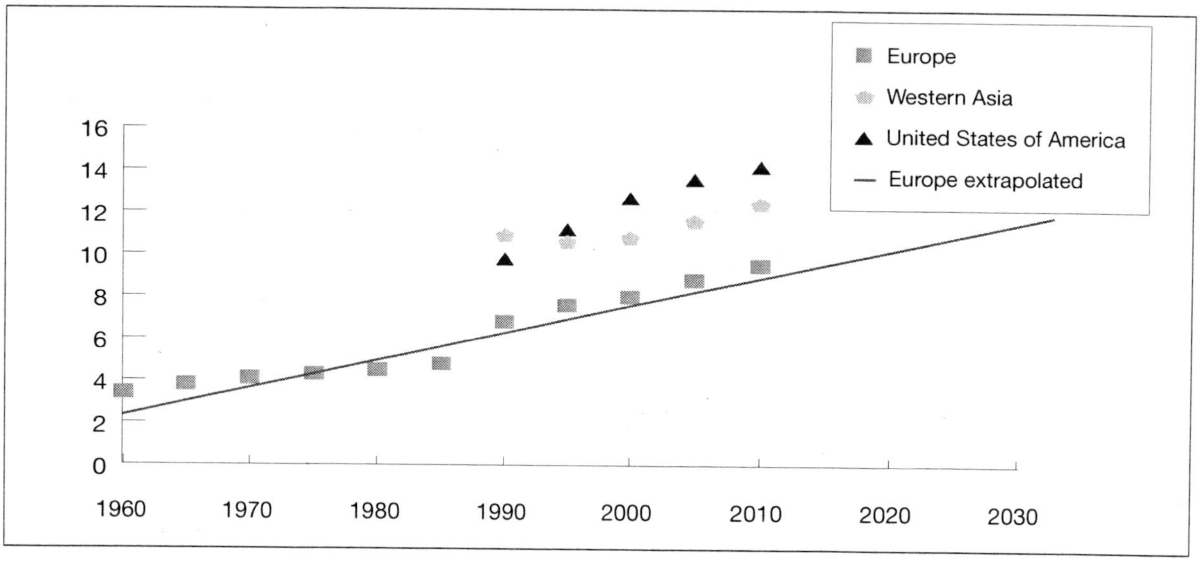

Note: 2010 estimated.

Source: Population Division of the Department of Economic and Social Affairs of the United Nations Secretariat, *Trends in Total Migrant Stock: The 2005 Revision*, 2006.

If this trend continues it could reach nearly 12% by 2030. Although European countries are generally tightening up on immigration from outside the European Union, this has been countered by increases into the more advanced economies from the new member countries of eastern Europe. Indeed, it is quite clear that the enlargement of the European Union and the integration processes involved has been a major driver of increasing migration without Europe. An important part of the migration debate is whether the incoming migrants are more or less skilled. Arguably, the tourism industry needs both types but the political impetus is behind favouring more skilled personnel.

One obvious impact of this in Europe is that such immigrants could be a magnet for visits from friends and relatives helping to boost VFR travel. Equally, there may be VFR visits from those who have emigrated and want to return home every now and then, or those who are maybe second or third generation inhabitants in non-European countries who are seeking to go 'back to their roots'.

The world region with the highest proportion of immigrants is Oceania with an estimated 16% of the population. This followed by the United States (14%) and then western Asia (12%) of which the majority involves countries of the Middle East.

But in terms of sheer numbers, the United States has the largest number of immigrants in the world as table 4.1 shows and immigration continues to grow there. This is fundamentally changing the make-up of the population as shown by the increase in the Hispanic group in this country. While this particular group may not be important for migration led tourism there could well be a growth in Europeans coming home to visit friends and relatives.

Table 4.1 Most important destinations for migrants: Top ten countries with the largest number of international migrants, 2005

	Number of immigrants (x 1000)	Share of international migrants (%)	Rank
United States of America	38,355	20.2	1
Russian Federation	12,080	6.4	2
Germany	10,144	5.3	3
France	6,471	3.4	4
Saudi Arabia	6,361	3.3	5

	Number of immigrants (× 1000)	Share of international migrants (%)	Rank
Canada	6,106	3.2	6
India	5,700	3.0	7
United Kingdom	5,408	2.8	8
Spain	4,790	2.5	9
Australia	4,097	2.2	10
Top ten total	**99,511**	**52.3**	
World	**190,634**	**100.0**	

Source: Population Division of the Department of Economic and Social Affairs of the United Nations Secretariat, *Trends in Total Migrant Stock: The 2005 Revision*, 2006.

The immigration into the United States of America could have far-reaching impacts on the structure of its outbound market. The Hispanic population (most of which come from South America) are likely to be visiting other destinations than those of traditional United States citizens and looking for other media as sources of inspiration and information. That said, there will be elements that still hanker over visiting their European roots (see case study).

Case Study 5 Scotland's *Big Homecoming* 2009

Migration has become a vital demographic and financial force in the modern world. A nation that has produced a significant Diaspora can generate considerable income by accessing the wealth represented by that Diaspora, either through remittances or through encouraging family based or 'nostalgic' tourism to the 'homeland'.

Scotland has embarked on a campaign to tap into the extremely lucrative visiting friend and relatives (VFR) market by encouraging the 40 million odd individuals worldwide who claim Scottish heritage to return 'home' for the 250th anniversary of the birth of Robert Burns. It was hoped that the campaign would help ease Scottish tourism through the potentially dramatic downturn as a result of the recession. There are signs that the campaign has been a success. In terms of web traffic the Scottish Government's website (www.scotland.gov.uk) stating that the period April 2008 to March 2009 saw a 51% increase in web traffic to the Visit Scotland website; in addition interest was being shown from countries not normally associated with the Diaspora, such as India with a 58% rise in traffic. Figures for actual tourist arrivals have yet to be released for 2009, but Scottish whisky has already claimed that distillery tours increased 21% on 2008 and saw a 12% increase in spend.

Overall, it can be seen that the VFR market is an important one. Certainly it has grown for every region as the figure 4.17 shows[5]. In 2008, international tourist arrivals for the purpose of VFR, health, religion and other were estimated to account for about a quarter of all arrivals globally.

5 These data should however be treated with some caution, as the category used is 'Visiting friends and relatives, health, religion, other' and some countries report a statistically significant figure under 'other', making the summary result unreliable.

Figure 4.18 Arrivals by purpose of visiting friends and relatives (VFR), health, religion and other (× 1000)

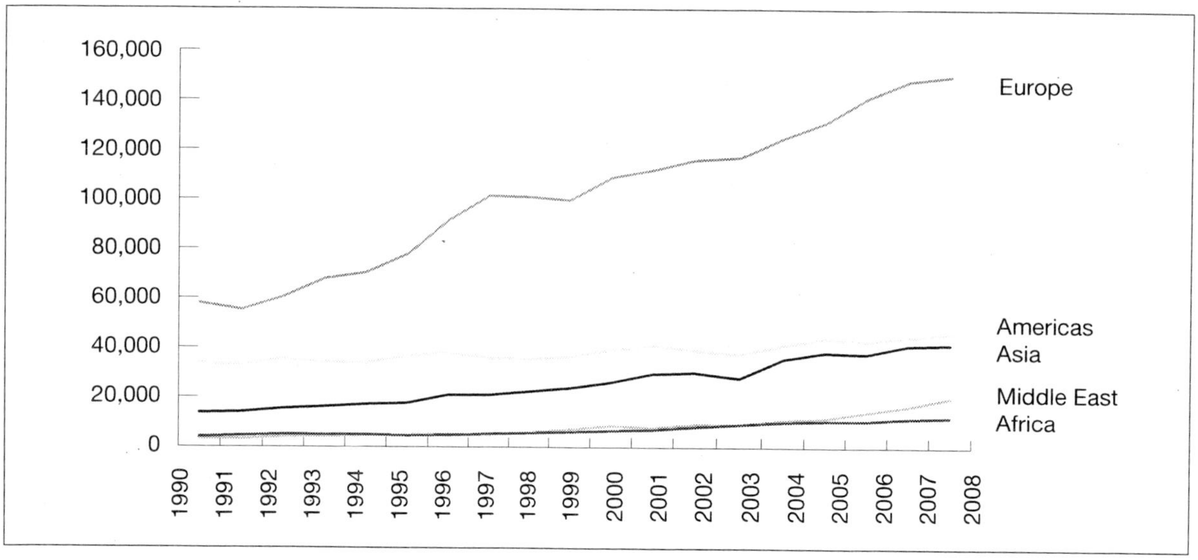

Source: World Tourism Organization (UNWTO).

Figure 4.19 International tourist arrivals by purpose of visit, 2008 (%)

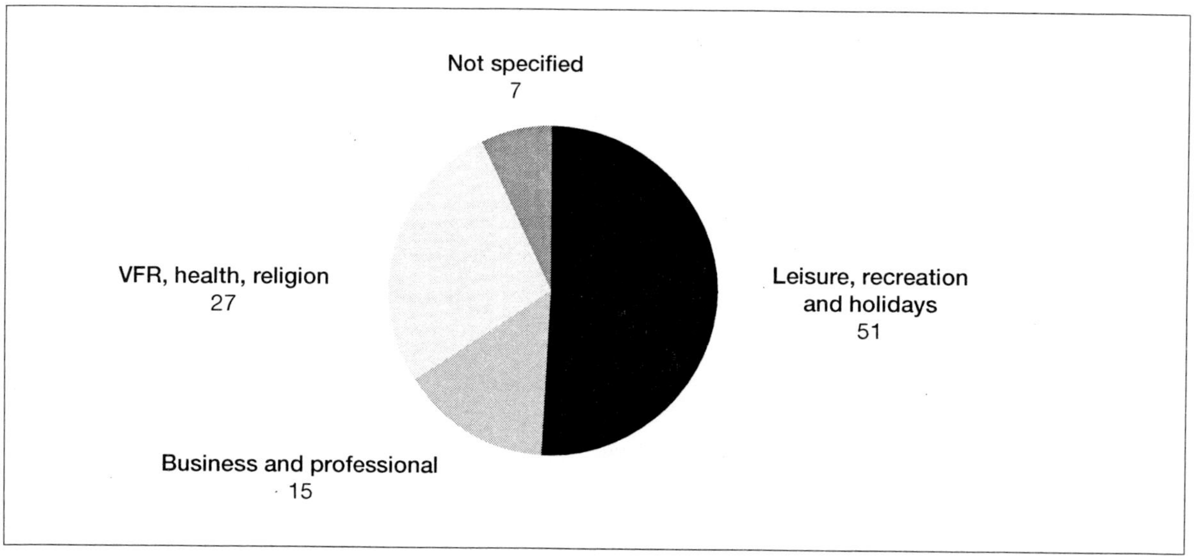

Source: World Tourism Organization (UNWTO), *Tourism Highlights, 2009 Edition.*

With families dispersed around the world, some tourism companies are seeing a significant opportunity in holidays that unite families in a convenient location – not necessarily one where any family member lives.

As Richard Bowden-Doyle, the Managing Director of @Beyond, a luxury safari lodge operator observed when interviewed for this project:

> *"More and more families are scattered around the world. A lot more of them see holidays as a way of bringing the family back together again. They come in to our lodges from Singapore and the United States of America and so on. We are seeing enough of this for it to be a notable part of our business."*

Summary of key location and migration trends

Population location

- The population of western developed nations will decline as a proportion of the total world population.
- The population of the Americas will remain stable as a proportion of the world total.
- Europe's will fall and Asia will gradually increase.
- The proportion of the world's population living in urban areas rather than rural areas is growing steadily and is forecast to increase to 2030.
- The future rate of growth of urbanisation is very different by country.

Migration

- In the recent past global levels of migration have remained stable, with migrants accounting for around 3% of global population between 1990 and 2005.
- However, if that rate were to remain constant, given the forecast growth in the world population there would be 42 million extra migrants in 2030 than today.
- Europe has seen a big increase in its migrant population from 4% in 1960 to 9% today. If this trend were to continue it would reach 12% by 2030.
- The United States of America has the largest number of the world's immigrants.

Chapter 5

Demographic Change

The World population is set to increase at a steady rate from just above 5 billion in 1990 to just over 8 billion in 2030. This is a result of several factors, notably the extension of life expectancy across most of the globe (from 63.2 to 72.1 between 1990 and 2030). In terms of fertility there will be a significant drop over the period, however the world will remain above replacement level at 2.5, down from 3.5 in 1990. As usual female life expectancy will lead male, though the difference will be less dramatic globally than within some nations. Male life expectancy lagged 4 years behind female in 1990 (61.2 compared with 65.2). By 2030 this will have extended to four and a half years at 69.9 compared to female expectancy of 74.4. The world age profile shows a gradual ageing process over the period. The majority of the populace were under 40 in 1990; they will be under 65 in 2010 and under 85 in 2030. It is well known that the world shifted from being mostly rurally to mostly urban in the last decade. Over the course of our period the urban population will shift from just above 40% to just below 60%. If we look at the correspondence maps we can see how the various countries we have identified will progress in age terms over four decades under analysis, and how this progression rates in relation to the others.

Figure 5.1 World population and the continent fertility

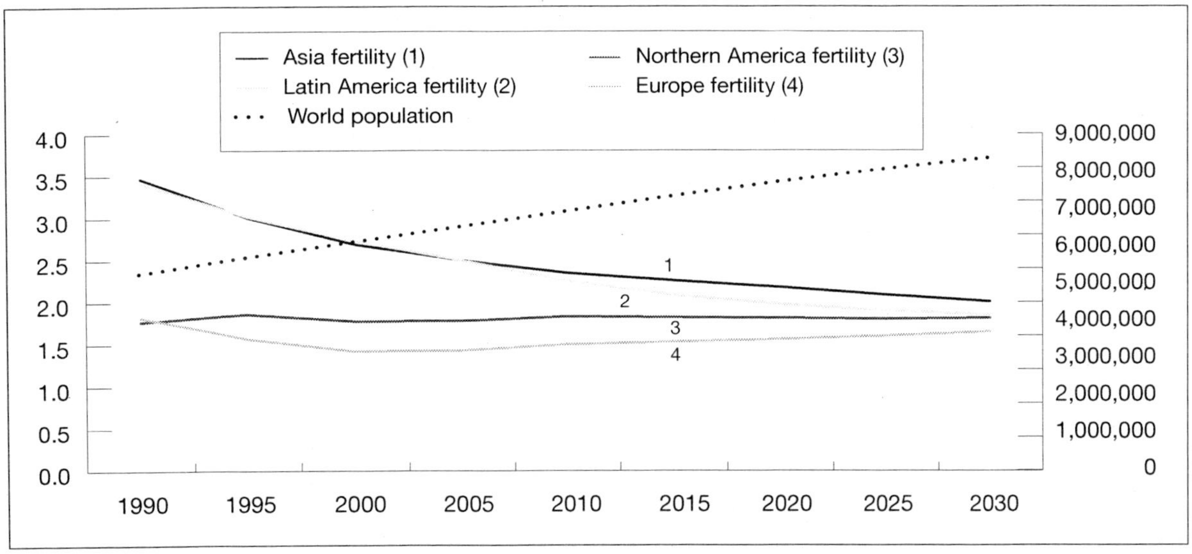

Source: Population Division of the Department of Economic and Social Affairs of the United Nations Secretariat, *World Population Prospects: The 2008 Revision*, 2009.

5.1 Regions

Continental patterns of fertility, ageing, life expectancy, urbanisation and gender disparity differ widely. However, as will be seen the differences within continents are often as stark as the difference between them. **Europe** however is probably the most coherent of all four continents when it comes to these factors. Europe displays an ageing population. This phenomenon is attributable to several different factors. Notable among them is the continent's low fertility when compared with places like Asia and Latin America. While it has recovered from a dramatic dip at the end of the last century, European fertility remains below replacement level (2.1 children per woman) and by 2030 it is expected to have levelled out at around 1.7 children per woman. This average disguises considerable differences however.

As Castles has pointed out, northern European nations like Norway and Sweden tend to have higher fertility than those of the South, despite having undergone a dramatic collapse in fertility earlier on in the 1960's and 70's. By contrast southern European nations, particularly those with a strong Catholic, patriarchal culture maintained higher fertility rates for longer following the growth of widely available female contraceptive technologies. Once their rates subsequently dropped they did so sharply and did not pick up in a similar manner to their northern European neighbours.[1] In terms of life expectancy, Europe has displayed a steady but slight increase which is set to continue for another two decades. Female life expectancy is set to reach 82.1 years up from 76.5 in 1990. Male life expectancy will reach 75.6 a gain of just over 6 years over the period, and the average will rise to 78.9 from 72.8. The graph of Europe's age structure displays a clear move to the right. Europe's proportion of the global population is set to decline significantly from 1990-2030 from 14% to around 9%. Europe has been predominantly urban for a considerable period; in 1990 it already stood at 70%, this is expected to increase to 78% by 2030. If we turn to the correspondence analysis of Europe's age we see it remains fairly uniform, most of the countries moving from a majority populace of around the middle in 1990, and moving to around the same point at the right of the chart 2030.

Figure 5.2 Europe's population and fertility

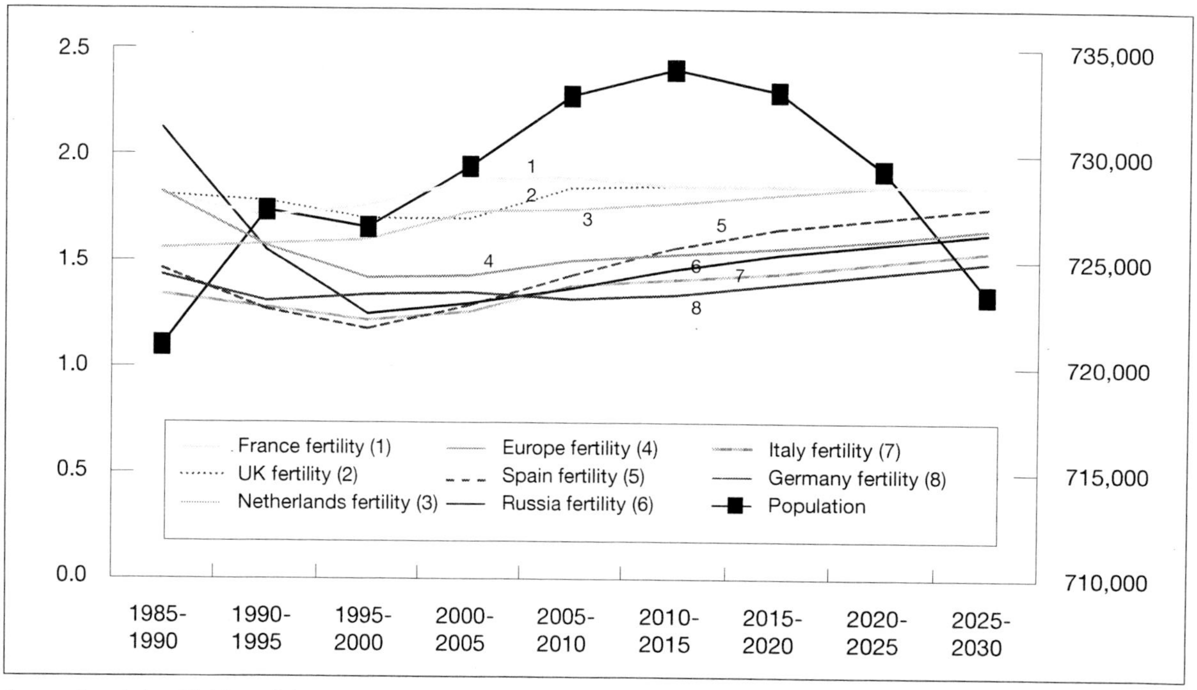

Source: Population Division of the Department of Economic and Social Affairs of the United Nations Secretariat, *World Population Prospects: The 2008 Revision*, 2009.

By contrast, **Asia** displays considerable intra-continental differences between developed and developing nations with regards to many demographic factors. Fertility is set to decline steadily from 3.47 children per woman in 1990 to 2.1 in 2030. While this is a steep decline it is notable that Asian fertility will not drop below replacement level during the time-period under review. Of course a smooth line in a graph conceals considerable differences between countries. China and India; the continent's two most populated nations display significantly divergent fertility models. China's population, though high is considered to be levelling off now whereas the point at which Indian fertility will stabilise continues to be pushed back by demographers and the total population of the country is projected to overtake China by 2050. Asian life expectancy is set to increase in line with global trends. In 1990 it stood at 62.7 years, with a low 2.5 year difference between male life expectancy (61.5) and female (64). However as the average life expectancy has increased, so male and female expectancy has become increasingly divergent. By 2030 the difference is set to reach a still relatively minor 4 years; with male expectancy standing at 71.6 and female at 75.7, the average will be 73.6. Asia's population is not projected to age to the degree that Europe's is. Throughout our period the majority of people in Asia will be under forty.

1 Castles, F. G. (2003), 'The World Turned Upside Down: Below Replacement Fertility, Changing Preferences and Family-Friendly Policy in 21 OECD Countries', *Journal of European Social Policy* (Online), vol. 13 (3), pp. 209-227.

Asia makes up a large portion of the global population (around 60%), mainly due to the size of India and China each of which amount to around 20%. Asia's shift from rural to urban has been one of the most dramatic trends of the last few decades. Between 1990 and 2030 the pattern of urban vs. rural habitation is set to shift from just 30% urban to almost 60%. Within this demographic shift the change in the profile of India and China are hugely significant. Both of these nations show a double-digit increase in their urban population, India's rising from 25% to just over 45% and China's moving from just under 30% to just fewer than 60%. A correspondence map for Asia reveals a clear disparity between the "developing" nations of India and China and post-industrial Japan. India still has a predominantly young population, Japan's populace begins in the middle of our graph and point and continues to move right eventually reaching the furthermost point of any country by 2030. China meanwhile falls roughly in the middle; a country with an ageing population and incipient pensions crises; it nonetheless remains just below the half-way mark in 2030.

Figure 5.3 Asia's population and fertility

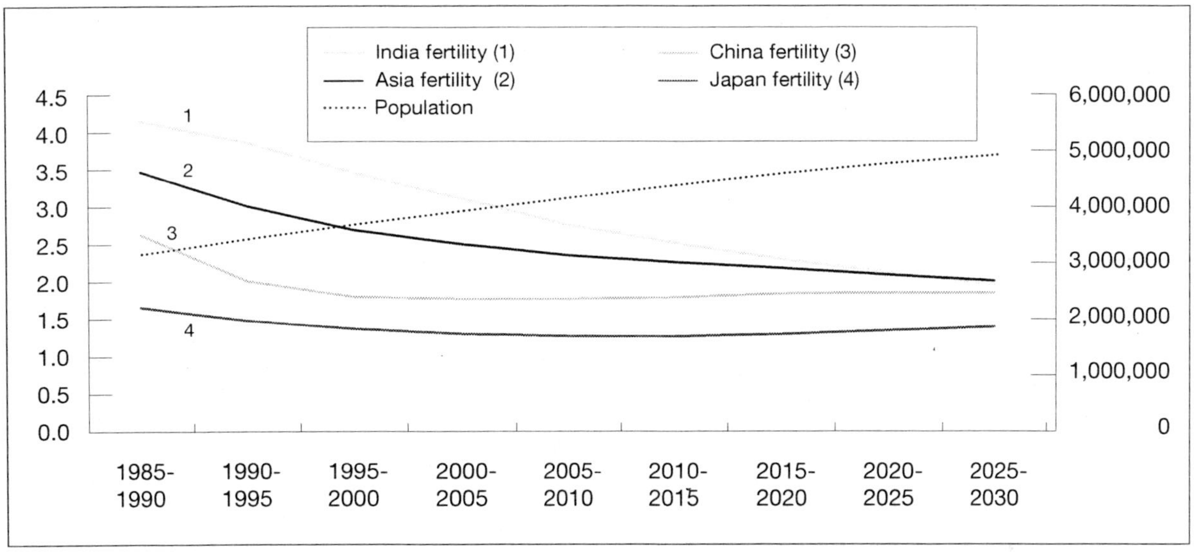

Source: Population Division of the Department of Economic and Social Affairs of the United Nations Secretariat, *World Population Prospects: The 2008 Revision*, 2009.

The fertility of the **Latin American and the Caribbean** region will follow a gentle curve from a high point of 3.5 children per woman in 1990 down to just about replacement level in 2030. This is a trend we have seen in Asia as well. In terms of life expectancy the region will witness a 10 year average increase over the 40 year period. Male and female expectancies have both increased at roughly the same rate and so will maintain the same level of divergence. Male expectancy is set to increase from 63.0 in 1990 to 74.3 in 2030, while female will increase to 80.4 from 70.5. Latin America and the Caribbean's population are projected to age over the period 1990-2030. However, the transition is set to be milder than that seen in Europe. A small majority of the population will be over 40 by 2030. This is a significant change from 1990, when the population graph shows a steep drop in numbers after the age of 25, a trend that is repeated in more moderate form in 2010. The region makes up around 9% of the world's population; at least a third of this is accounted for by Brazil alone, this will remain the case throughout the period 1990-2030. In terms of a rural to urban shift, the region has been urbanised for a significant period, but will become more so; going from 70% to over 85% between 1990 and 2030. This is a trend that is mirrored within Brazil's population trajectory.

Northern America (United States of America and Canada): a dramatic divergence in many demographic factors especially considering their similarity in levels of development. The fertility of northern America shows a violent peak then trough in fertility, this was then followed by a modest rise in the period 2025-2030 returning the level to 1.82. This pattern is a result of the significantly divergent fertility levels between the two nations. The age profile of the region is similar to that of Europe. Over the four decades under analysis the largest section of the population will progress from age 20-24 in 1990, to 45-49 in 2010 and finally reaching 65-69 in 2030. Life expectancy in the region, like in western Europe and in much of the rest of the world is set to increase over the period. The average will increase from 76 in 1990 to 82.25 in 2030. As with most regions, female expectancy will lead male, however this differential is projected to moderate significantly over the period. At the start of the period the difference between the two was 7 years standing at 79.4 and 72.6 respectively. By 2030 this gap will have shrunk to 4 years; 84.5 and 80.5. This pattern covers a significant difference between the two nations. As a study produced by the Institut National D'Etudes Démografiques revealed, intra-national differentials within the countries are far starker within the United States of America, where the poorest 20% is not only far worse off than the richest, but also far worse off than their equivalents in Canada or Europe.[2] The study also noted that life expectancy had improved at a faster rate over a similar period in Canada than in the United States of America. The northern Americans constitute about 6% of the global population, a figure that is projected to remain stable till 2030. This figure is largely due to the size of the United States, while Canada's contribution amounts to less than 1%. Northern American urban density, like Europe's, has been high for a prolonged period, it is projected to rise from just under 76% in 1990 to just under 86% in 2030. When we look at the correspondence analysis we can see the impact of the differences in life-expectancy and fertility within northern America. Canada's profile is considerably more elongated, covering a broader age-span than in the United States of America where the limits on gains in health and life-expectancy as well as higher fertility means the population is set to remain younger.

Figure 5.4 Americas' population and fertility

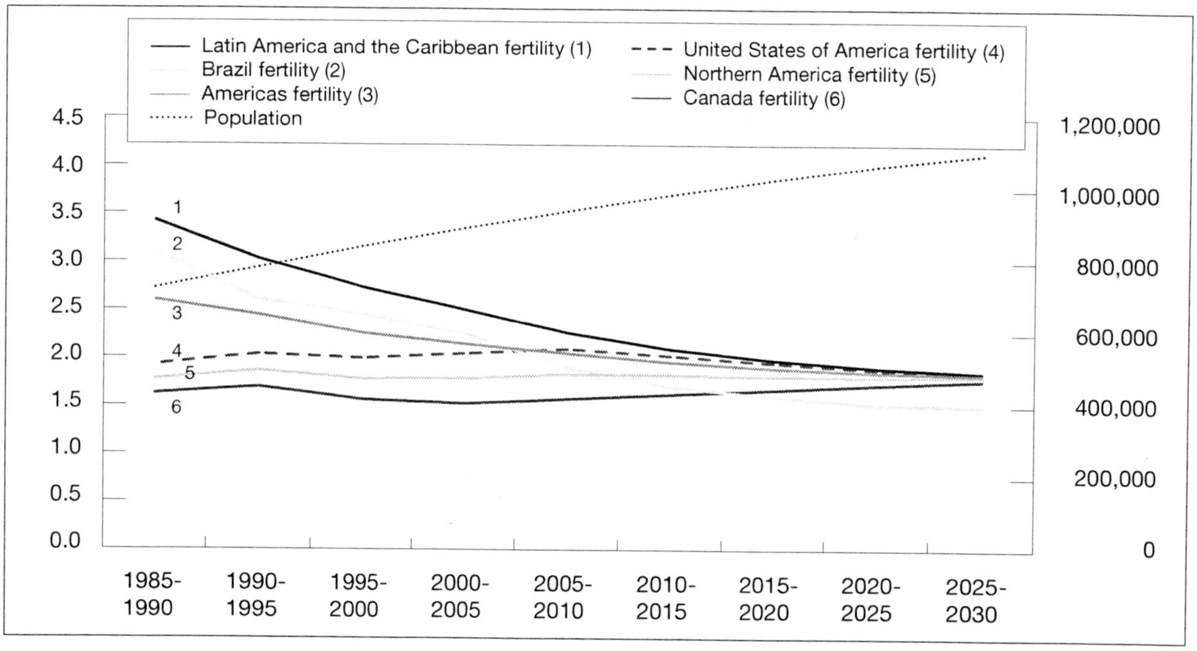

Source: Population Division of the Department of Economic and Social Affairs of the United Nations Secretariat, *World Population Prospects: The 2008 Revision*, 2009.

5.2 Countries by Region

5.2.1 Americas

The total fertility rate for **Brazil** will decline over the period eventually dropping well below replacement level. In 1990 it stood at 3.1 children per woman (still a considerable drop from the 6.15 in 1950) however the next five years saw a dramatic 0.5 drop to 2.6 in 1995. This decline will continue at a more modest pace for the rest of the period. Life expectancy is predicted to rise from 65.3 in 1985-1990 to 76.9 in 2025-2030. As usual however, this hides stark differences between male and female life

2 Institut National D'Etudes Démographiques (2008), 'Population and Societies', *Population Trends in the United States and Europe: Similarities and Differences*, no. 440.

expectancy. The difference between the two remained around eight years in women's favour from 1985-1990 until 2000-2005 at which point it reduced to seven years (going from 61.9/69.0 to 67.2/74.9). By the end of the period the difference is still seven years at 73.4 and 80.3 respectively. The ageing of the population seen in many European nations will not be such a significant factor for Brazil. In 1990 the largest sector of the Brazilian populace was in the younger end of the age spectrum; with the largest groups being under 14 years of age. Over the period to 2030 this moves towards the middle with the group aged 10-14 in 1990 remaining dominant in each subsequent decade. Despite this however the younger age groups remain well represented and the population graph displays a clear downward slope to the right (i.e. towards the older end of the spectrum. Therefore though the older population does increase in Brazil it does not have such a sizeable impact on overall demographic structure due the size of the younger population. The gender ratio of Brazil is set to become increasingly unequal over the course of our period. In 1990 it stood at 98.7 men per 100 women, however this declines rapidly by 1995 it has fallen to 98.2 and by the end of our period it fallen all the way to 95.5. If you look at Brazil's age progression (it's on the BRIC correspondence map) you will see that Brazil maintains a reasonably youthful population compared to the rest of the BRIC countries, even more so than China, it remains in the centre of the map along with the Russian Federation throughout the period.

In terms of fertility **Canada** also follows the pattern laid out in Europe, though it does differ from that in the United States of America. Canadian fertility has historically been low and certainly during the 4 or so decades under review, however it is projected to improve. Canadian fertility stood at 1.6 children per woman in 1990, plunging to a low of 1.45 in 1995-2000. After this it is projected to rise until reaching 1.85 (still well below replacement level) in 2030. Canadian life expectancy is set to follow the trend seen in most other countries, that of continual improvement. Like other developed nations the gap between male and female life expectancy is projected to narrow in Canada. In 1990 it stood at around seven years, 73.7 and 80.3 respectively. However, after 1995 the female rate of increase reduced slightly while the male increased bringing the two closer together. By 2030 male and female expectancies are set to be only 4 years apart standing at 81 and 85.3 respectively with a national average of 83.1. Canada's age profile is set to follow a similar path to that of Europe and the United States of America. As the period under analysis progresses the majority of the population will move from being under 25 in 1990, to being under 50 in 2010 and finally just under 70 in 2030. Looking at the age chart we see a similar lengthening of the graph lines indicating that the population's age range will spread out for most bands before dropping off quite steeply after the age of 74.

Fertility rose in the **United States of America** between 1985-1990 to two children per woman, before briefly slumping to 1.95 and rising again up to a peak of 2.5 children per woman in the time period 2005-2010. It is project to slump after this point hitting 1.85 by 2030. Life expectancy in the United States of America will rise though not as far as in other countries, the Institut National D'Etudes Démographiques attributes this to the average being dragged down by the considerable intra-national disparities in wealth and healthcare provision within the country.[3] The average expectancy in the United States of America will rise from 75 to 81.4. Female expectancy will go from 78.4 to 83.7 while male will increase significantly more, going from 71.5 to 79.1. The United States of America has an age profile which is fairly standard for western nations: Three Peaks each progressively older than the last. In 1990 the largest group was aged between 24 and 34, in 2010 this space was filled by the 44-54 age group, by 2030 the peak will have become so broad and shallow that it covers all the ages between 40 and 70. Fertility in the United States of America is higher than many other western countries however; largely as a result of the large scale migration to the country particularly from Latin America. In terms of urban population the United States of America, already predominantly urban will become more, though less than the United Kingdom, going from 74% to 86% urban between 1990 and 2030.

3 Institut National D'Etudes Démographiques (2008), 'Population and Societies', *Population Trends in the United States and Europe: Similarities and Differences*, no. 440.

5.2.2 Asia

China's fertility is set to level out, from a high point of above 2.5 children per woman in 1990 to just below 1.9 for the rest of the period. Life expectancy will rise steeply from an average of 67.4 in 1990 to an average of 76.6 in 2030. Over this period however, male and female expectancy is set to become increasingly divergent. In 1990 there was just less than three years difference between male and female life expectancy at 66 and 68.8. However by 2030 this will have extended to four years difference at 74.7 and 78.6. China's age profile is also set to follow the Three Peaks formula we have seen in Europe and the United States of America; however the transitions between these 'peaks' will be considerably more abrupt in China than elsewhere. At the start of our period the largest age group in China was considerably younger than in many other nations aged just 20-24. By 2010, this group had been replaced by those in the 40-44 bands, though another slightly smaller peak is still visible within the early 20-something. By 2030 this group will have been replaced by the 60-64 age groups, though once again we can see a slightly smaller secondary peak this time in the 40-44 age groups. The story of China's urbanisation has been one of the most dramatic of the last two decades. Between 1990 and 2030 China's urban population is projected to rocket from just under 30% to just under 60%.

India's fertility is set to decline over the period from a high point of above 4 children per woman in 1990 down to just below 2.5 in 2030 still above replacement level. Indian life expectancy is projected to improve from an average of just below 75 in 1990 to just above 82 in 2030. As usual female life expectancy is greater than male, going from 78.2 to 84.9 and 71.7 to 79.6 respectively. In line with much of Asia and the developing world, India's age profile displays a clear downward slope across the four decades between 1990 and 2030. At no point is the majority of the population projected to be older than 45. In 1990 the largest section of the population was below 15. In 2010 this group will have moved up and the largest section will be aged 20 and below. It should be noted that this will be a smaller group amounting to 10% of the population compared to the 14% in 1990. Finally in 2030 the peaks will have once again modified and the largest section of the populace will be aged 40 and below. India's level of urbanisation is set to increase dramatically by 2030, however it will remain a predominantly rural nation with just under 45% of the populace living in cities by the end of our period.

Japanese fertility has been low for some time and, it is projected to decline gently from just over 1.6 in 1990 to a low of 1.2 in 2010 before a gentle rise to 1.4 by 2030. Life expectancy in Japan is set to increase as in much of the world, however it will remain relatively divergent compared to other countries. The average life expectancy will increase from 78.5 to 85.3. As usual female life expectancy will remain longer than male going from 81.3 to 88.9 years and 75.5 to 81.7 years respectively. Notably, rather than moderating the difference between the two is set to increase over the period from around 6 years to just under 9 years. Japan's age profile is similar to western Europe's except that it shows a double-peak for each year. In 1990 the largest groups were in the 15-19 and the 40-44 age brackets. By 2010 these will have shifted to the 35-39 and the 60-64 brackets. Finally in 2030 the largest groups will be in the 55-59 and the 80-84 brackets (though this group will be notably smaller).

5.2.3 Europe

France saw a dramatic dip in fertility at the beginning of the period, followed by an equally dramatic upswing from a low of 1.7 to a 1.9 children per woman by 2005. This will subsequently level off to a steady 1.85 children per woman, a figure which remains unchanged till 2030. Life expectancy in France, as in much of the world is set to improve over the four decades being reviewed, though the relatively high starting point means that its progress will be more moderate than some other countries. Average life expectancy in France is projected to rise from 76 to 83.9 years. Once again female life expectancy will lead male throughout the period, though the difference will moderate from a stark eight years in 1990 (71.9 compared to 80.1) down to five years in 2030 (81 compared to 86.8). The age profile of France is similar to that of much of Europe, though the peaks are gentler in this case, covering a broader age range than is typical. In 1990, for instance the majority of the population was under 50, however it stretched from the 10-14 to the 40-44 age groups with little difference between them. This pattern continues, though the groups involved will become older; in 2010 the majority of the populace will be aged between 39 and 64. By 2030 this will have progressed to cover the ages 55-84, though there will be a gradual slope downwards from 6% of the population down to 4%.

Germany has relatively low fertility compared with places like France and the United States of America. After 1990 it dipped to a low of just over 1.3 children per woman, before rising again to 1.35. Between 2005 and 2010 it dipped again down to 1.3; it is projected to rise to a still modest 1.5 by 2030. German life-expectancy is projected to make a relatively sharp improvement from an already high level in 1990. At the start of the period average life expectancy in Germany was 75 years. This is projected to climb to 82 years in 2030. The typical divergence between male and female life expectancy is projected to remain at around a 6 year gap throughout the period with only very little movement downwards. At the beginning of the period male life expectancy stood at 71.7 years, while female was 78.2, by 2010 this gap had been moderated slightly to 77.8 years compared to 83.1, finally by 2030 it is projected to have been reduced to about 5 years, at 79.6 and 84.9 respectively. Compared to France, Germany displays a more conventional 'three-peaks' age profile. In the 1990's the majority of the population was within the 14-24 age group. By 2010 this will have shifted to the 35 to 50 age group and by 2030 the largest part of the population will be aged between 60 and 70.

Italian fertility during this period will remain quite low, starting at just under 1.4 it will raise from a year 2000 dip (1.2 children per woman) to reach around 1.6 children per woman in 2030. The average life expectancy in Italy will rise from a little above 75 years in 1990 to a little above 83 years in 2030. The age profile of Italy show a classic 'three-peaks' formation; in 1990 the largest segment of the population was aged 25 and under. In 2010 this peak had moved to the 35 to 45 age band, finally in 2030 the largest section of the population will be aged 59-70.

Though somewhat erratic, fertility in the **Netherlands** provides a good example of Castle's analysis of the history of European fertility. Beginning our period with a very low 1.55 children per woman, this is followed by a steep rise to 1.75 in 2000-2005, then a brief plateau before a steady rise to 1.85 (about the highest point that European fertility reaches in our period). Life expectancy in the Netherlands began the period, quite divergent for a developed European nation; the national average stood at 76.7 which would eventually rise to 82.4. Male and female expectancy in 1990 was separated by a gap of 6.4 years, at 73.5 and 79.9 respectively, however by 2030 this will have decreased to a 4 years at 80.2 and 84.2. The Netherlands' age profile follows that of most western nations, falling into the usual three-peaks. In 1990 the largest age group was the 15-24 year olds, by 2010 it will be the 45-54 year olds, and finally in 2030 it will be those aged 60-65.

Fertility in the **Russian Federation** dropped steeply in the early 1990's, however it is projected to steadily return to just below replacement level reaching 1.63 children per woman by 2030. Unlike the rest of Europe and much of the rest of the world Russian life expectancy is not predicted to grow very much in the coming decades. Between 1990 and 2010 it dipped significantly from 69 to 66 years. After this it is set to recover but by 2030 the average expectancy will still only be 71.6 years. As usual female life expectancy will lead male, but this time the difference will remain a stark 10 years; going from 73.6 vs. 63.8 in 1990 to 76.5 vs. 66.5 in 2030. Unsurprisingly, given these differentials, Russian Federation's gender ratio is heavily skewed in favour of women, a trend which exacerbates over our period; moving from 88 men per 100 women, to 84 men per hundred women in 2030. The age profile of the Russian Federation is erratic. At the beginning of our period the largest age group was the 25-34 group. Along with this group there were smaller sharper peaks in the groups aged 45-49 and 55-59 before a fairly steep decline after the age of 60. By 2010, and somewhat uniquely, this age profile has shifted backwards slightly; the first peak is now in the group aged 20-24 with another slightly smaller in the group 45-49 who made up one of the earlier peaks, aside from these groups no age cohort reaches the size of those we saw in 1990, and we see a steep decline after the age of 60. Finally in 2030 the population has significantly aged; the largest group is now aged 40-55 but after this there is a significantly smaller group aged 65-69 but after this the numbers decline steeply. The Russian Federation is set to decline as a proportion of the World's population, from 3% in 1990 to 1.5% in 2030. At the same time its urban percentage will increase from 73% to 77%. Looking at the BRIC correspondence map we can see that the Russian Federation maintains a balanced population, in age terms, remaining around the centre of the Map, though not as neatly as does Brazil.

Case study 6 Russian tourism in Turkey

Europe's population has declined relative to the rest of the world, and this trend has started to be matched to some extent in the financial sphere. As the BRIC (Brazil, the Russian Federation, India and China) nations, in particular have come to dominate in many resorts that previously moulded their offer to match western European preferences, they have now had to start adapting to new tastes, new cuisines and of course new languages.

The Turkish beach resort of Kemer by the Taurus Mountains provides an excellent example of a destination which has adapted its offer to emerging markets. The resort had previously been popular with German tourists attracted by the good weather, fine views and affordable price tag. However with the emergence of the Russian Federation as a major economic power and tourism source market Kemer has adapted its offer and is now primarily focused around attracting Russian tourists.

As a result of this change the staff employed in resorts have switched to speaking Russian from German, signs are now printed in Cyrillic script and the local nightclub now plays Russian pop music. Other changes, as might be expected, have included the types of food and drink on offer. Cheap flights are now available daily from the Russian Federation and the Ukraine. There are other attractions for Russian and Ukrainian tourists – not only are flights relatively cheap to Turkey but they can be issued visas at the airport on arrival. These kinds of adaptations have been taking place all over Turkey.

In **Spain** absolute fertility declined throughout the 1990's from 1.46 children per woman between 1985-1990 to a low of 1.18 between 1995 and 2000. However after this it began to pick up again and is set to reach 1.85 by 2030, still below replacement level. Life expectancy over this period follows a continual curve upward, with the female advantage in life-expectancy being moderated though never removed. In 1985-1990 the average total life expectancy stood at 76.6 years; however the difference between the two was a stark seven years (73.3-80.2 for men and women respectively). Throughout the time scale the difference remains high – dropping down to around six years after 2015, it reaches an average of 5 years by 2025. During this period the average total life expectancy will rise to 83.6, but as is clear this conceals considerable differences. The largest section of the populace throughout our period will be those that were aged 10-14 in 1990. One startling trend which is notable in all countries is the ageing of the population. To take an extreme example the over 100 years population is set to increase from 2000 in 1990 to 41,000 in 2030.

Fertility in the **United Kingdom** has historically been low since the 1970's, though it has recovered. It dipped once more between 1995 and 2000 when it fell from 1.8 to 1.65 children per woman. It is expected to return to 1.85 by 2030. Historically life-expectancy has been high in the United Kingdom; the average extending from 75 to 82 between 1990 and 2030. The gap between female and male life expectancy is projected to shrink over the period, from a little under six years: 72.3 years vs. 78 years in 1990 to 79.6 years vs. 84. The age profile of the United Kingdom, like much of Europe follows the three-peaks formation. In 1990 the largest group within the population was aged 44 and under, though after that there is a slow and steady decline unlike the steep drops we see in places like the Russian Federation. This pattern is repeated, though slightly with older age groups in 2010, and again in 2030. Predominantly urban for many years (like much of Europe) the United Kingdom is set to reach 92% urban population by 2030.

Chapter 6

Lifestyle and Tourism

Other issues not directly covered by the project brief become relevant when considered in the context of changing demographics. Examples include attitudes to, and usage of, technology, environmental concerns and the degree of an internationalist outlook. If younger or older people have different views on these then their importance may become more or less as the demographic profile of the world or regions change.

But we start with one of the major drivers of value and behavioural change, increasing affluence across the globe.

6.1 Increased Prosperity and Attitudes towards Work, Leisure and Travel

As incomes rise in most countries in the world, both developed and developing, so people's values, aspirations, motivations and behaviour do too. Generally, this applies to all demographic groups whether they are older tourists or young singles or families. Apart from making more products and services affordable, it also changes people's attitude to work, leisure and the relationship between the two.

So, across the world – through changes in legislation and individual preference – there has generally been a reduction in working hours and greater free time that can be spent on leisure, travel, and personal development. An increase in leisure preferences can be seen not only in western Europe, where there has been a strong decline in average working hours since the 1970s, but also in the United States (where working hours have yet to fall on a long-term basis but there is evidence of them starting to do so in response to the current recession) as well as in Latin America and South Asia. The continuing decline of working hours is likely to provide substantial support to the growth of the worldwide tourism industry, in particular in regions such as the United States and East Asia where existing average work hours remain high by international comparison.

According to the OECD, the Republic of Korea has the longest working hours of the countries it covers at 2316 per employee per year (down from 2876 in 1980). The United States meanwhile has 1794, down from 1810. France is typical of a European country at 1573 (down from 1842 in 1980).

Figure 6.1 Proportion of the public who agree that 'reducing the importance of work in our lives would be a good thing' (%)

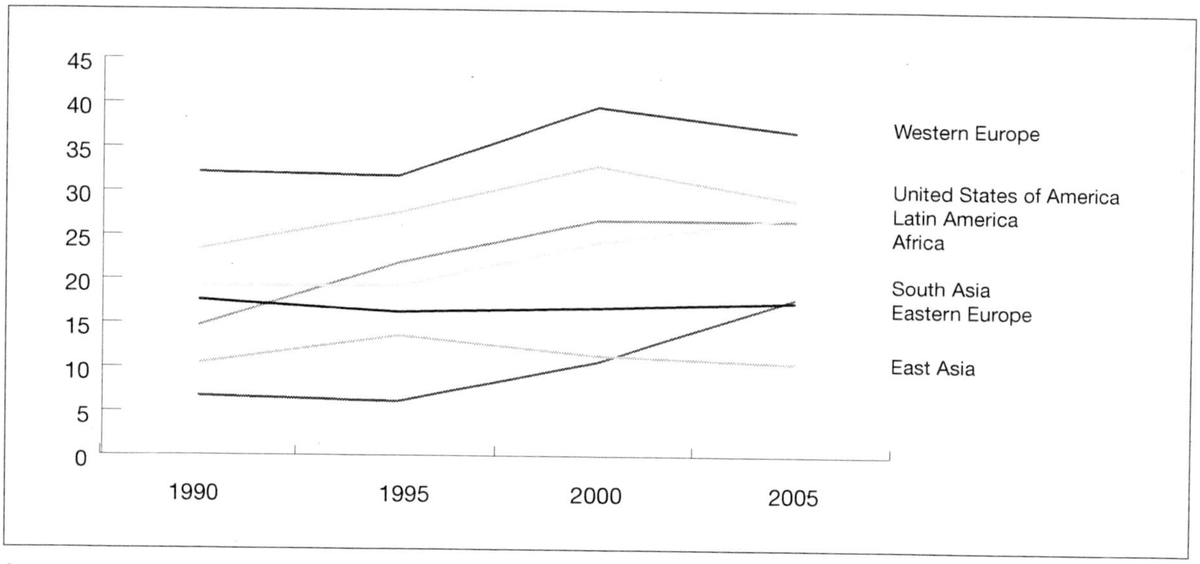

Source: World Values Survey.

Economic development is a major factor in encouraging this transition, such that a growing 'leisure society' can be expected to develop in coming years in the emerging economies of Asia, eastern Europe, and Latin America. This association is clearly illustrated by the strong cross-sectional relationship between income per capita and attitudes to leisure (see charts, below).

Figure 6.2 Importance of leisure in life by GDP per capita: Proportion saying leisure is important in life

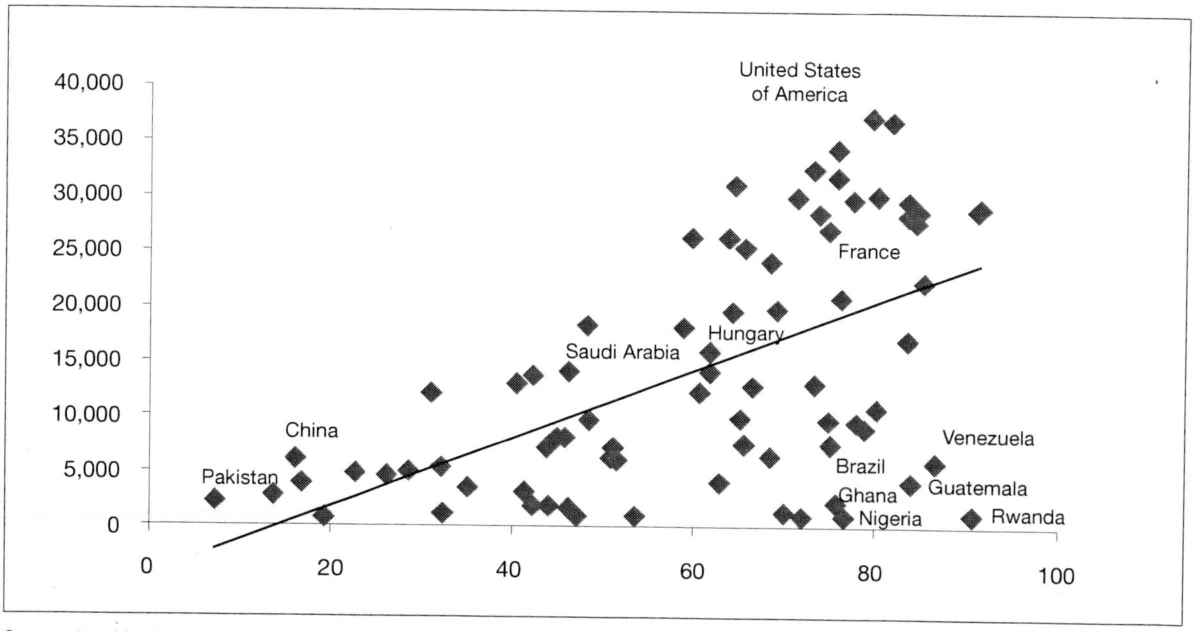

Source: World Values Survey.

But, the impact in increases in prosperity is not a straight line effect. Beyond a certain level people may continue to be better off and may well behave to that effect but may not necessarily feel so. Thus, research shows that there has been little change over the last twenty years in people's satisfaction with their financial situation. Responses to questions on satisfaction with household finances suggest many consumers in western societies remain dissatisfied by the state of their household finances, in particular in the United States (see chart) where median incomes have stagnated in the new millennium despite rising healthcare and fuel costs. Further pressures on household finances due to weak employment and credit constraints may further encourage growth towards the lower end of the tourism market in future years.

Figure 6.3 How satisfied with financial situation (1 = completely dissatisfied; 10 = completely satisfied)

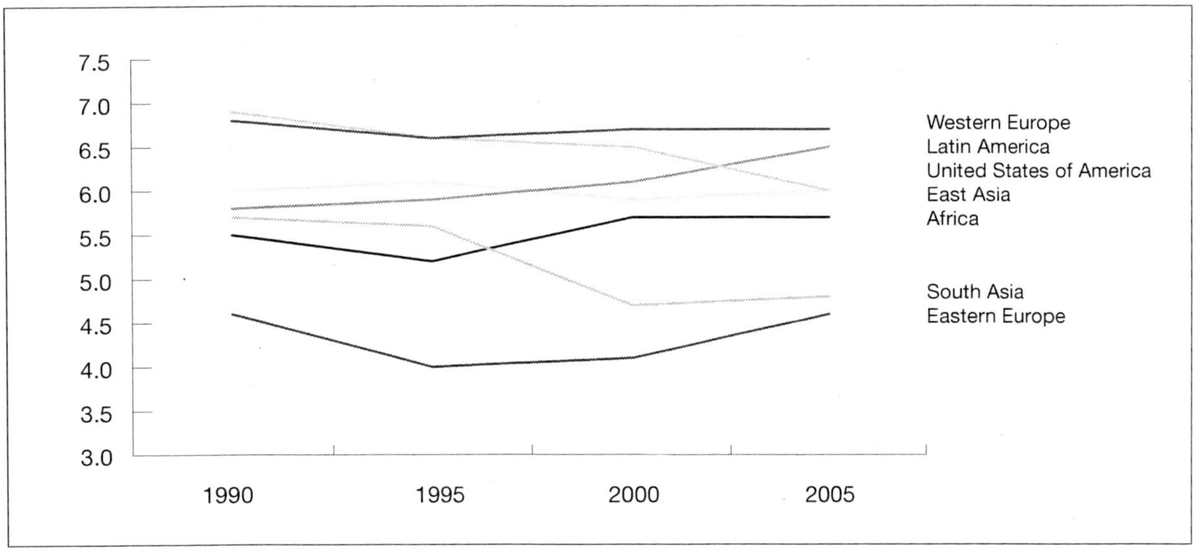

Source: World Values Survey.

Related to this is the growing feeling of time pressure as time, not money, becomes the constraint on what people can do. So, although (on average) there is more leisure time and greater affluence there is a continued feeling of pressure.

This balancing between time and money is a critical issue for the tourism industry. The key now may be to endeavour to provide 'value for time'. This can be done by providing more efficient delivery of services to the traveller – transfer and check-in times, for example – and maximisation (and perhaps intensification) of any activities that are embarked upon. It could also include a further increase in the demand for short (and again perhaps intensive) breaks which have already grown partly as a result of this phenomenon.

Of course, the current recession (at the time of writing) in many parts of the world has hardened the money and time-money value equations in people's minds. Hence it may be that the main areas of tourist market growth in future years may include substantial growth in the budget tourism and weekend breaks over the near term. Add to this the fact that a lot of growth in the world tourist market over the next twenty years will be originating from developing countries in Asia and that should provide growth in the budget too but also the traditional sightseeing categories.

Of course, within this overall picture, higher end tourism will still be in demand from affluent households. However, even within more affluent households there is likely to be a 'mix' of holiday types that will include budget elements on some occasion.

Case Study 7 Low-end tourism market

Over the last two decades people in the developed world came to expect at least one foreign holiday a year. In response to this appetite, a range of low-end or budget travel options sprung up to provide cheap, and therefore frequent travel, which cut costs by cutting 'unnecessary' frills like free meals. In Europe, airlines such as Ryanair, Vueling and Wizzair have already established themselves in the market providing this low-end air-travel for tourists on a budget. Now part of the developing world has also begun to follow this trend. In recent years, the rapid expansion of the Asian middle class has seen the growth of low-cost air lines in countries such as India and Malaysia providing cheap flights often over relatively short distances around the continent, though also from Europe.

In 2007, Richard Branson, owner of Virgin Atlantic Airlines announced his entry into this segment with his purchase of a share in Kuala Lumpur based Fly Asian Express. The move prompted speculation that the company could float on the market, valued at around US$ 1 billion.

Recession inspired cost-cutting has already seen Britons moving outside of Europe to places where the exchange rate is more favourable; and this will only encourage the trend which has seen a host of low-cost carriers such as Phuket Air, One-Two Go, Nok Air and Thai Air Asia from Thailand, as well as Tiger Airlines, Valueair and Jetstar from Singapore and Jet Airways and Kingfisher Airlines from India.

6.2 Values and Attitudes

Values and attitudes are changing in a range of ways – almost too many to describe here. So, we concentrate on four areas where there is (or potentially is) a major demographic difference across age groups. These are: the growth of more internationalist and cosmopolitan attitudes; ethical issues (and related to that environmental concerns, covered separately); and an increasing sense of adventure and willingness to try things.

6.2.1 The Rise of the Cosmopolitan Internationalist

In addition to economic development, the globalisation of social networks, whether through multinational companies, higher education, or international civil society, can be expected to drive further growth of tourism and travel. Evidence of this trend can be found in the recent World Values Surveys, which indicate a rising proportion of individuals viewing themselves as global citizens and increasing numbers involved in international civic networks, for example through humanitarian organisations concerned with international development or global human rights (see section 6.2.3).

Leading this more cosmopolitan and international outlook are younger generations. For example, they are more interested in solving many of the world's problems. Figure 6.4 for example, shows that, in general, successive generations are more likely to be concerned about this issue (in this case world poverty).

Figure 6.4 Across the world: young are more internationalist than the elderly

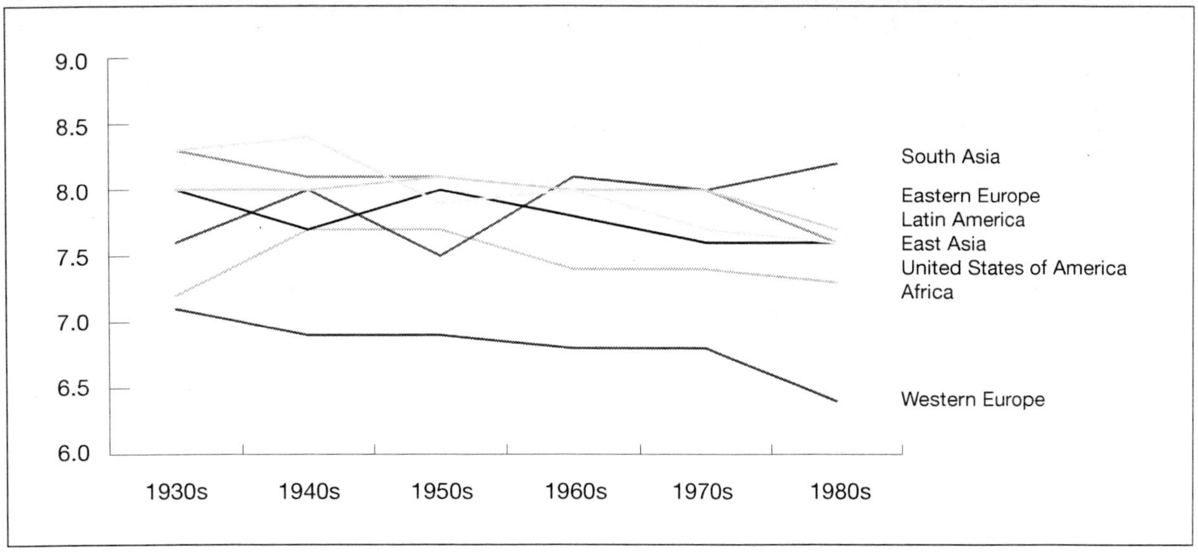

Note: Figures are by generational age cohort (respondents born in 1930s, 1940s, 1950s, 1960s, 1970s and 1980s).
Top priority: To solve poverty in the world versus deal with own country first – a lower score = world poverty more important.

Source: World Values Survey.

There is not consistency across the world however with two important trends being identified. These could be termed 'the rise of global Asia' and indications of the 'retreat' of 'global America'. Evidence for the emergence of a new 'global Asia' can be found in the responses of younger East Asians. East Asians register higher responses than the peoples of any other region with the youngest cohort having the highest. This may reflect the growing tendency of East Asians to study abroad in foreign universities, have family members based in several continents, and work for leading multinational companies with operations spread across Asia, Europe and the United States.

By contrast, 'global America' is in retreat. Younger Americans are less likely than older generations of Americans to say that they trust the peoples of other countries; they are also less likely to identify as global citizens, indeed are less likely to offer this description of themselves than the youth of any other region anywhere in the world. The difficulty of American workers in adapting to global competition and the response to September 11th may both play a role in this recent trend.

Figure 6.5 Young East Asians are the most likely to see themselves as global citizens*, young Americans least so

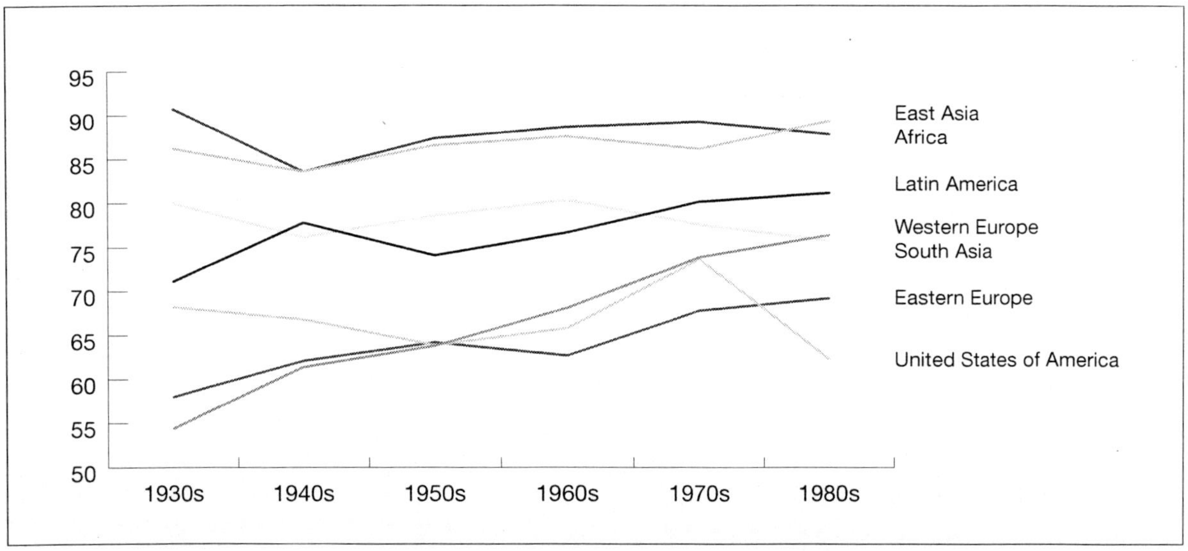

* When asked regarding their attachment to local, national, or supranational units of identity.

Source: World Values Survey.

6.2.2 Ethical Concerns

Heavily linked with this increasingly international outlook is the growth in ethical concerns with younger generations again exhibiting slightly more cosmopolitan attitudes than their elders, for example in their greater support for foreign aid. (Such attitudes are particularly prevalent in western Europe, suggesting that Europeans may continue to be an important contributor to outbound travel in the twenty-first century, as they have been in the late twentieth.)

However, there is also some evidence of a general trend over time to increasing engagement with international development issues, affecting those of all ages. A demographic breakdown of membership of organisations concerned with development and human rights for 2005 shows all age groups are well represented, and not simply younger age cohorts. This suggests that any development benefits associated with increasing tourism will help to encourage further tourism. Furthermore, this would generate important positive stories about the contribution of tourism to global sustainability to help counteract the negative ones associated with air travel.

Figure 6.6 Support for increasing level of foreign aid (%)

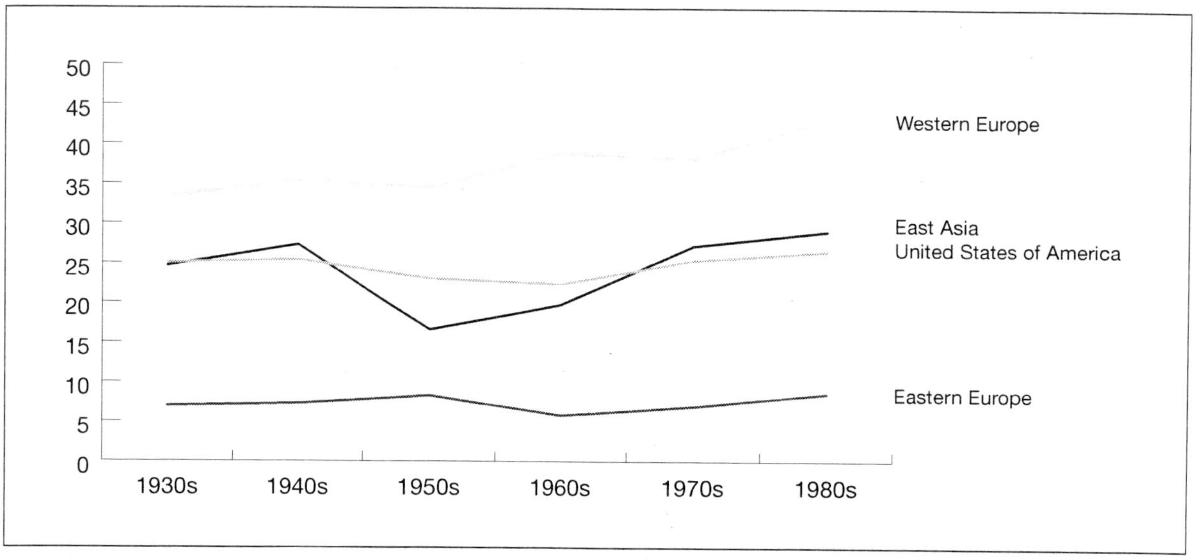

Note: Percent agreeing would be willing to pay higher taxes for increased foreign aid.
Source: World Values Survey.

Figure 6.7 Membership of organisations concerned with international development or human rights is demographically balanced (%)

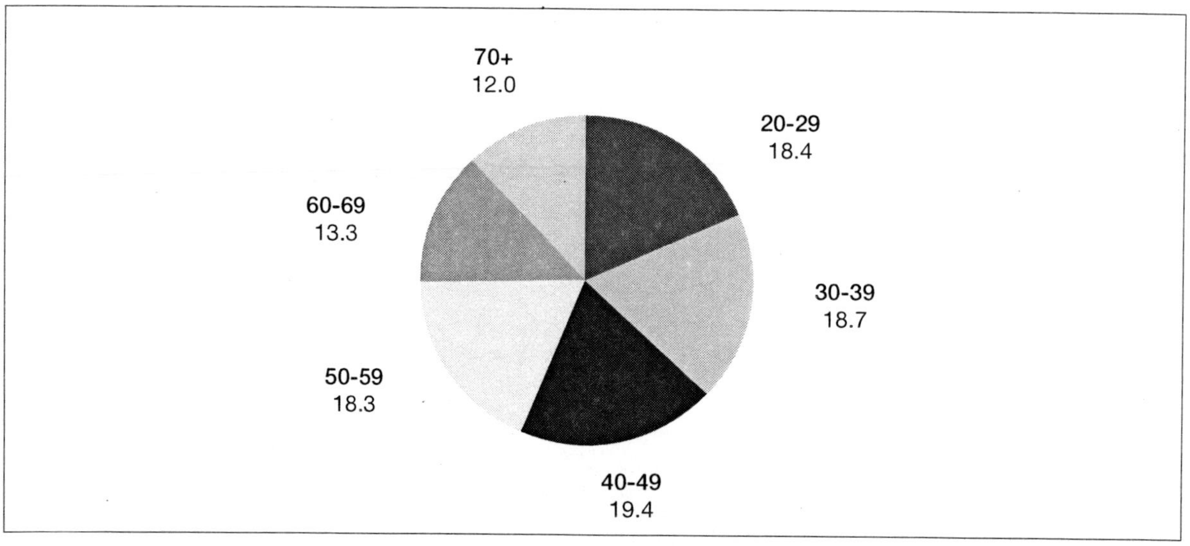

Source: World Values Survey.

6.2.3 Environmental Issues

Concern about the environment has grown significantly as is well known and particularly among the younger population. There is a cohort effect here so people who have grown up over the last ten years are more concerned about environmental issues. This suggests that green factors will be important for those up to, say, 50 years old by 2030. So destinations and companies attempting to appeal to such age groups need to take account of this.

Attitudes to the environment also pattern the nature of tourist activities, with the growth for example of ecotourism, which aims to reduce to a minimum the impact of tourist activities on the natural habitat. Data from the World Values Survey show a rising degree of environmental conscientiousness, as evinced, for example, through the engagement of respondents in organisations concerned with environmental issues.

Across the world, membership of environmental organisations has risen in every region since 1995 except for the United States, which has seen a slight fall; and the sharpest rise has been seen in East Asia. As a result, it is estimated that membership of environmental movements across Europe, the Americas, and East Asia has risen from 1.3 billion to 1.4 billion over the decade.

Figure 6.8 Membership of the global environmental movement is disproportionately weighted to the young (%)

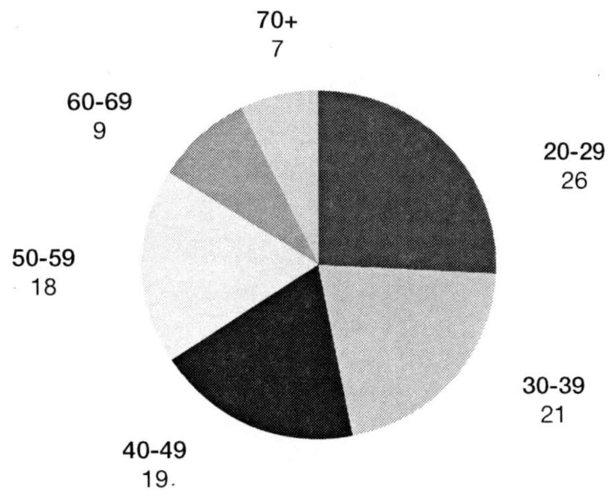

Source: World Values Survey.

Consistent with the view of a recent trend toward environmental activism, data also show that membership of the environmental movement is disproportionately heavy among the young: indeed, those aged 20-29 constitute over a quarter of the membership of such groups. Unlike the example of attitudes to risk and excitement, it seems plausible that a 'cohort effect' will exist when it comes to attitudes to the environment and sustainability. That is, a presumption that today's younger age groups who are more concerned about the environment will maintain this level of concern as they age.

Case Study 8 Kapawi Lodge Ecuador

As awareness and concern for environmental issues has spread through much of the globe, often in conjunction with the desire for a more unique less 'packaged' holiday experience, a niche in the travel market has sprung up that combines both these trends.

Eco-tourism obviously trades on the environmentally responsible aspect of its offer. However, it often combines this with an appeal to the individualist traveller who wishes for experiences that are unavailable to the mainstream, and is willing to pay a premium to get them.

One such example is the Kapawi Lodge which is staffed and owned by the Achuar tribe, and is situated in the middle of the Ecuadorian Amazon twenty days' walk from the nearest town. Visitors to the lodge are provided with accommodation and food, as well as opportunities to learn about the ecology and wildlife of the Amazonian jungle. The money brought in by these tourists not only goes to supporting the Achuar in their daily life, but it supports their campaign to prevent millions of acres of Amazon from being exploited by oil and logging companies who potentially have rights to the region.

The Kapawi Lodge therefore provides a perfect example of the trends in experience led, ecotourism that are likely to increase in the coming years as habitats such as the Amazon increasingly come under threat and a wider variety of tourists seek to differentiate their holiday experiences. The lodge is not only a break from the more conventional comfort based holiday packages but it provides the opportunity for travellers to support their ecological concerns via their consumption choices. So far the Kapawi Lodge has received numerous prizes including Second Prize in the Sustainable Award for Conservation in 2004, the Ecotourism Awards in 1998, and in 2009 was designated one of the top 50 Ecolodges in the world by the editors of National Geographic Adventure Magazine.

However, against this trend toward greater environmental activism, among ordinary consumers the surveys since 1990 also show that the imperative to protect the environment has become tempered by a desire to save money, with consumers steadily less willing to agree that they would 'give part of their income' to help 'protect the environment'. This is a potentially key issue for tourism where many parts of the industry seek to charge more for environmentally friendly products and services. In the future there must be a question mark over whether this can endure – especially where consumers increasingly understand that some environmental measures actually save money for the businesses in question.

This countertrend has been strongest in the United States, where household financial satisfaction has deteriorated most rapidly as shown earlier, but has also affected eastern Europe and Latin America. On the other hand, East and South Asians remain willing to contribute to protect the environment, a response that may in part be determined by the very visible environmental challenges (poor air and water quality, pollution) affecting daily life in these regions.

Figure 6.9 Declining willingness to 'give part of one's income' to protect the environment (%)

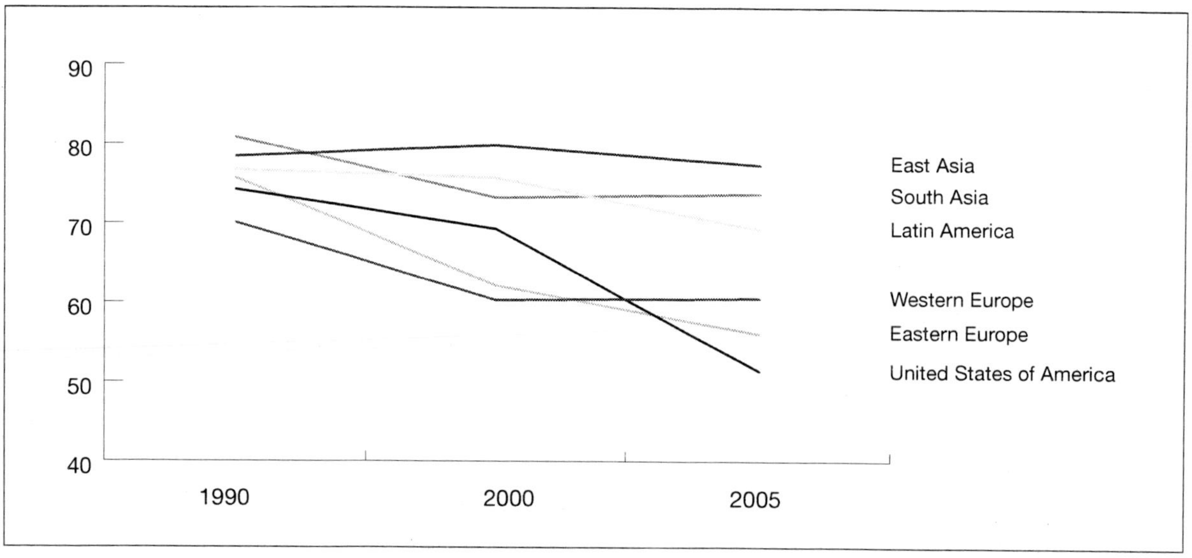

Source: World Values Survey.

6.2.4 A More Adventurous Outlook

Generally there has been an increase in developed countries towards what might be called 'adventure tourism'. Not surprisingly, this is particularly prevalent among younger travellers. An ageing population may well slow down this trend.

Data from the World Values surveys also allow speculation on the sub-sectoral growth of different aspects of the tourism market. For example, while adventure tourism has grown as a tourism category in the last decade due to the increase of younger travellers from western Europe, the increasing importance of new Asian tourists may encourage further growth in future years around traditional tourism segments such as sightseeing and hiking. The assumption here is that attitudes to risk and excitement are subject to an age effect (rather than a cohort effect). That is to say, people's attitudes to risk will change as they get older and, in this regard, older people of the future will be as risk averse as older people today.

There are also significantly different attitudes to risk and excitement by region. In response to a question in the recent values surveys, for example, which asked whether 'adventure and taking risks' and 'to have an exciting life' were part of their personality, East Asians of all ages were far less likely than other peoples to respond in the affirmative.

Figures 6.10 Across the world, the young are more favourable to adventure (%)

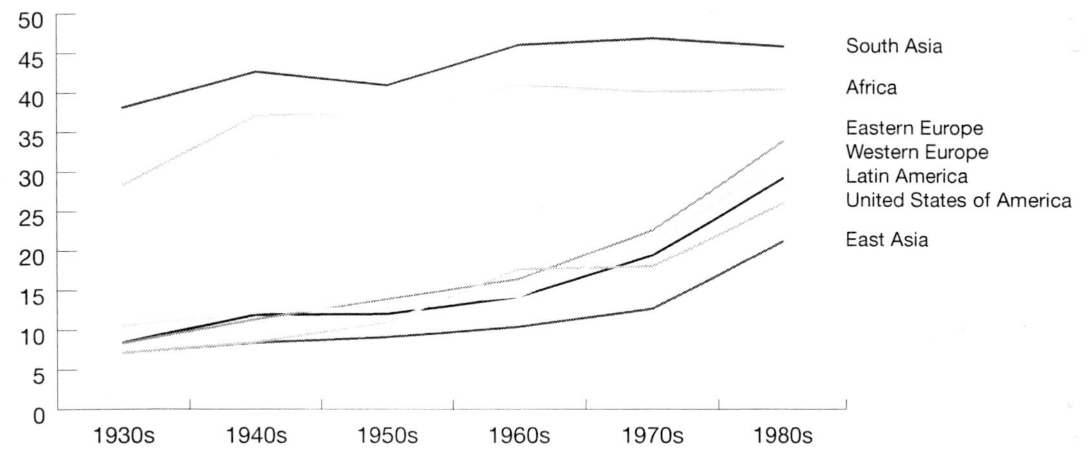

Note: Figures are by generational age cohort (respondents born in 1930s, 1940s, 1950s, 1960s, 1970s and 1980s).
Source: World Values Survey.

6.3 Technology

The growing access to technology is one of the main factors in driving awareness of other countries and other cultures and hence an interest in travel and tourism. It is also important within the tourism industry itself, of course, as a communication and sales medium as people use the internet to research for ideas, search for offers or even purchase services.

Across the globe, internet access is growing particularly in developing countries. Between 2005 and 2007 penetration (as measured by internet connections per 100 people) nearly doubled in places like China and (albeit from a very small base) India. Already higher in Brazil, it increased 65% to 35 connections per 100.

Figure 6.11 Internet penetration (number of connections per 100 people)

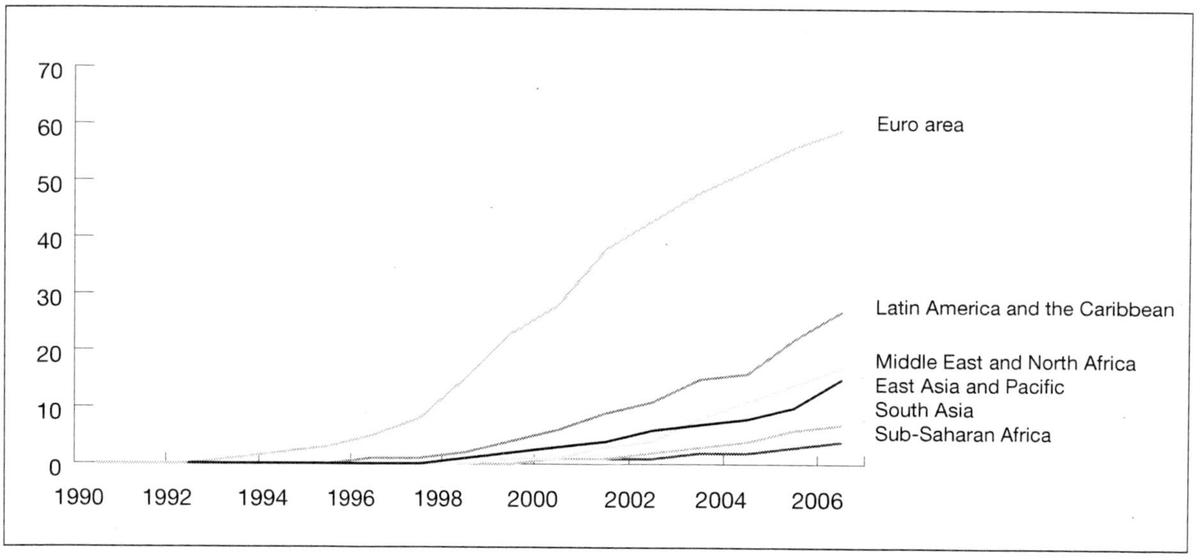

Source: World Bank.

As important, and perhaps more so, is the movement to mobile internet. This is particularly so in developing countries where people are switching straight to mobile and by-passing fixed line connections.

Figure 6.12 Mobile phone penetration (number of mobiles per 100 people)

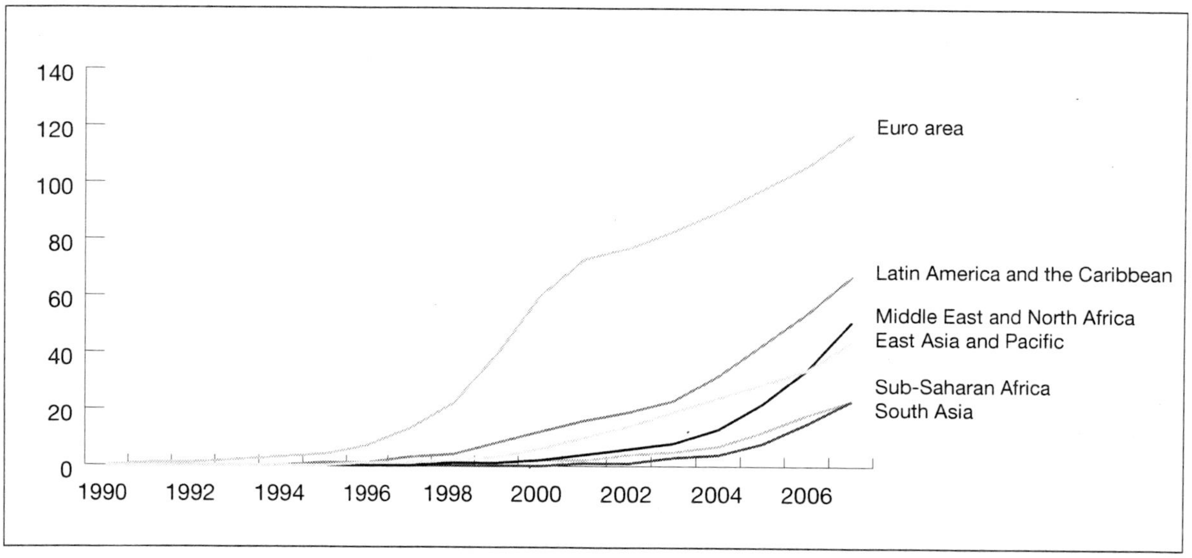

Source: World Bank.

This is important not just because the internet will become increasingly important as a sales and marketing medium as the numbers with access to it grow but also because of the demographic distribution of usage. Not surprisingly, younger people are much more likely to frequently use a personal computer (figure 6.13). As these people take their technology skills with them as they age, so online activity will become ever more important for travel and tourism.

Figure 6.13 Proportion of the population using a personal computer 'frequently' (%)

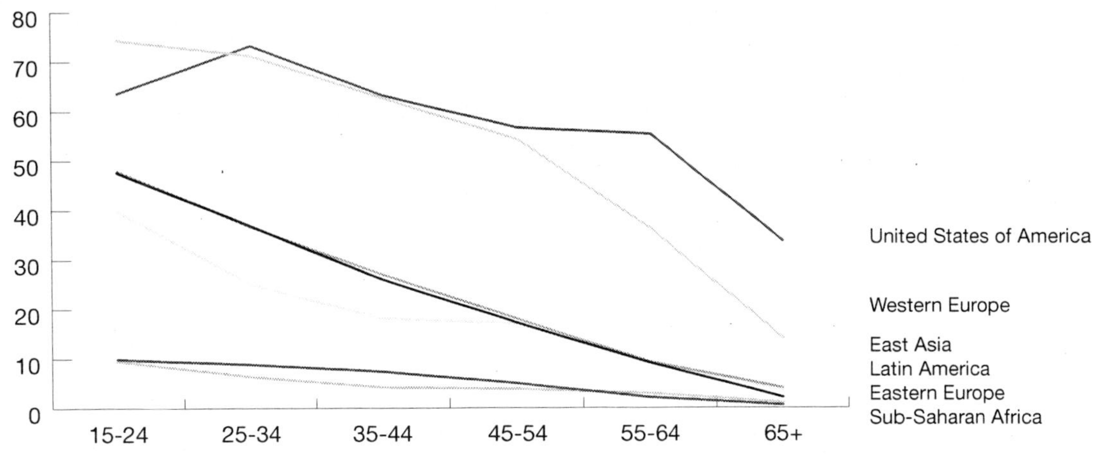

Source: World Values Survey.

6.4 The Fragmentation of Tastes

Taken together, the factors mentioned above (increased prosperity, growing interest in leisure and the consequent time versus money debate. An increasing internationalist outlook, a more adventurous attitude – and related to internationalism increasing cultural curiosity, ethical and environmental concerns and greater access to technology) are all in their own way leading to a growing fragmentation of tastes.

This growing variation in consumer tastes and interests is already a clear trend in developed nations, and is starting to emerge in developing ones too as such countries get richer, leisure time increases, offers get more creative and as globalisation (and the media) expose people to other ideas and possible ways to use their time. While not strictly a demographic trend there are demographic aspects as we have shown in this section. And it is very relevant to the types of holidays people take and the groups they go in. This includes sporting holidays (ranging from those hooked on skiing to those who have become expert climbers, kayakers or scuba divers); educational holidays (learning about Romanesque church architecture – and in the process visiting them – or studying oil or watercolour painting, for example); and cultural holidays (like wine tasting or theatre going or visiting art galleries). While this is already a minority interest it is growing steadily in developed nations and could well become important over time for tourists from other countries, although note the point made earlier about visitors from places like India or China having potentially more 'conservative' tastes in destinations and activities.

> *"Asian tourists (Chinese and Indian particularly) might wanting slightly different types of tourism because they are relatively new, almost they would be more like the tourism world was 20 or 30 years ago in the developed world. [They are] going to the more conventional sites and packages."*
>
> Professor Ralf Buckley,
> *Director, International Centre for Ecotourism Research, Griffith University, Australia*

For marketing and communications it is important to recognise that in the future there will be an ever-growing set of tourism needs and aspirations and new segments (or 'tribes') that need to be catered for.

Summary of key lifestyle trends

- The appeal of increased leisure time will remain strong in developed markets and will grow in developing markets, resulting in more time available for tourism and travel.
- In the longer term emerging markets like Asia will become 'leisure societies' like those in the West.
- However, people in general, and in established markets particularly, do not **feel** wealthier. This sense of financial constraint will sustain an increased interest in budget travel (even, occasionally among affluent travellers).
- People also feel an increased sense of time pressure (despite in many cases having more leisure time). This puts an increased focus on the 'value for time' offered by travel and tourism.
- The trend towards increased globalisation will boost tourism, as people are increasingly 'international' and 'cosmopolitan' in their outlook. This is true in emerging markets as well as developed ones (the United States of America may be a slight, temporary exception here as a reaction to 9/11).
- We expect to see increasing concern about ethical issues in future as younger people tend to be more concerned about issues such as global poverty and more supportive of foreign aid.
- Similarly, there will be increased concern about the environmental and sustainability in future, as today's younger consumers who are more concerned about these issues, form a bigger proportion of the tourist market.
- The ageing of the population and the growth of inexperienced tourists from emerging markets may boost traditional tourism activities and limit the growth of some of the more extreme aspects of adventure tourism.
- In emerging, as well as developed markets, access to information technology is now a key driver of awareness of other countries and their tourism offers.
- All of these developments, in combination, suggest an increasing fragmentation of tastes, in both developed and emerging markets.

Chapter 7

Summary and the Implications for Tourism

The analysis has shown that there are major changes and challenges presented by the demographic developments the World faces over the next twenty years. Fundamentally, these involve population growth and age structure change driven by differential fertility rates and vastly improved health care. Alongside this, and related to it, are global movements of people – either from rural to urban environments within countries or migration related between countries. Finally, there are important changes in values, attitudes and lifestyles which are directly affected by some of these demographic changes. Some of the implications of these for tourism are considered below.

7.1 Population and Ageing

Broadly speaking, the trends point to two developments in future tourism related to population and age structure. The first is the rise in tourism from the ends of the age spectrum. The second is the rise of Asian and developing-world tourism more generally. These two factors interrelate in the following manner. While populations across the world are growing, and growing older, this is predominantly a feature of the developed world's demography, though it is also increasingly significant in China. This means that tourism will increasingly have to take account of the needs and preferences of older travellers. This will necessarily impact upon accommodation offers, travel arrangements, the organisation of tours and cruises and timing of offers – for instance some moves away from the links to school summer holidays will be possible.

While Europe and the developed world is rapidly ageing – fuelled by the trends discussed earlier – the developing world has maintained a far more youthful population. In addition it has taken up a proportionately greater portion of the world's populace. It is, therefore, an increasingly important market for world tourism. The impacts of this are complicated but broadly they will include the need for an adjustment in holiday packages to cater for travellers from more traditional or conservative cultures, less interested in the hedonistic packages, with more focus on history and culture than has been prominent in much of recent European and western tourism. There may also have to be a reorganisation to take account of the preponderance of groups of young Asian and South American couples, given the tendency of people from these cultures to marry younger than has become the custom in Europe and northern America. Similarly the rise of the global South in tourism terms will have an impact on the timing of infrastructural factors such as flights from countries of origin.

The other important thing to remember about any older tourists is that they are likely to be fitter and younger looking in outlook.

The implications for travel and tourism include:

- The current market in developed countries is ageing and an increased amount of attention should be given to the needs of older tourists from these source markets (see also section on life expectancy).
- Tourists from developing countries are likely to be younger with very distinctive needs from the older tourists from more traditional source markets.
- This could force a stark choice for tourism destinations in their marketing, communications and product development. Do you choose to attract older or younger tourists? Or try to attract both and run the risk of not satisfying either segment?

- Within resorts in particular, balancing the needs and wants of different age cohorts from different cultures could be a source of competitive advantage (see also section below on changing family structures).
- This also presents a challenge for marketing and communications within tourism, which must address the needs of younger less experienced tourists in developing markets and the needs of experienced tourists in developed markets.
- For the transport and accommodation, the tension between designing products and services for older and younger tourists may not be so stark. Design that takes into account the needs of older tourists (for example providing greater ease of use) might simply come to be seen as examples of good design for all.
- There may be a radical challenge in current assumptions about the implications of ageing for tourism needs and wants. For example, we may see younger tourists who are still working full time looking for time to relax on holiday, whilst older tourists who generally have more time on their hands go on holiday to try new activities.

7.2 Life Expectancy

Life expectancy is extending across the world. In developing countries this is driven (as it was in developing countries in the last century) by reductions in infant mortality. In developed countries it is progress in countering infectious diseases and later life illnesses (like cancer) that is prolonging life. It can be assumed that the developing countries will move in this direction over the next 20 years. Of course, increased life expectancy is one of the two major factors altering both the size and the age structure of the global population but it has some impacts in its own right. So, the implications for travel and tourism include:

- Increased life expectancy will mean there are larger numbers of older tourists from existing markets in developed countries. The needs of these consumers may be many such as the need for proximity to medical care (this is important given the forecast increase in conditions such as obesity and allergies in future).
- Fortunately, developments in telemedicine should help facilitate travel and tourism for older (and younger) tourists with chronic medical conditions – but access to reliable information and communications technology will be expected by these tourists in future.
- Today, older consumers are much less likely to have access to the internet and use the latest mobile communications devices.
- Within the next 10 years this will change radically, with more technology literate older consumers looking for technology to enhance every aspect of the tourism experience from research to purchase, to the actual experience and on-going relationship with tourism providers.
- Older tourists will have a 'younger' outlook than previous generations of older tourists and may well be more adventurous wanting to try new things.
- Despite this, greater numbers of these older tourists will have minor disabilities (such as difficulties climbing stairs etc). Both the accommodation and transport sectors of the industry need to take account of this in terms of design and staff training.
- Older tourists (at least when they are not looking after their grand children!) will have greater freedom than younger adults to travel outside of school holidays. This could help change the traditional seasonality of some vacations.
- Increased longevity should increase the period over which people are active travellers and tourists. Potentially, this increases the return on effective marketing techniques (especially customer

relationship management programmes) that capture tourists at an early age and maximise the 'life time value' of the relationship. For example, we may need to see more lateral thinking in terms of industry staples like loyalty programmes (such as loyalty schemes that operate across sectors, or even 'country' loyalty schemes).

- Finally, 'life stage' and recent key 'life events' could become more important as indicators of the needs and wants of tourists, rather than just age along. As people live longer, and are exposed to a range of social changes (such as divorce, second families, more access to education, career changes – see section 7.3 below), so the life course becomes less 'linear'. In these circumstances, segmentations based on age will be less useful indicator of the likely needs of a tourist than those based on life stage or most recent significant life event.

7.3 Household Composition and Family Structures

The impact of longer lives and reducing fertility is significant. First, family structures become longer, yet leaner – they move from more 'horizontal' with fewer generations to more 'vertical' structures with more generations. Potentially this can affect family dynamics (greater intergenerational interaction) and travel parties themselves (more multi-generational ones). Add to this other social changes such as increases in divorce in some parts of the world or a longer (and in some instances new) period of singledom and new travel groupings emerge. Changes in life-stages and more family transitional stages suggest a potential increase in singles tourism, added to by the still growing young adult markets of Asia and Brazil. This might include more gap year travellers. Equally, there may well be more inter-generational travel groups (grandparents and grandchildren) and multi-generational family groups.

The implications for travel and tourism include:

- Overall, as households and families become more diverse – more multi-generational, more singles, more 'second' families and so on – the whole of the tourism sector will have to respond to this diversity.
- Marketing and communications will have to address new needs and wants that result from these emerging family and household structures. For example, communications will have to demonstrate an understanding of the diverse needs of those travelling in multi-generation parties.
- Multi-generation parties are also likely to face a more complex array of options and choices when booking their holidays. The best communications and marketing will help to intelligently 'edit' this choice on behalf of the consumer.
- New, attractive segments also emerge for marketers in the tourism sector as a result of increased diversity (for example the style and design conscious gay market that tend to have relatively high disposable incomes).
- Transportation could respond by providing new ticketing packages (the three generations 'family ticket') and new services to support the needs of divorced and single parents.
- Accommodation providers also need to respond to this new demographic diversity through more flexible accommodation (especially adjoining rooms designed for the needs of three generations).
- Accommodation pricing might also seek to tap into (rather than alienate) the growing singles markets. This might involve more attractive pricing for single people or improved childcare and babysitting for single parents in hotels and resorts.
- Multi generation and diverse party sizes will also put an increased emphasis on staff training where the focus must be on anticipating needs and increasing cultural sensitivity to new groups of travellers.

- A key challenge for those providing services for both multi-generation and singles travellers alike will be to understand when their customers need formal entertainment (within or outside their group) and when they wish to have some quiet time alone (away from the group and/or family).
- Single tourists may welcome the sensitive introduction of opportunities to participate in groups, whilst those travelling in large groups will appreciate the opportunity to spend some time alone.
- The growth of the singles market suggests strong opportunities for educational and 'interest-based' tourism, as these offers tend to provide 'safe' and reassuring environments for single tourists.

7.4 Population Location

There are two aspects of population location that are important: the increasing proportion of the world's citizens that reside in the developing countries and, conversely, the decreasing proportion in Europe in particular; and second the global shift from rural to urban communities.

The implications for travel and tourism include:

- The changing distribution of the population across the globe (along with changes in the economic centre of power) will see an increase in the importance of Asian tourists to the European market.
- This requires all elements of the industry to be sensitive to the cultural and religious needs of these tourists.
- The growth of the urban population is a positive development for tourism, as data suggest that urban dwellers have a greater propensity to travel than those living in rural areas.
- Among urban dwellers in developed markets the experience of urban life might create a demand for rural tourism experiences (for a change of scene and a change of pace).
- For these groups we envisage a strong appeal for tourism products that offer a 'back to nature' element (perhaps experiences on farms that put tourists in touch with the realities of food and drink production).
- There could also be a market for urban-rural house swaps.
- However, it seems likely that urban dwellers in emerging markets will still be more likely to visit cities and to indulge in more traditional site seeing and shopping as they travel in to Europe for the first time. But as we, know as tourists become more experienced they are likely to seek a greater diversity of experiences.

7.5 Migration

The other critical aspect of population location is the impact of globalisation on the travel of people between countries and continents. Migration has been around for much of the world's history but seems to have accelerated somewhat in the last 40 years as the globalisation agenda has progressed. Some regions are particularly affected. Those experiencing significant and increased inflows include the United States, the Middle East and Europe. Much of this impacts on tourism either because workers are relocating to work in the tourist industry or because having relatives of friends in other countries promotes visits to them (VFR).

Finally, there is a long-term nature to this with the growth, and the history, of immigration being a potentially important factor in maintaining visits to friends and relatives or nostalgic 'visiting roots' travels.

The implications for travel and tourism include:

- In the recent past migration into Europe has increased significantly. This looks set to continue, as migration does within parts of Europe.
- This will give a strong boost to the VFR and migration led tourism markets.
- These tourists will have a diverse set of needs depending on their circumstances. Most economic migrants will be relatively poor and dependent on low cost forms of travel such as budget airlines or coach travel.
- However, there will be a significant minority of relatively wealth migrants (and their families) working in the great financial centres of Europe or whose children are located in Europe for their education. These tourists will have very different needs and may use premium travel options and stay in premium accommodation.
- Migrants within Europe will become an increasing source of labour for the European tourism industry.
- An increase potential for family reunions.
- It will be important to stress non-accommodation services and facilities as in many cases VFR tourists will use private accommodation.

7.6 Other Issues

There are a number of other factors related to demographics which are also important. For example, younger Asians are more cosmopolitan than their elders and than those in many other parts of the world. That, together with rising discretionary spending is forecast to rise in coming decades as Asian economies shift from an export-led growth model to one driven by domestic consumption suggest a growing importance of such consumers in tourism markets. But note that as consumption preferences among Asian consumers are more conservative than among western consumers, this may drive continued growth in the traditional (historical, sightseeing, hiking) segment of the market.

Survey data show no sign of any retrenchment in the trend toward a more 'leisure-oriented' society, with strong proportions of the public across many societies continuing to favour reductions in average working hours and greater time for personal leisure activities. The current global economic crisis may provide an opportunity for a steady increase in leisure time, in particular in economies such as the United States where working hours remain high, workers are favourable to working hours' reductions, and companies face problems of structural overcapacity. This would parallel the experience of Japan in the 1990s, which saw sharp reductions in working hours as companies responded to an economic slump by offering employees free time in exchange for wage freezes and cutbacks. With an increase in average leisure time, consumers will have greater flexibility to engage in international travel and tourism activities.

But, modern day consumers have ethical and environmental concerns that cannot be ignored. While temporarily halted to some extent by the current recession, this is a long running trend that will, certainly at the margins, have a continued impact going forward.

And because it is so age-related, new technology will too. Younger people, that is tomorrow's consumers, are much more likely to use (or indeed demand) internet, mobile and interactive solutions and communications. As these cohorts age and as technology penetration increase, particularly in the developing world where usage currently can still be very low, the idea of not embracing technology for communications and service provision will be unacceptable.

All of these factors add to the growing fragmentation of tastes which will require more differentiated and sophisticated solutions.

The implications for travel and tourism include:

- The attractions of leisure, tourism and travel remain strong. Tourism and holidays will remain a high priority for consumers in developed markets and will increase as a priority for consumers in emerging markets.
- Though having more leisure time, people will not necessarily feel wealthier. This sense of financial constraint should boost demand for budget travel and tourism (even among some affluent consumers, some of the time).
- As will the faster growth of tourism in less affluent and less experienced emerging markets will not only boost budget travel but also more traditional tourism activities (like sightseeing and shopping).
- People feel an increased sense of time pressure and time constraint. This means that tourism has to offer 'value for time'. This goes for the whole process of purchase, transportation (quick check-in and transfer) and the maximisation of time use whilst on holiday (offering the right balance of activities and relaxation to maximise the 'benefit' of the experience).
- Given that younger consumers are more concerned about international development issues and global poverty, the tourism industry should do all it can to communicate the development benefits of tourism.
- Further, any tourism offer that is seen to be in anyway unethical (exploitative of local people and environments) is likely to be more severely rejected by consumers in future than is currently the case.
- Linked to this, environmental issues and concerns will play a greater role in consumer decision making in future.
- Meeting minimum environmental standards will be an expectation, and will not necessarily be a long term source of competitive advantage for businesses operating in travel and tourism.
- Further, concern about the environment does not necessarily translate into a willingness to pay a premium price for environmentally friendly products and services. The ability to charge a premium for 'green' tourism offers may diminish in future.
- The overall ageing of the population may limit the growth of some of the more extreme aspects of adventure tourism in the future.
- The effective use of the internet and mobile technologies will be increasingly important to the success of tourism offers in future. These technologies are particularly embraced and most enthusiastically used by today's young consumers. In future, they will expect to be able to use these technologies to make their tourism purchases more efficient and to enhance their tourism experiences.
- Finally, all of these factors combined, suggest an increasing fragmentation of tastes and markets in future. This trend is already well established in developed markets, but it will also spread to emerging markets as they become more prosperous. This will make accurate segmentation and accurately targeted marketing and communications even more important (and ever more challenging!).

Chapter 8

Data

8.1 Global Demographic Trends

Table 8.1 World population (× 1000)

Year	World population
1990	5,290,452
1995	5,713,073
2000	6,115,367
2005	6,512,276
2010	6,908,688
2015	7,302,186
2020	7,674,833
2025	8,011,533
2030	8,308,895

Source: Population Division of the Department of Economic and Social Affairs of the United Nations Secretariat, *World Population Prospects: The 2008 Revision*, 2009.

Figure 8.1 World fertility

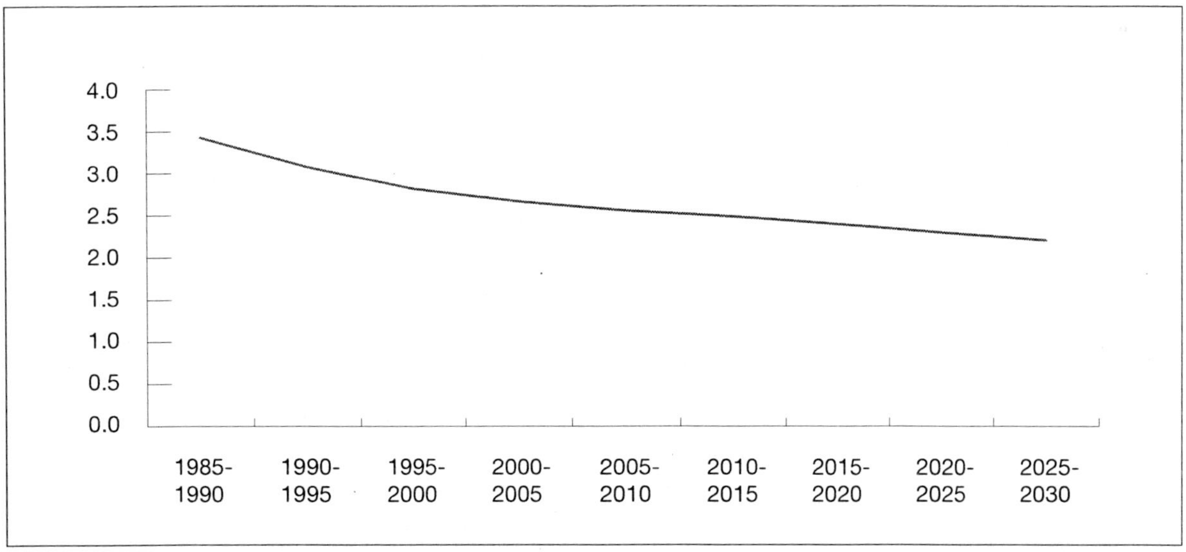

Source: Population Division of the Department of Economic and Social Affairs of the United Nations Secretariat, *World Population Prospects: The 2008 Revision*, 2009.

Table 8.2 World life expectancy (years)

Year	All	Male	Female
1985-1990	63.2	61.2	65.2
1990-1995	64.0	61.9	66.2
1995-2000	65.2	63.0	67.4
2000-2005	66.4	64.2	68.6
2005-2010	67.6	65.4	69.8
2010-2015	68.9	66.7	71.1
2015-2020	70.1	67.9	72.3
2020-2025	71.1	68.9	73.4
2025-2030	72.1	69.9	74.4

Source: Population Division of the Department of Economic and Social Affairs of the United Nations Secretariat, *World Population Prospects: The 2008 Revision*, 2009.

Figure 8.2 World population by age band (%)

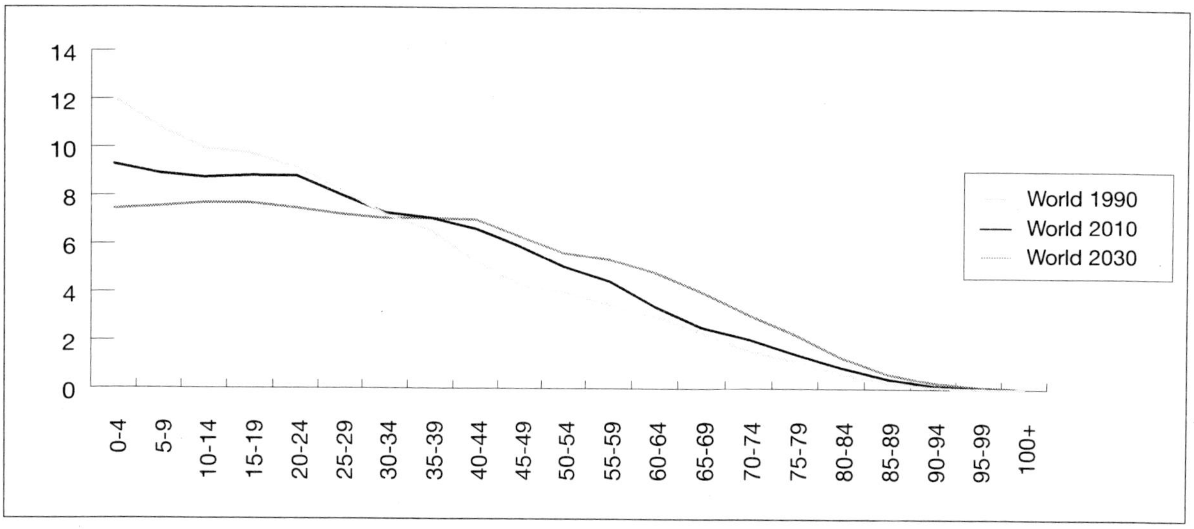

Source: Population Division of the Department of Economic and Social Affairs of the United Nations Secretariat, *World Population Prospects: The 2008 Revision*, 2009.

Figure 8.3 World population by gender (males per hundred females)

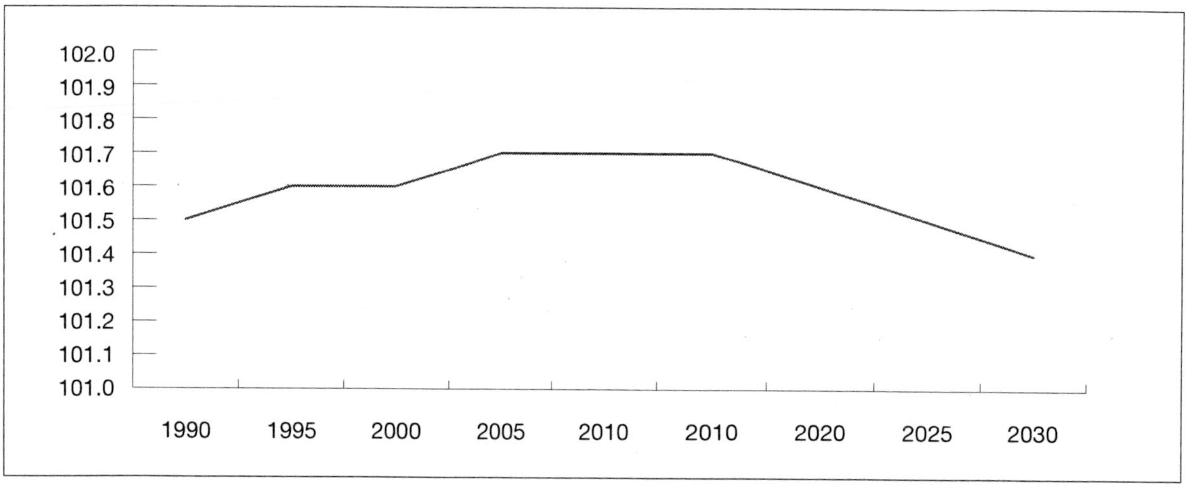

Source: Population Division of the Department of Economic and Social Affairs of the United Nations Secretariat, *World Population Prospects: The 2008 Revision*, 2009.

Table 8.3 World urban population (%)

Year	Urban population
1990	43
1995	45
2000	47
2005	49
2010	51
2015	53
2020	55
2025	57
2030	60

Source: Population Division of the Department of Economic and Social Affairs of the United Nations Secretariat, *World Population Prospects: The 2008 Revision*, 2009.

Figure 8.4 Age correspondence map: world

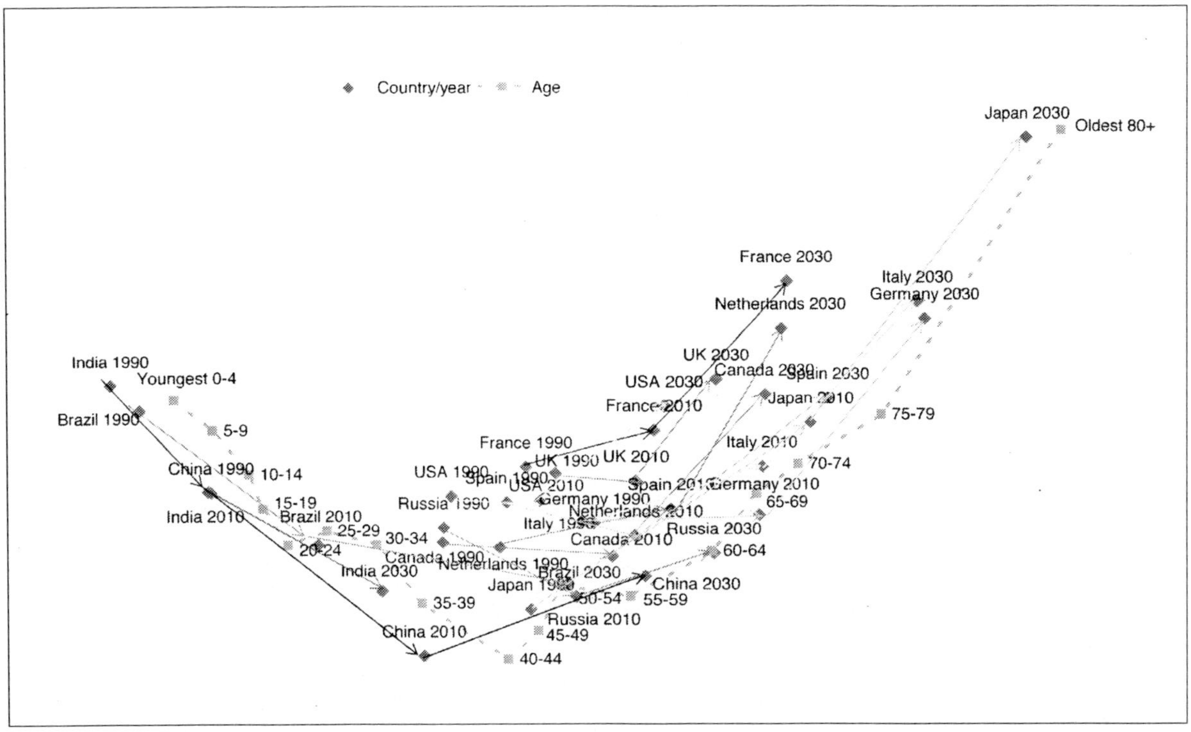

Source: Population Division of the Department of Economic and Social Affairs of the United Nations Secretariat, *World Population Prospects: The 2008 Revision*, 2009.

8.2 Regional Demographic Trends

8.2.1 Europe

Figure 8.5 European fertility

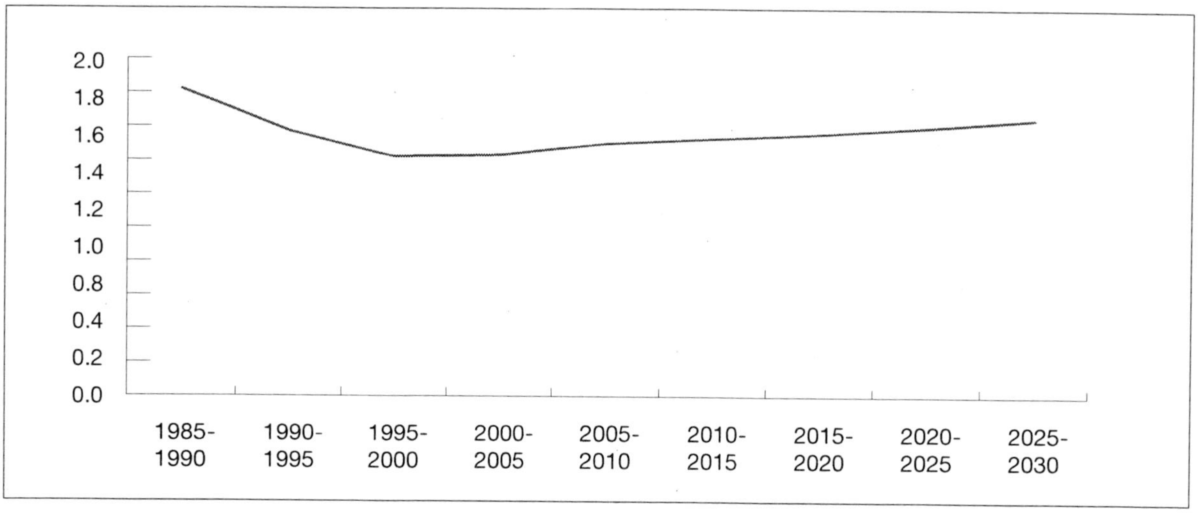

Source: Population Division of the Department of Economic and Social Affairs of the United Nations Secretariat, *World Population Prospects: The 2008 Revision*, 2009.

Table 8.4 European life expectancy (years)

Year	All	Male	Female
1985-1990	72.8	69.0	76.5
1990-1995	72.6	68.3	76.8
1995-2000	73.1	68.9	77.3
2000-2005	73.8	69.6	78.0
2005-2010	75.1	71.1	79.1
2010-2015	76.1	72.3	79.9
2015-2020	77.1	73.5	80.7
2020-2025	78.1	74.6	81.4
2025-2030	78.9	75.6	82.1

Source: Population Division of the Department of Economic and Social Affairs of the United Nations Secretariat, *World Population Prospects: The 2008 Revision*, 2009.

Table 8.5 European population by age band (%)

Age	1990	2010	2030
0-4	6.7	5.7	5.0
5-9	6.9	6.7	5.7
10-14	6.9	6.9	6.8
15-19	7.2	6.9	7.0
20-24	7.3	7.1	6.9
25-29	7.8	7.3	7.1
30-34	7.8	7.7	7.3
35-39	7.4	7.7	7.7
40-44	6.7	7.2	7.6
45-49	5.4	6.5	7.1
50-54	6.3	5.2	6.3
55-59	5.4	5.9	5.0
60-64	5.5	5.1	5.6
65-69	4.4	4.9	4.6
70-74	2.7	3.8	4.2
75-79	2.8	2.2	3.0
80-84	1.8	1.9	1.5
85-89	0.8	0.9	1.0
90-94	0.2	0.3	0.4
95-99	0.04	0.05	0.07
100+	0.00	0.01	0.01

Source: Population Division of the Department of Economic and Social Affairs of the United Nations Secretariat, *World Population Prospects: The 2008 Revision*, 2009.

Figure 8.6 European population by age band (%)

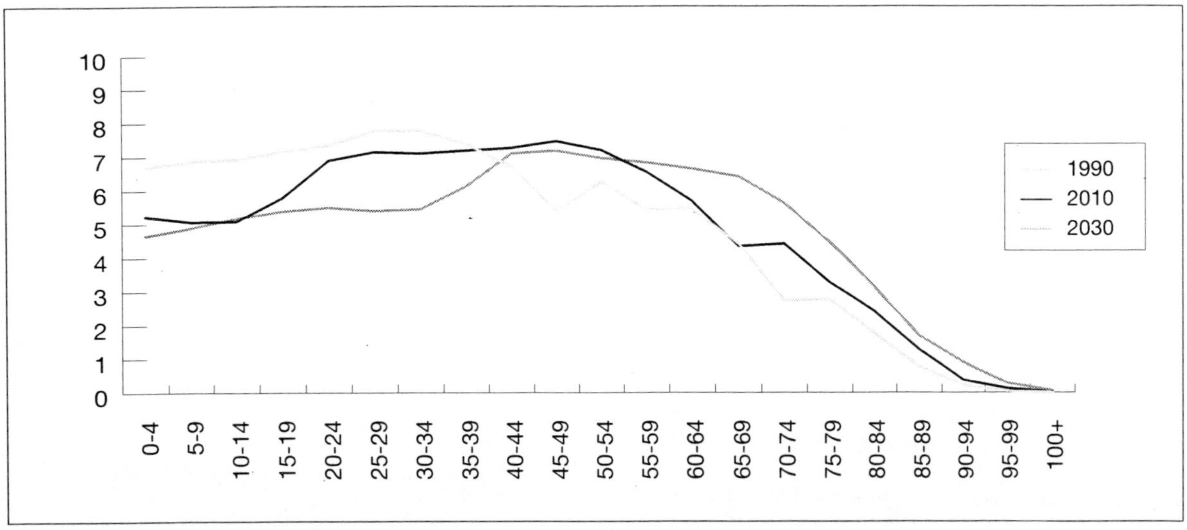

Source: Population Division of the Department of Economic and Social Affairs of the United Nations Secretariat, *World Population Prospects: The 2008 Revision*, 2009.

Figure 8.7 World population in Europe (%)

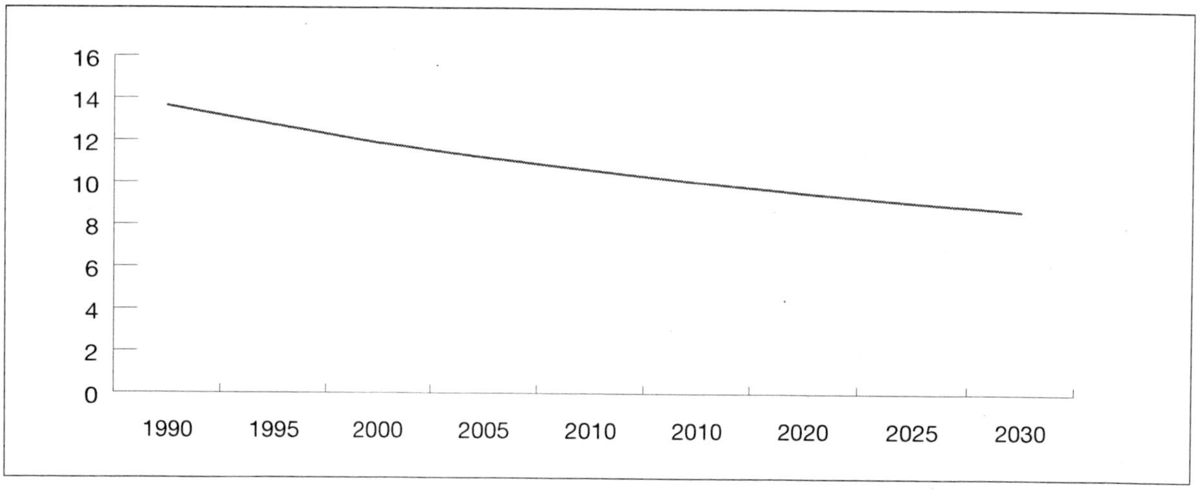

Source: Population Division of the Department of Economic and Social Affairs of the United Nations Secretariat, *World Population Prospects: The 2008 Revision*, 2009.

Figure 8.8 European urban population (%)

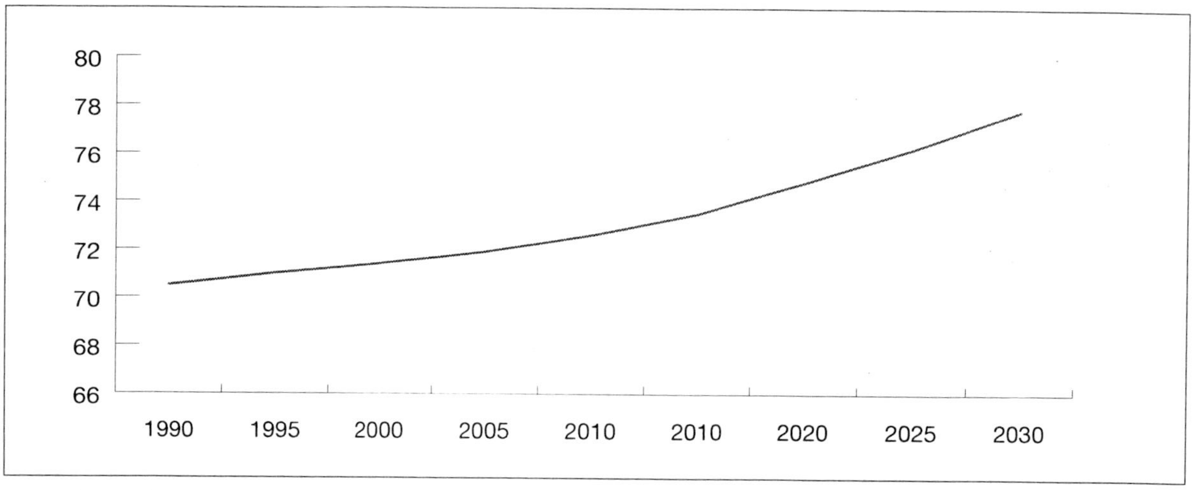

Source: Population Division of the Department of Economic and Social Affairs of the United Nations Secretariat, *World Population Prospects: The 2008 Revision*, 2009.

Figure 8.9 Age correspondence map: Europe

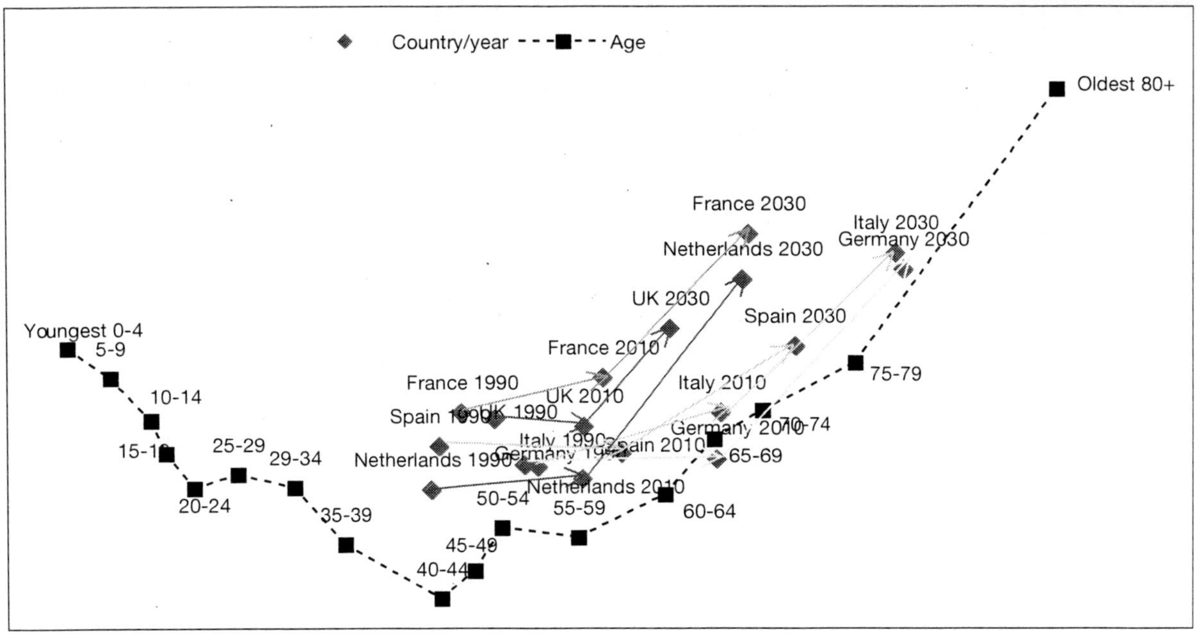

Source: Population Division of the Department of Economic and Social Affairs of the United Nations Secretariat, *World Population Prospects: The 2008 Revision*, 2009.

8.2.2 Asia

Figure 8.10 Asian fertility

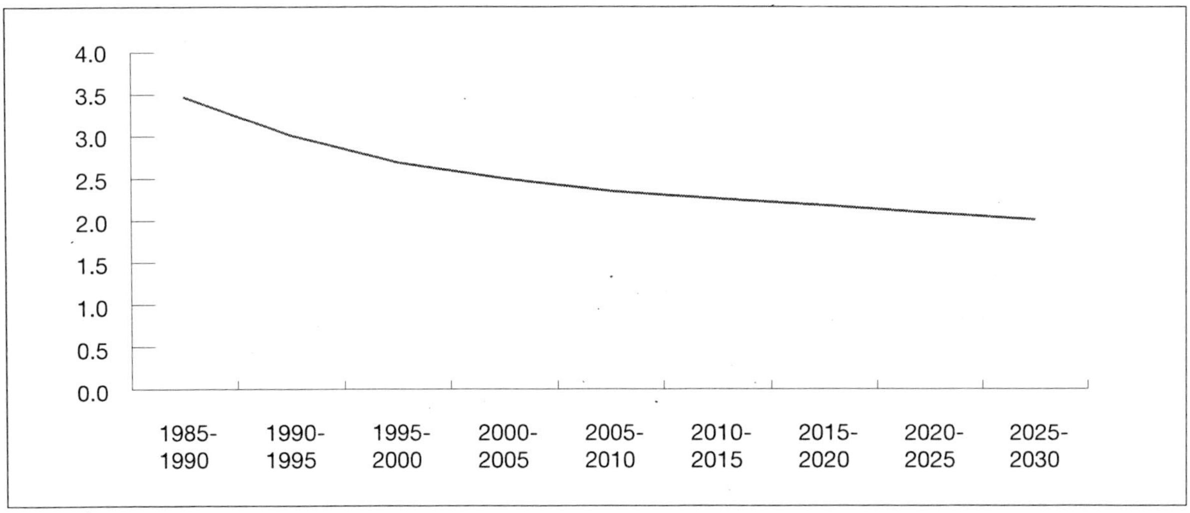

Source: Population Division of the Department of Economic and Social Affairs of the United Nations Secretariat, *World Population Prospects: The 2008 Revision*, 2009.

Table 8.6 Asian life expectancy (years)

Year	All	Male	Female
1985-1990	62.7	61.5	64.0
1990-1995	64.2	62.8	65.7
1995-2000	65.9	64.3	67.5
2000-2005	67.6	65.9	69.3
2005-2010	68.9	67.1	70.8
2010-2015	68.9	68.4	72.3
2015-2020	71.5	69.6	73.5
2020-2025	72.6	70.6	74.7
2025-2030	73.6	71.6	74.7

Source: Population Division of the Department of Economic and Social Affairs of the United Nations Secretariat, *World Population Prospects: The 2008 Revision*, 2009.

Table 8.7 Asian population by age band (%)

Age	1990	2010	2030
0-4	12.5	8.8	6.8
5-9	11.2	8.7	7.0
10-14	10.2	8.7	7.3
15-19	10.3	9.0	7.4
20-24	9.8	9.1	7.3
25-29	8.5	8.2	7.2
30-34	7.2	7.4	7.2
35-39	6.6	7.5	7.4
40-44	5.1	7.1	7.4
45-49	4.1	6.0	6.6
50-54	3.8	5.0	5.9
55-59	3.3	4.5	5.8
60-64	2.6	3.2	5.3
65-69	2.0	2.4	4.2
70-74	1.3	1.9	3.0
75-79	0.8	1.3	2.2
80-84	0.4	0.7	1.2
85-89	0.1	0.3	0.5
90-94	0.04	0.1	0.2
95-99	0.01	0.02	0.1
100+	0.00	0.00	0.01

Source: Population Division of the Department of Economic and Social Affairs of the United Nations Secretariat, *World Population Prospects: The 2008 Revision*, 2009.

Figure 8.11 Asian population by age band (%)

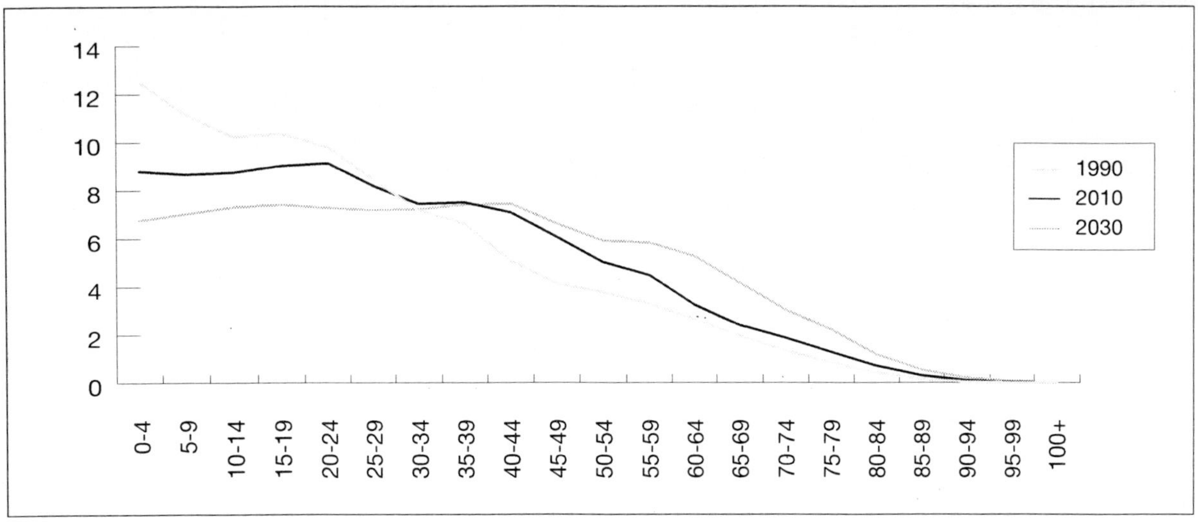

Source: Population Division of the Department of Economic and Social Affairs of the United Nations Secretariat, *World Population Prospects: The 2008 Revision*, 2009.

Figure 8.12 Asian population by gender (males per hundred females)

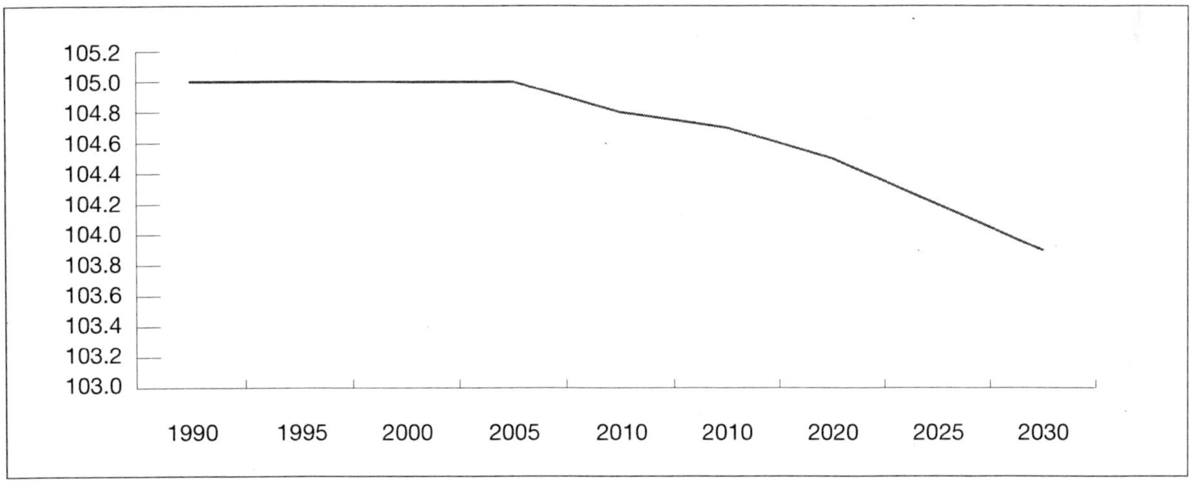

Source: Population Division of the Department of Economic and Social Affairs of the United Nations Secretariat, *World Population Prospects: The 2008 Revision*, 2009.

Figure 8.13 World population in Asia, India and China, 1990-2030 (%)

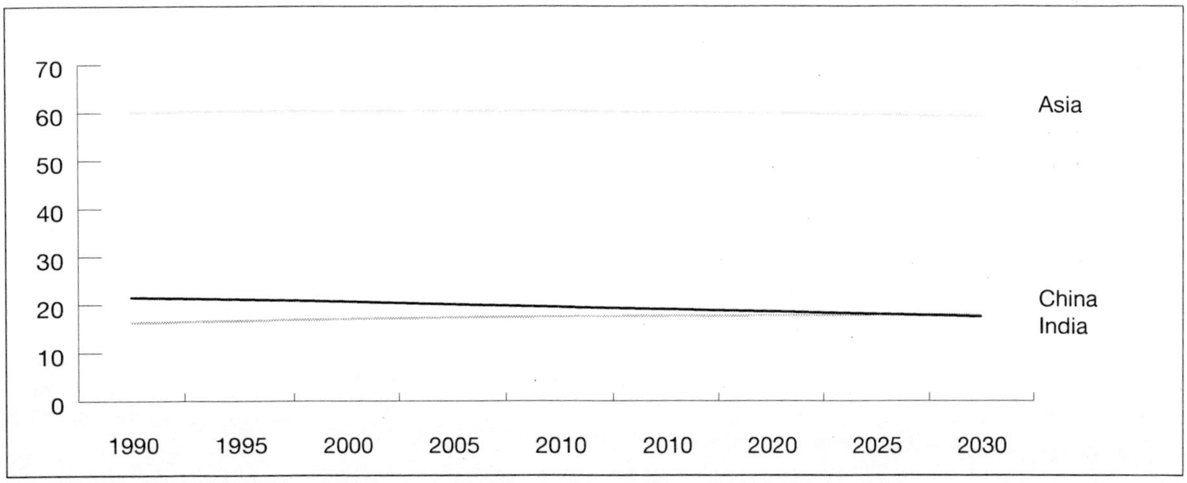

Source: Population Division of the Department of Economic and Social Affairs of the United Nations Secretariat, *World Population Prospects: The 2008 Revision*, 2009.

Figure 8.14 Asian Urban Population (%)

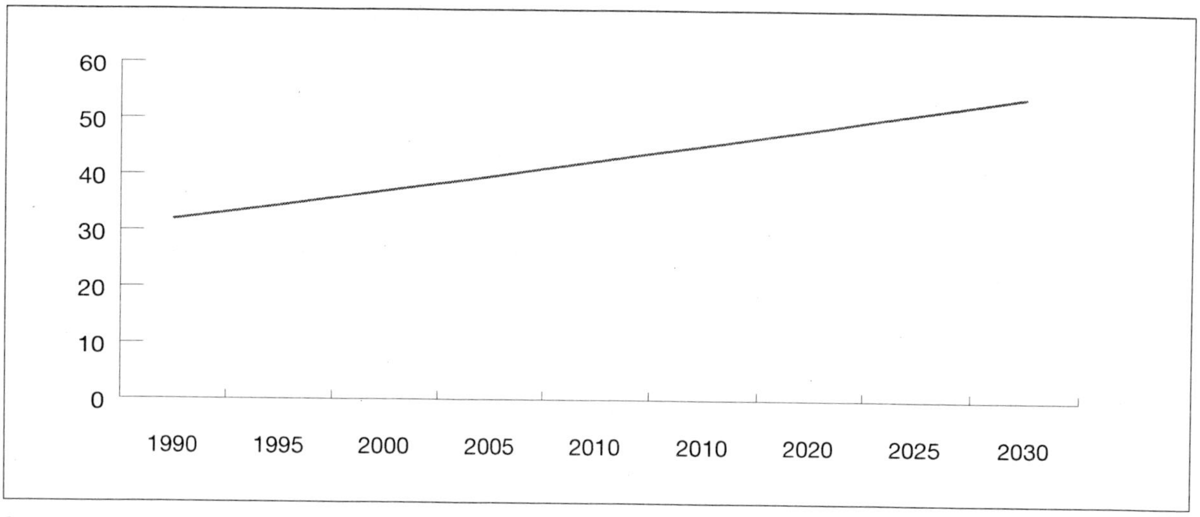

Source: Population Division of the Department of Economic and Social Affairs of the United Nations Secretariat, *World Population Prospects: The 2008 Revision*, 2009.

Figure 8.15 Age correspondence map: Asia

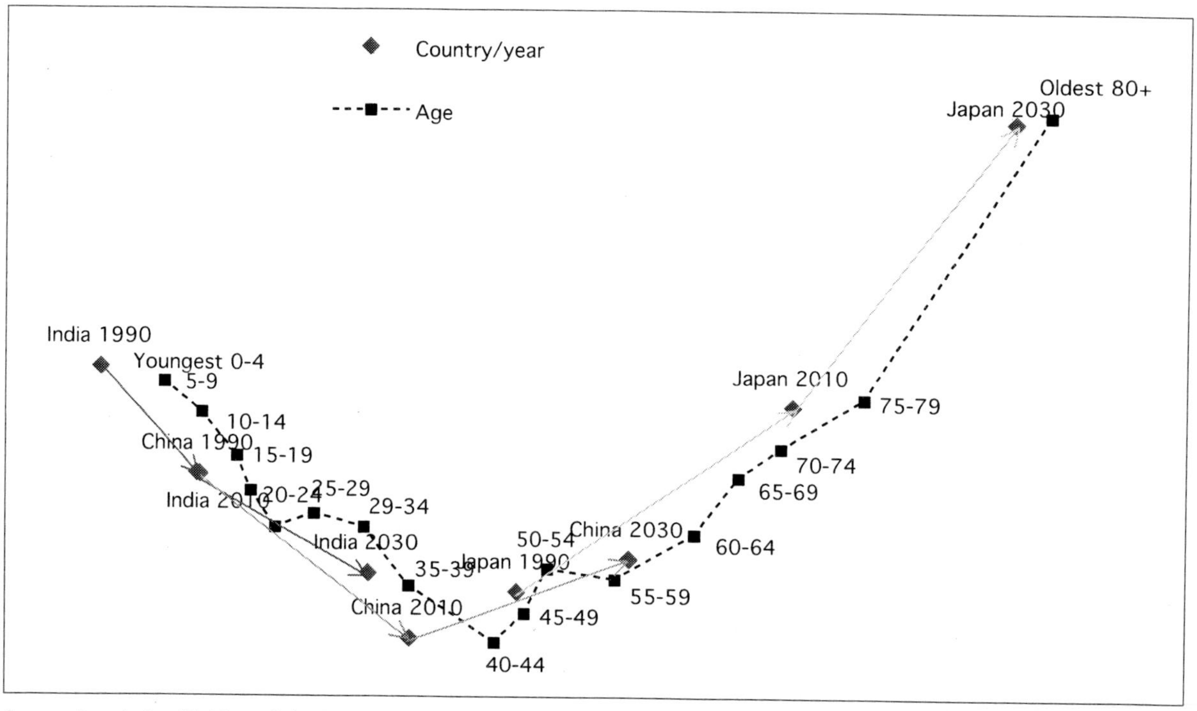

Source: Population Division of the Department of Economic and Social Affairs of the United Nations Secretariat, *World Population Prospects: The 2008 Revision*, 2009.

8.2.3 Latin America and the Caribbean

Figure 8.16 Latin American and the Caribbean fertility

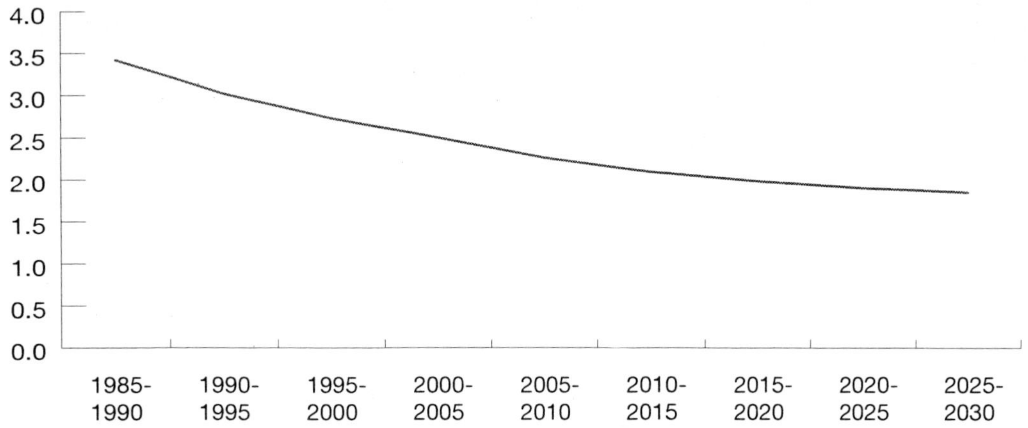

Source: Population Division of the Department of Economic and Social Affairs of the United Nations Secretariat, *World Population Prospects: The 2008 Revision*, 2009.

Table 8.8 Latin American and the Caribbean life expectancy (years)

Year	All	Male	Female
1985-1990	67.1	63.9	70.5
1990-1995	68.9	65.6	72.3
1995-2000	70.7	67.4	74.1
2000-2005	72.1	68.9	75.5
2005-2010	73.4	70.2	76.7
2010-2015	74.5	71.3	77.7
2015-2020	75.6	72.4	78.7
2020-2025	76.5	73.4	79.6
2025-2030	77.3	74.2	80.4

Source: Population Division of the Department of Economic and Social Affairs of the United Nations Secretariat, *World Population Prospects: The 2008 Revision*, 2009.

Table 8.9 Latin American and the Caribbean population by age band (%)

Age	1990	2010	2030
0-4	12.5	9.0	6.7
5-9	12.2	9.3	6.8
10-14	11.4	9.3	7.0
15-19	10.4	9.1	7.2
20-24	9.3	8.8	7.3
25-29	8.4	8.4	7.5
30-34	7.1	7.8	7.5
35-39	6.1	7.1	7.3
40-44	4.9	6.4	7.0
45-49	4.0	5.8	6.7
50-54	3.4	4.9	6.2
55-59	2.8	4.0	5.5
60-64	2.4	3.1	4.8
65-69	1.8	2.4	4.1
70-74	1.3	1.8	3.2
75-79	0.9	1.3	2.3
80-84	0.5	0.8	1.4
85-89	0.2	0.4	0.7
90-94	0.07	0.2	0.3
95-99	0.01	0.05	0.1
100+	0.00	0.01	0.04

Source: Population Division of the Department of Economic and Social Affairs of the United Nations Secretariat, *World Population Prospects: The 2008 Revision*, 2009.

Figure 8.17 Latin American and the Caribbean population by age band (%)

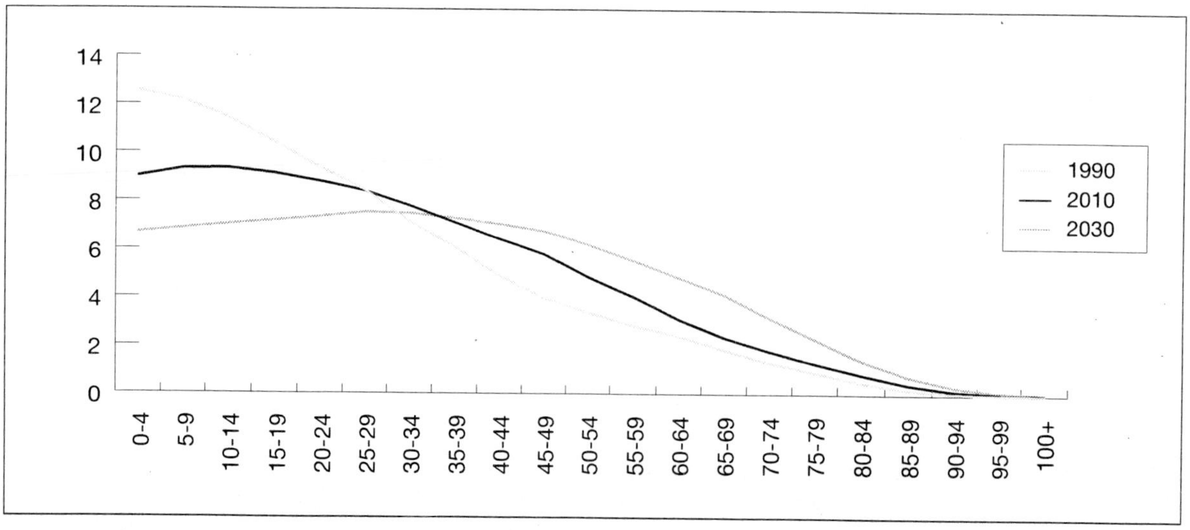

Source: Population Division of the Department of Economic and Social Affairs of the United Nations Secretariat, *World Population Prospects: The 2008 Revision*, 2009.

Figure 8.18 World population in Latin America and the Caribbean and in Brazil, 1990-2030 (%)

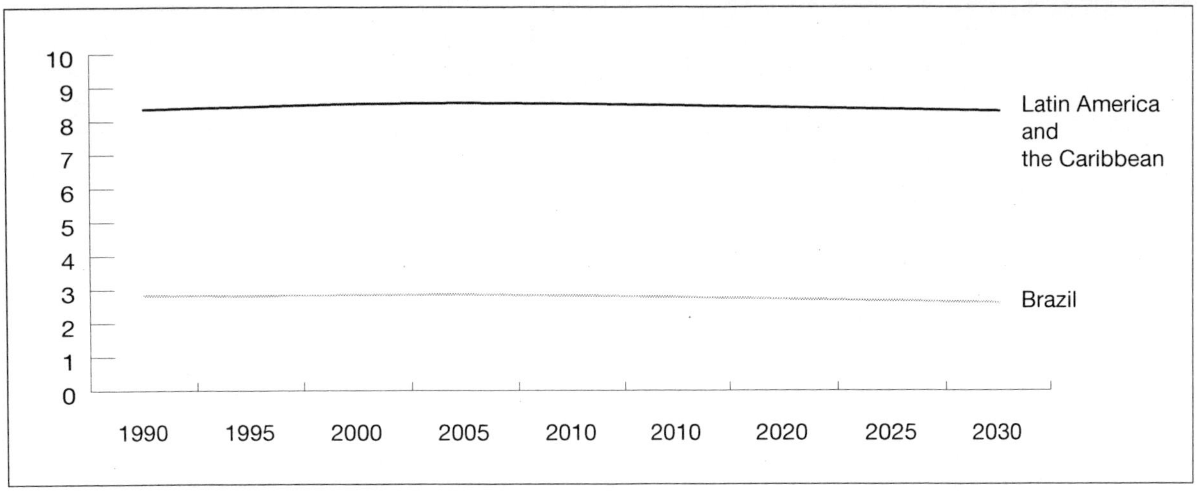

Source: Population Division of the Department of Economic and Social Affairs of the United Nations Secretariat, *World Population Prospects: The 2008 Revision*, 2009.

Figure 8.19 Latin American and the Caribbean urban population (%)

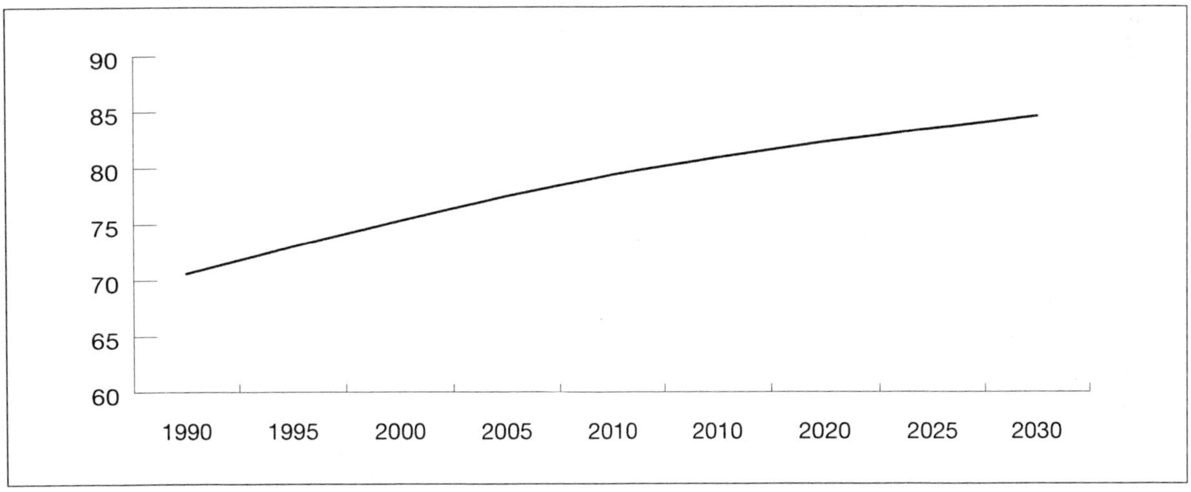

Source: Population Division of the Department of Economic and Social Affairs of the United Nations Secretariat, *World Population Prospects: The 2008 Revision*, 2009.

Figure 8.20 Age correspondence map: Brazil, Russia, India and China (BRIC countries)

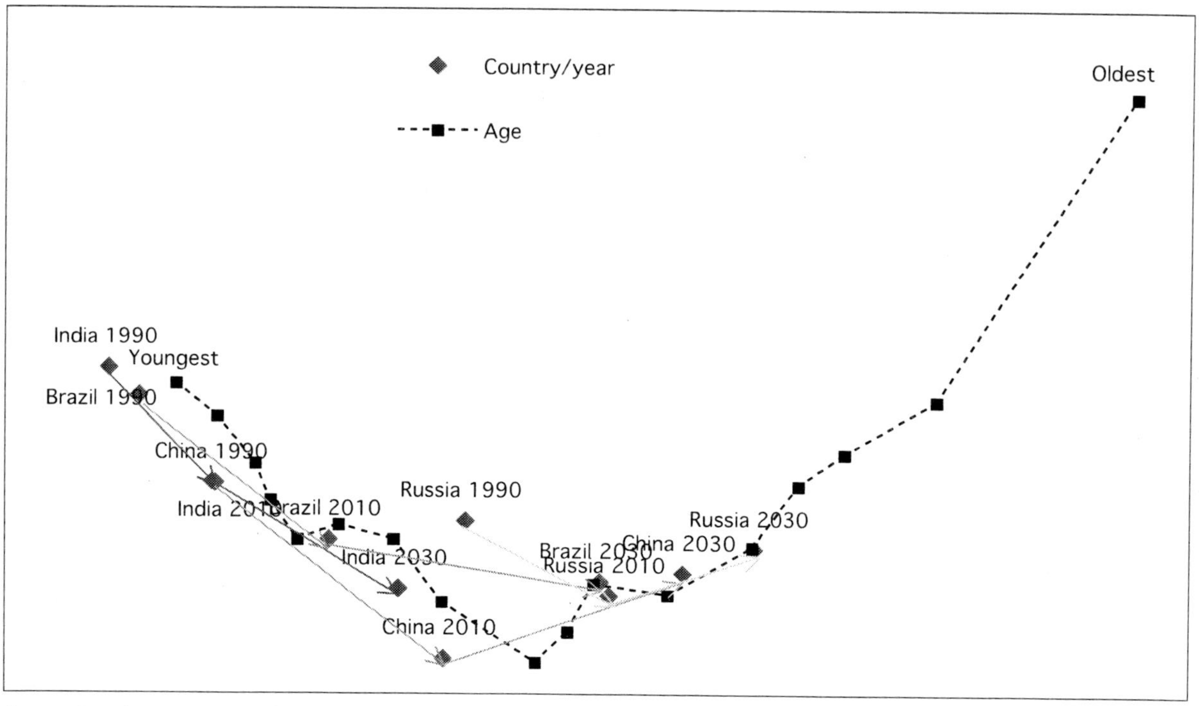

Source: Population Division of the Department of Economic and Social Affairs of the United Nations Secretariat, *World Population Prospects: The 2008 Revision*, 2009.

8.2.4 Northern America: United States of America and Canada

Figure 8.21 Northern American fertility

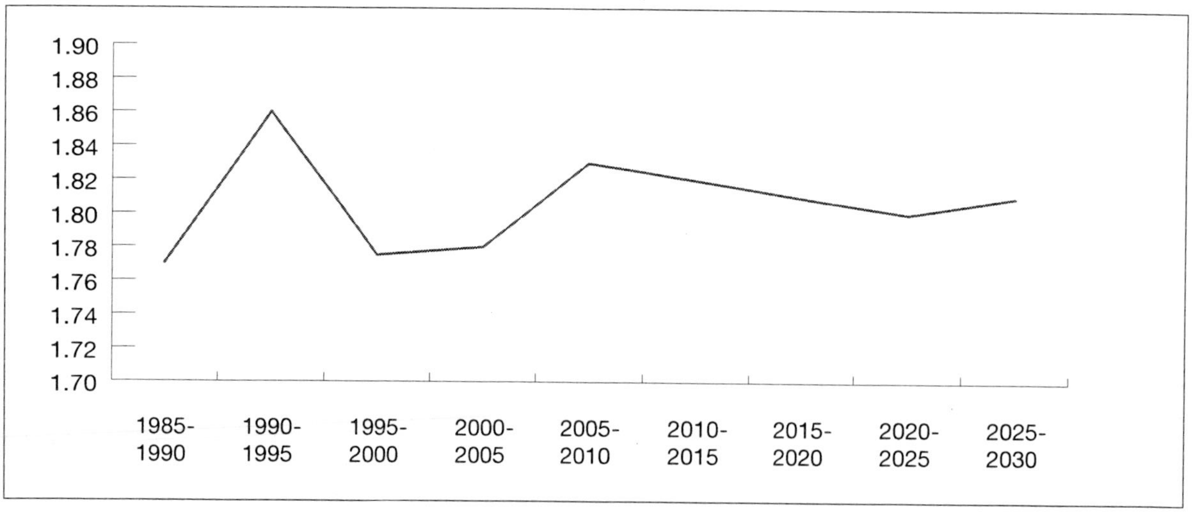

Source: Population Division of the Department of Economic and Social Affairs of the United Nations Secretariat, *World Population Prospects: The 2008 Revision*, 2009.

Table 8.10 Northern American life expectancy (years)

Year	All	Male	Female
1985-1990	76.0	72.6	79.3
1990-1995	76.8	73.6	79.9
1995-2000	78.1	75.5	80.6
2000-2005	79.0	76.5	81.4
2005-2010	79.9	77.6	82.1
2010-2015	80.6	78.4	82.8
2015-2020	81.2	79.1	83.4
2020-2025	81.8	79.6	83.9
2025-2030	82.2	80.0	84.5

Source: Population Division of the Department of Economic and Social Affairs of the United Nations Secretariat, *World Population Prospects: The 2008 Revision*, 2009.

Table 8.11 Northern American population by age band (%)

Age	1990	2010	2030
0-4	6.5	6.0	5.5
5-9	6.2	5.9	5.7
10-14	6.3	6.1	5.7
15-19	6.8	6.8	5.7
20-24	7.2	6.9	5.9
25-29	7.8	6.9	5.9
30-34	7.9	6.7	6.2
35-39	7.5	6.7	6.8
40-44	7.1	7.0	6.7
45-49	6.9	7.8	6.5
50-54	6.2	7.4	6.2
55-59	5.5	6.5	5.9
60-64	5.0	5.6	5.8
65-69	4.1	4.1	6.1
70-74	3.2	3.1	5.4
75-79	2.5	2.5	4.2
80-84	1.7	1.9	3.0
85-89	1.0	1.2	1.6
90-94	0.4	0.5	0.7
95-99	0.1	0.3	0.3
100+	0.02	0.03	0.06

Source: Population Division of the Department of Economic and Social Affairs of the United Nations Secretariat, *World Population Prospects: The 2008 Revision*, 2009.

Figure 8.22 Northern American population by age band (%)

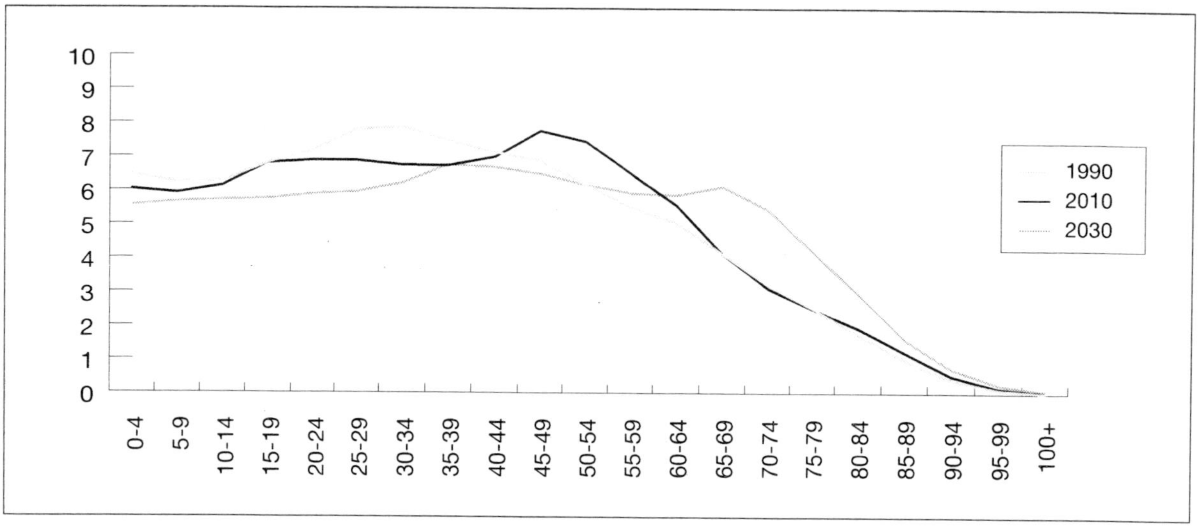

Source: Population Division of the Department of Economic and Social Affairs of the United Nations Secretariat, *World Population Prospects: The 2008 Revision*, 2009.

Figure 8.23 World populations in northern America, 1990-2030 (%)

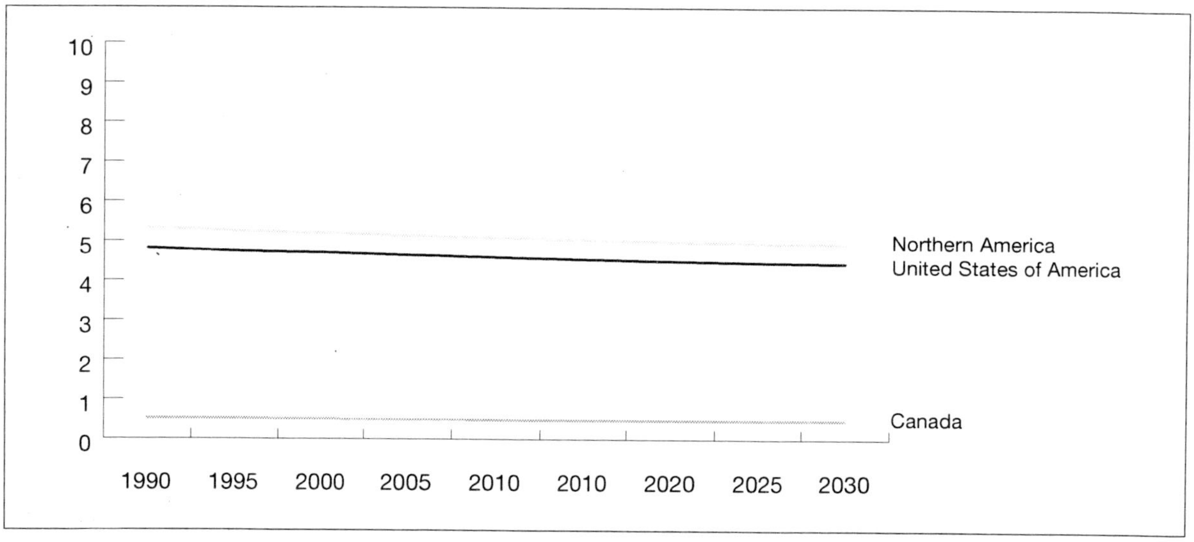

Source: Population Division of the Department of Economic and Social Affairs of the United Nations Secretariat, *World Population Prospects: The 2008 Revision*, 2009.

Figure 8.24 Correspondence map: Northern America

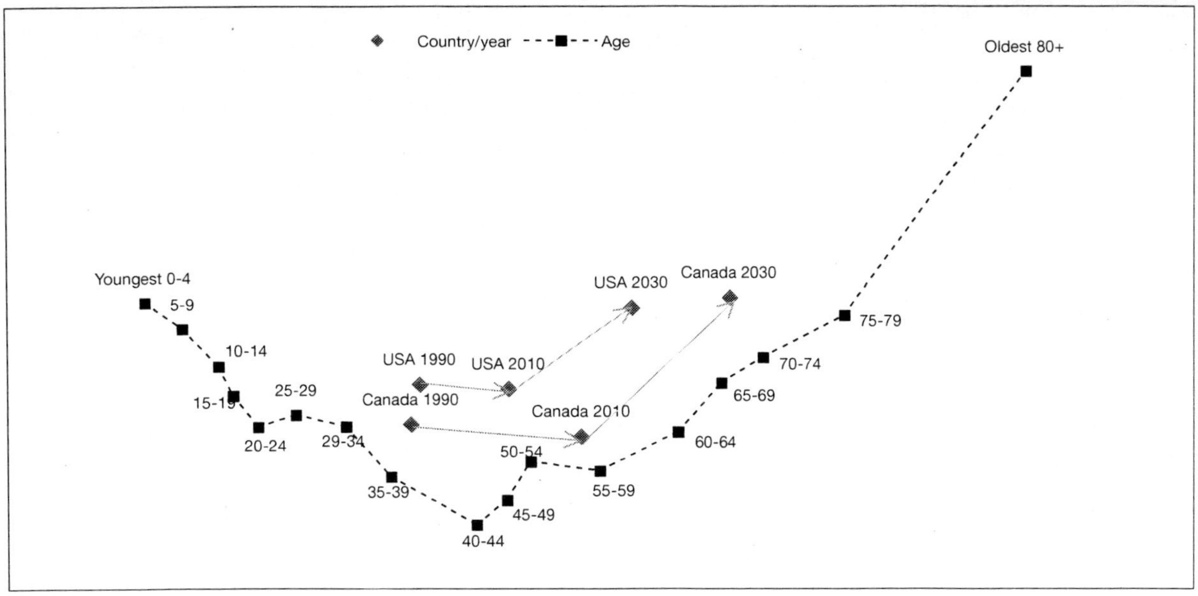

Source: Population Division of the Department of Economic and Social Affairs of the United Nations Secretariat, *World Population Prospects: The 2008 Revision*, 2009.

8.3 Country Specific Data

8.3.1 Brazil

Figure 8.25 Brazilian fertility

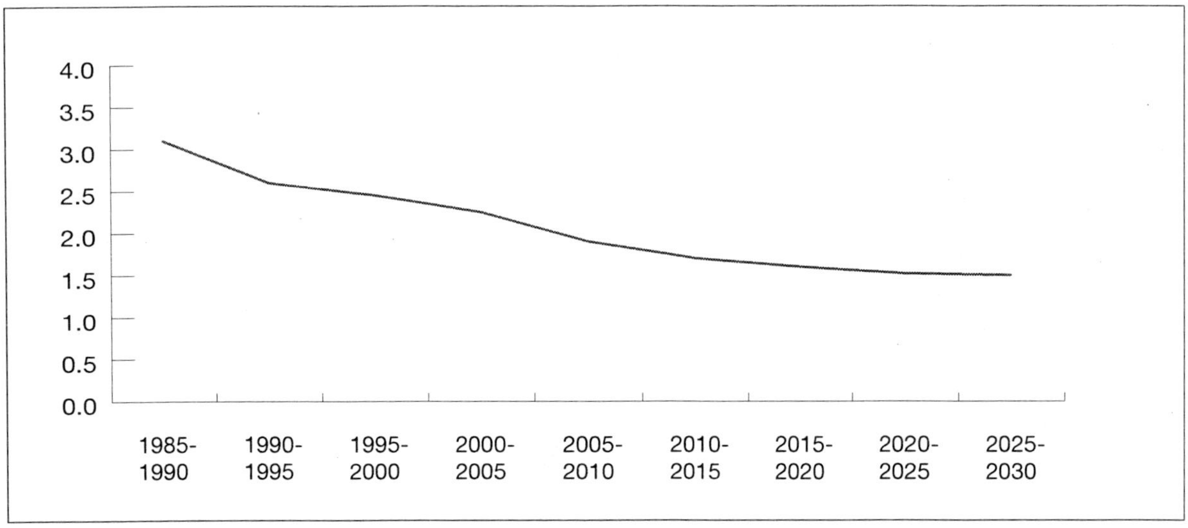

Source: Population Division of the Department of Economic and Social Affairs of the United Nations Secretariat, *World Population Prospects: The 2008 Revision*, 2009.

Table 8.12 Brazilian life expectancy (years)

Year	All	Male	Female
1985-1990	65.3	61.9	69.0
1990-1995	67.2	63.5	71.2
1995-2000	69.3	65.5	73.3
2000-2005	71.0	67.2	74.9
2005-2010	72.3	68.7	76.0
2010-2015	73.5	69.9	77.2
2015-2020	74.8	71.4	78.4
2020-2025	75.9	72.5	79.4
2025-2030	76.9	73.4	80.3

Source: Population Division of the Department of Economic and Social Affairs of the United Nations Secretariat, *World Population Prospects: The 2008 Revision*, 2009.

Table 8.13 Brazilian population by age band (%)

Age	1990	2010	2030
0-4	11.8	7.8	5.4
5-9	12.2	8.8	5.6
10-14	11.2	8.9	6.0
15-19	10.0	8.4	6.3
20-24	9.3	8.8	6.9
25-29	9.0	9.1	7.8
30-34	7.6	8.2	7.7
35-39	6.4	7.2	7.3
40-44	5.1	6.7	7.6
45-49	4.0	6.3	7.7
50-54	3.5	5.3	6.9
55-59	2.8	4.3	5.9
60-64	2.4	3.5	5.2
65-69	1.7	2.4	4.7
70-74	1.2	1.8	3.5
75-79	0.8	1.2	2.5
80-84	0.4	0.8	1.5
85-89	0.2	0.4	0.8
90-94	0.05	0.2	0.4
95-99	0.01	0.1	0.1
100+	0.00	0.01	0.04

Source: Population Division of the Department of Economic and Social Affairs of the United Nations Secretariat, *World Population Prospects: The 2008 Revision*, 2009.

Figure 8.26 Brazilian population by age band (%)

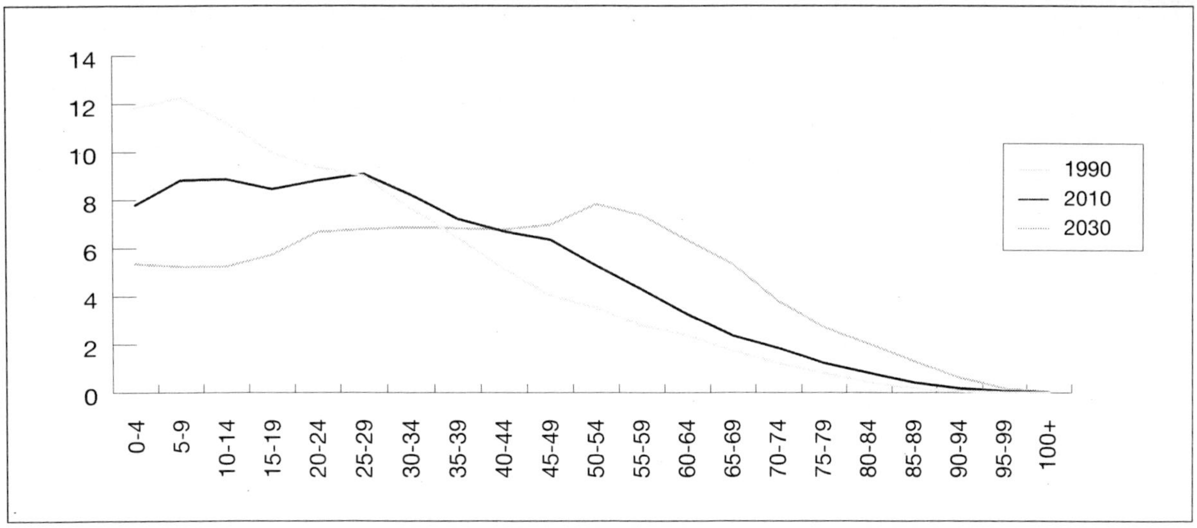

Source: Population Division of the Department of Economic and Social Affairs of the United Nations Secretariat, *World Population Prospects: The 2008 Revision*, 2009.

Figure 8.27 Brazilian population by gender (males per hundred females)

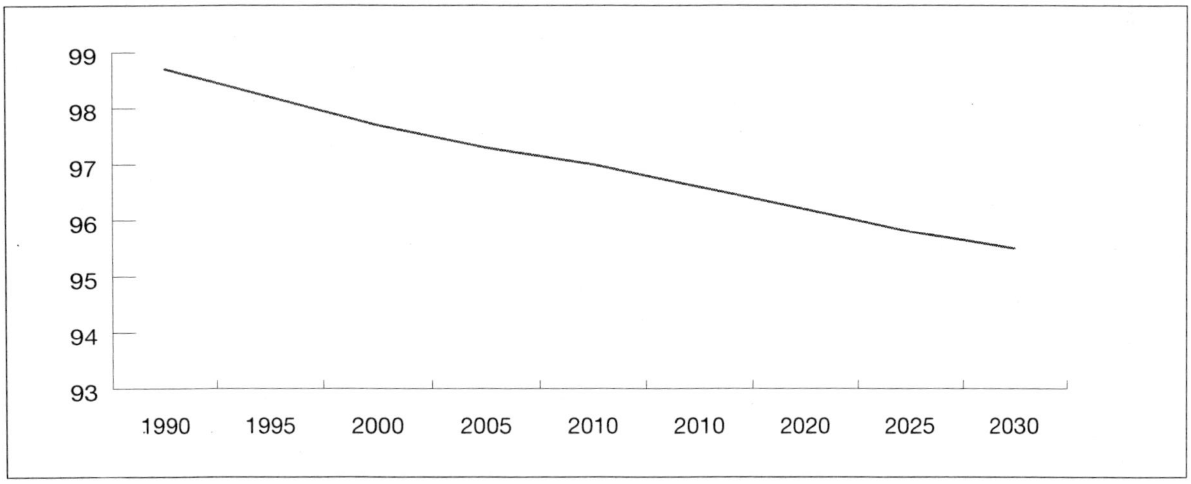

Source: Population Division of the Department of Economic and Social Affairs of the United Nations Secretariat, *World Population Prospects: The 2008 Revision*, 2009.

Figure 8.28 Brazilian urban population (%)

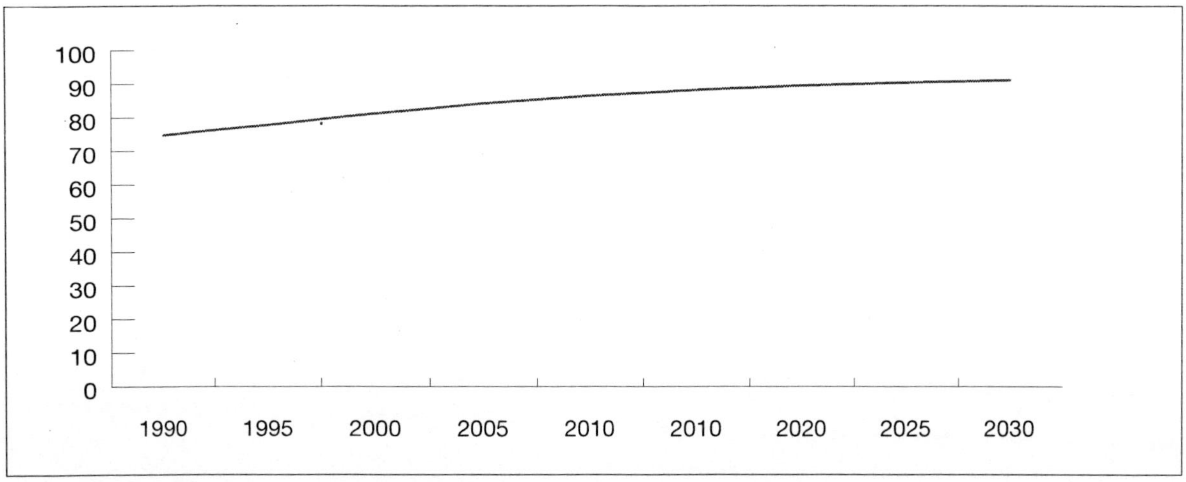

Source: Population Division of the Department of Economic and Social Affairs of the United Nations Secretariat, *World Population Prospects: The 2008 Revision*, 2009.

8.3.2 Canada

Figure 8.29 Canadian fertility

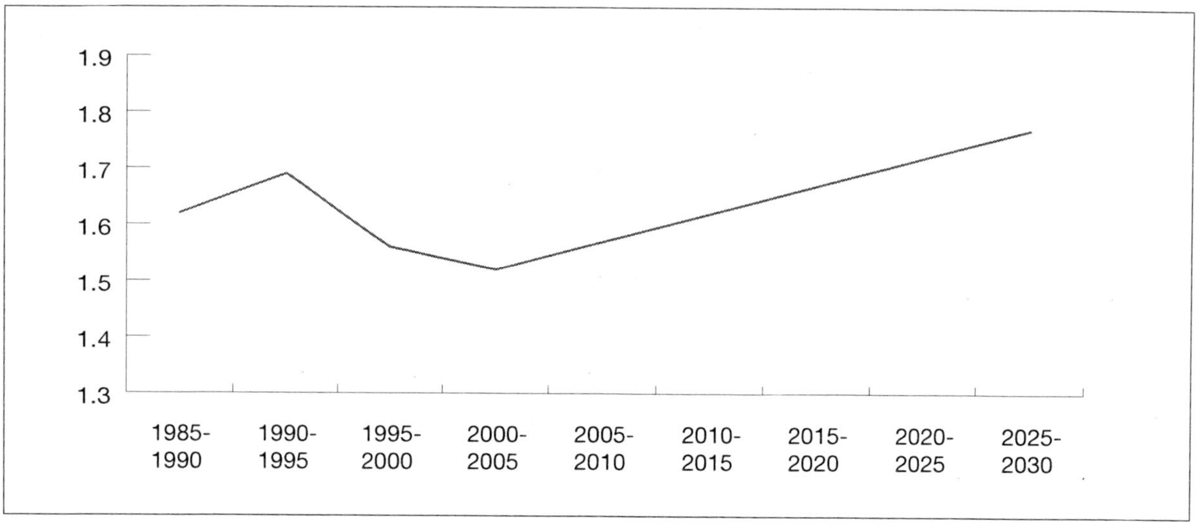

Source: Population Division of the Department of Economic and Social Affairs of the United Nations Secretariat, *World Population Prospects: The 2008 Revision*, 2009.

Table 8.14 Canadian life expectancy (years)

Year	All	Male	Female
1985-1990	77.0	73.7	80.3
1990-1995	77.9	74.8	81.0
1995-2000	78.7	75.9	81.4
2000-2005	79.8	77.3	82.3
2005-2010	80.7	78.3	82.9
2010-2015	81.4	79.2	83.6
2015-2020	82.0	79.9	84.1
2020-2025	82.6	80.5	84.7
2025-2030	83.1	81.0	85.3

Source: Population Division of the Department of Economic and Social Affairs of the United Nations Secretariat, *World Population Prospects: The 2008 Revision*, 2009.

Table 8.15 Canadian population by age band (%)

Age	1990	2010	2030
0-4	7.0	5.3	5.3
5-9	6.9	5.3	5.4
10-14	6.8	5.7	5.4
15-19	7.0	6.6	5.3
20-24	7.7	6.7	5.3
25-29	9.3	6.8	5.5
30-34	9.2	6.8	6.0
35-39	8.3	6.8	6.8
40-44	7.4	7.2	6.8
45-49	5.8	8.2	6.7
50-54	4.7	7.7	6.5
55-59	4.5	6.8	6.2
60-64	4.3	5.8	6.1
65-69	3.9	4.3	6.5
70-74	2.9	3.3	5.7
75-79	2.2	2.7	4.4
80-84	1.3	2.0	3.2
85-89	0.7	1.2	1.7
90-94	0.2	0.5	0.8
95-99	0.1	0.1	0.3
100+	0.01	0.02	0.06

Source: Population Division of the Department of Economic and Social Affairs of the United Nations Secretariat, *World Population Prospects: The 2008 Revision*, 2009.

Figure 8.30 Canadian Population by age band (%)

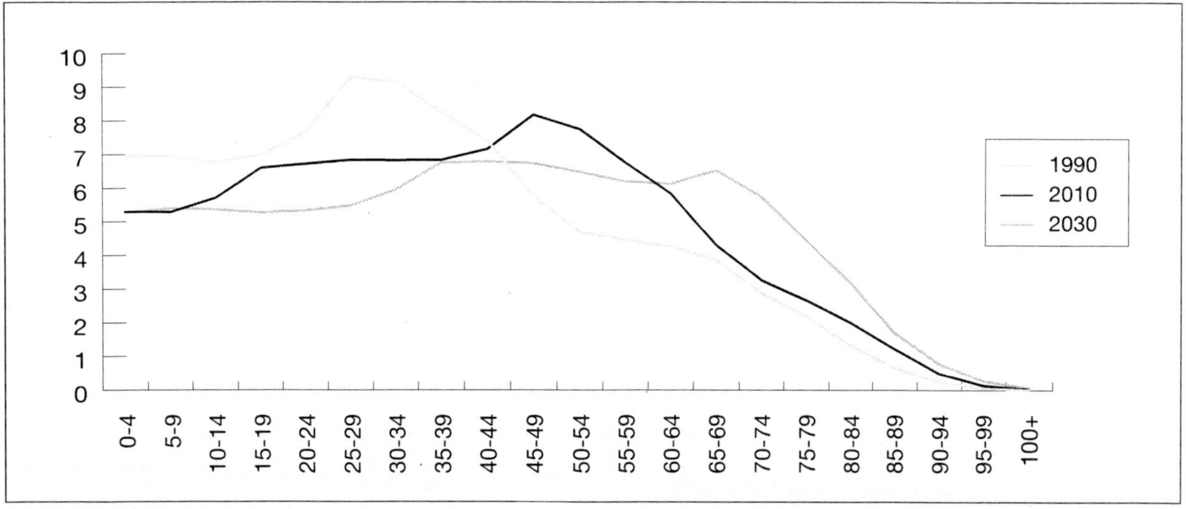

Source: Population Division of the Department of Economic and Social Affairs of the United Nations Secretariat, *World Population Prospects: The 2008 Revision*, 2009.

Figure 8.31 Canadian population by gender (males per hundred females)

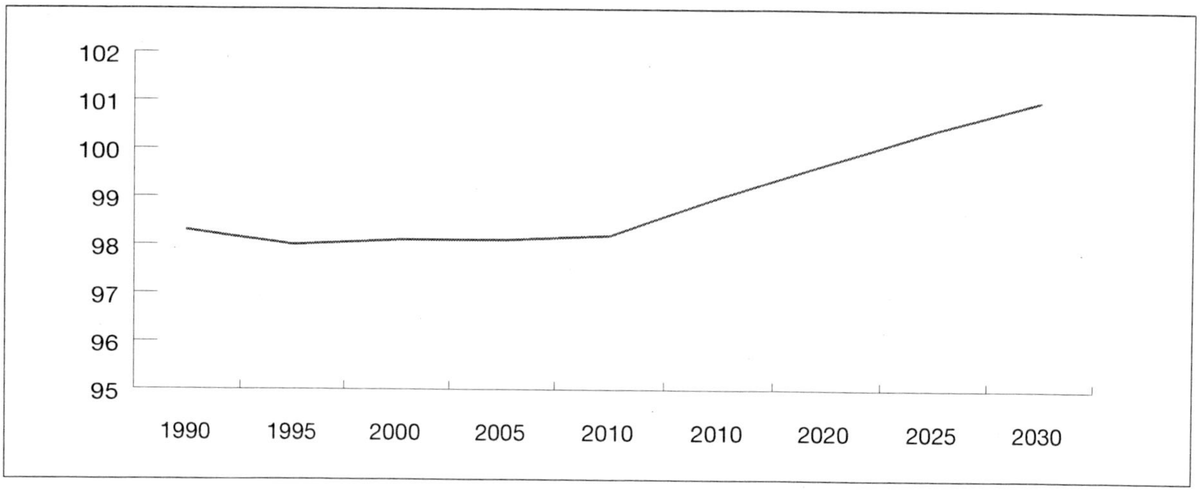

Source: Population Division of the Department of Economic and Social Affairs of the United Nations Secretariat, *World Population Prospects: The 2008 Revision*, 2009.

Figure 8.32 Canadian urban population (%)

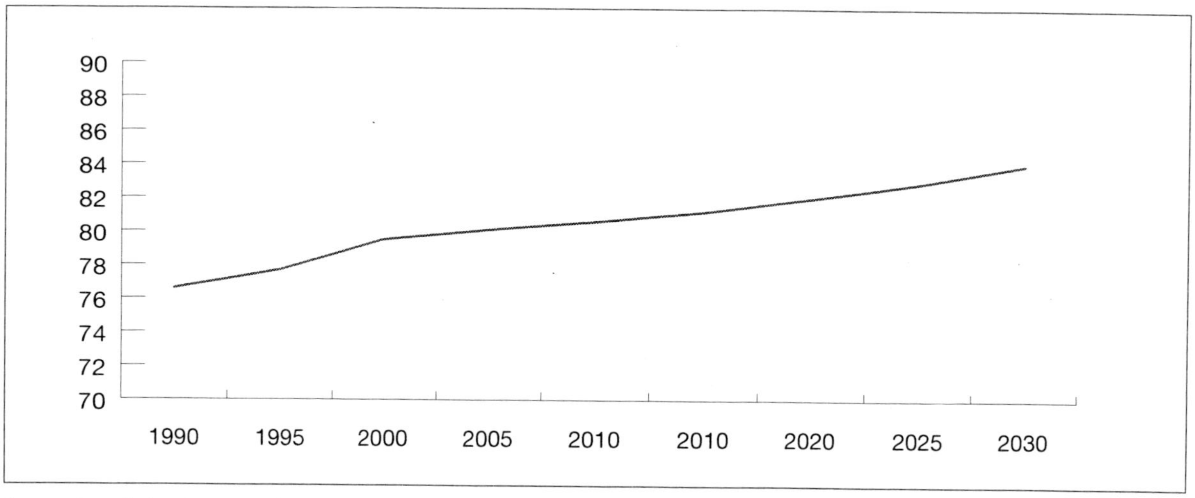

Source: Population Division of the Department of Economic and Social Affairs of the United Nations Secretariat, *World Population Prospects: The 2008 Revision*, 2009.

8.3.3 China

Figure 8.33 Chinese fertility

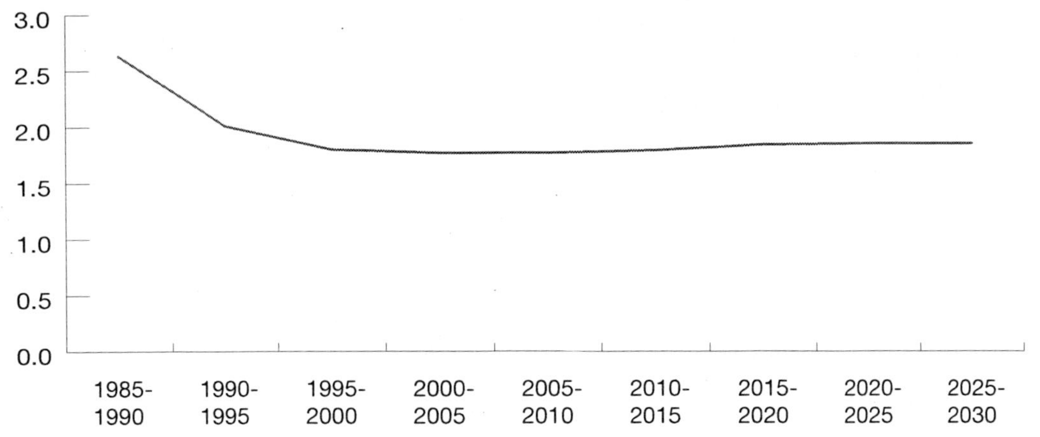

Source: Population Division of the Department of Economic and Social Affairs of the United Nations Secretariat, *World Population Prospects: The 2008 Revision*, 2009.

Table 8.16 Chinese life expectancy (years)

Year	All	Male	Female
1985-1990	67.4	66.0	68.8
1990-1995	68.8	67.4	70.3
1995-2000	70.4	69.0	72.0
2000-2005	72.0	70.5	73.7
2005-2010	73.0	71.3	74.8
2010-2015	74.0	72.3	75.9
2015-2020	74.9	73.1	76.9
2020-2025	74.9	74.0	77.8
2025-2030	75.8	74.7	78.6

Source: Population Division of the Department of Economic and Social Affairs of the United Nations Secretariat, *World Population Prospects: The 2008 Revision*, 2009.

Table 8.17 Chinese population by age band (%)

Age	1990	2010	2030
0-4	11.0	6.5	5.2
5-9	9.0	6.4	5.2
10-14	8.4	7.0	6.1
15-19	10.6	7.8	6.2
20-24	11.1	9.0	5.9
25-29	9.2	7.4	5.8
30-34	7.3	6.9	6.3
35-39	7.5	8.6	7.1
40-44	5.5	9.0	8.1
45-49	4.3	7.4	6.6
50-54	4.0	5.8	6.1
55-59	3.6	5.8	7.5
60-64	3.0	4.1	7.5
65-69	2.3	2.9	5.8
70-74	1.6	2.3	4.0
75-79	1.0	1.6	3.3
80-84	0.5	0.9	1.7
85-89	0.2	0.4	0.7
90-94	0.02	0.1	0.3
95-99	0.00	0.02	0.1
100+	0.00	0.00	0.01

Source: Population Division of the Department of Economic and Social Affairs of the United Nations Secretariat, *World Population Prospects: The 2008 Revision*, 2009.

Figure 8.34 Chinese population by age band (%)

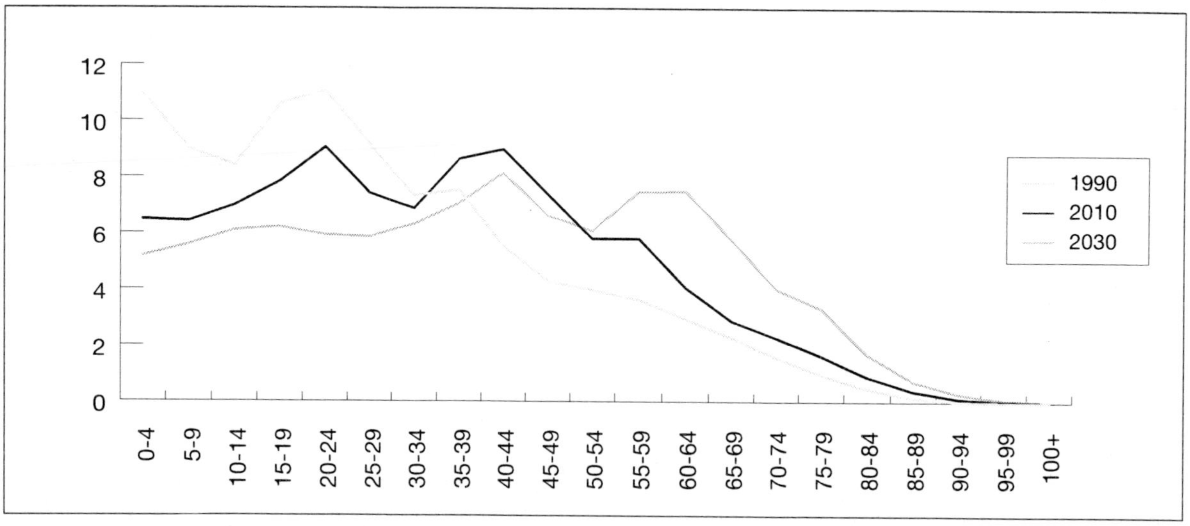

Source: Population Division of the Department of Economic and Social Affairs of the United Nations Secretariat, *World Population Prospects: The 2008 Revision*, 2009.

Figure 8.35 Chinese population by gender (males per hundred females)

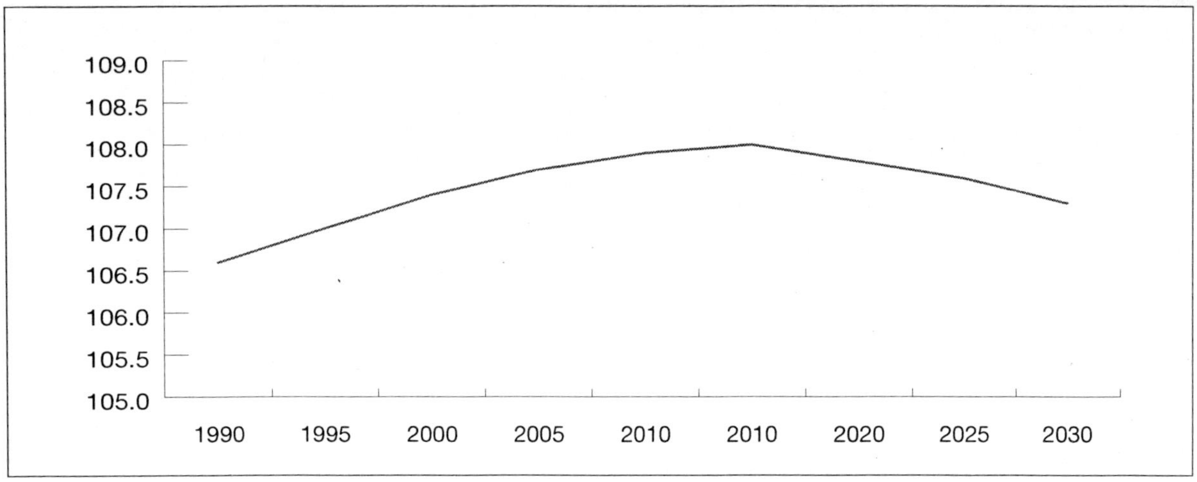

Source: Population Division of the Department of Economic and Social Affairs of the United Nations Secretariat, *World Population Prospects: The 2008 Revision*, 2009.

Figure 8.36 Chinese urban population (%)

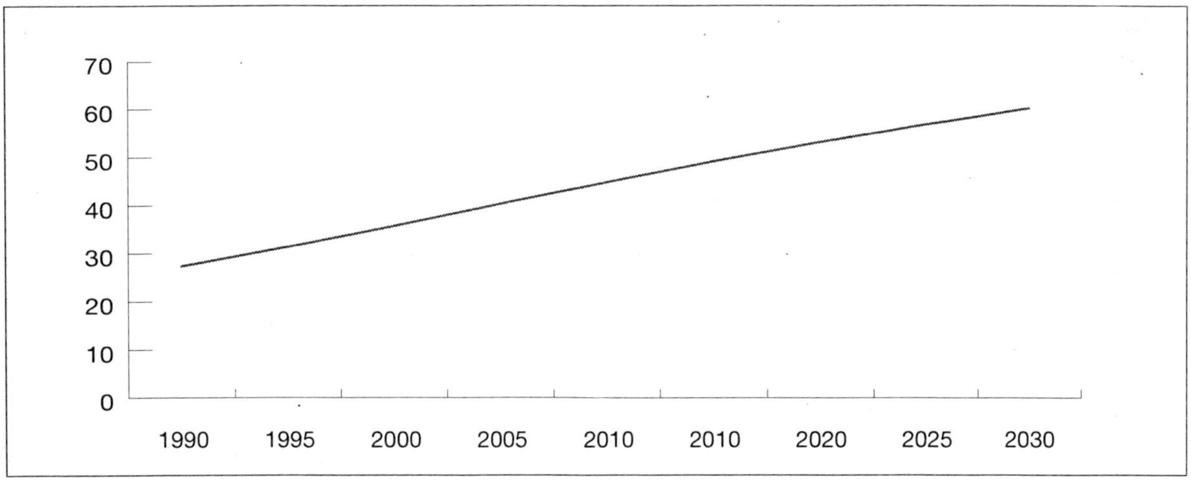

Source: Population Division of the Department of Economic and Social Affairs of the United Nations Secretariat, *World Population Prospects: The 2008 Revision*, 2009.

8.3.4 France

Figure 8.37 French fertility

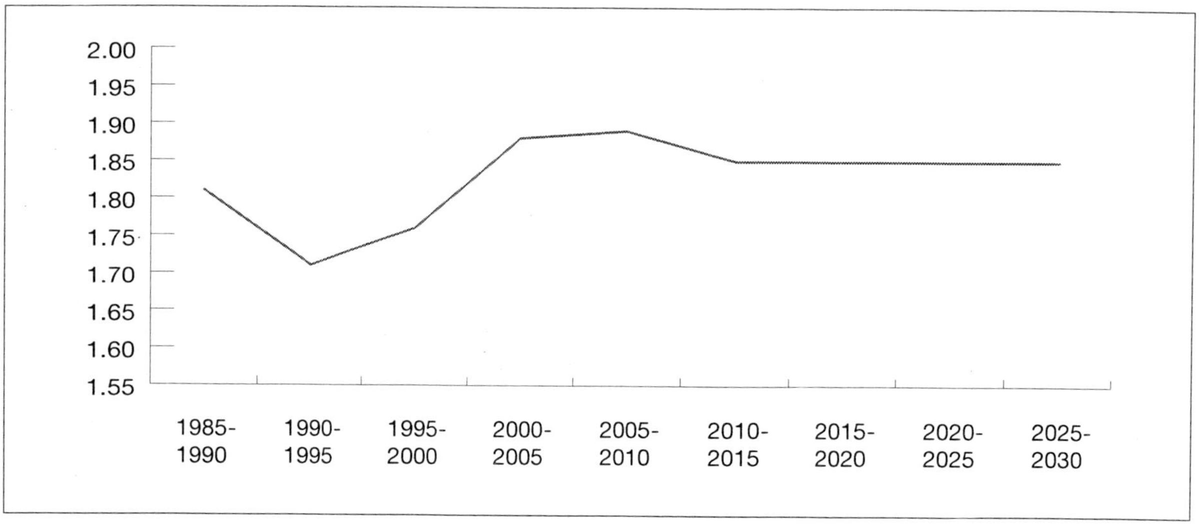

Source: Population Division of the Department of Economic and Social Affairs of the United Nations Secretariat, *World Population Prospects: The 2008 Revision*, 2009.

Table 8.18 French life expectancy (years)

Year	All	Male	Female
1985-1990	76.0	71.9	80.1
1990-1995	77.2	73.1	81.4
1995-2000	78.3	74.4	82.3
2000-2005	79.5	75.8	83.1
2005-2010	81.2	77.6	84.7
2010-2015	81.9	78.6	85.1
2015-2020	82.7	79.5	85.7
2020-2025	83.3	80.3	86.2
2025-2030	83.9	81.0	86.8

Source: Population Division of the Department of Economic and Social Affairs of the United Nations Secretariat, *World Population Prospects: The 2008 Revision*, 2009.

Table 8.19 French population by age band (%)

Age	1990	2010	2030
0-4	7.0	6.1	5.3
5-9	6.8	6.3	5.5
10-14	6.6	6.0	5.6
15-19	7.5	6.0	5.8
20-24	7.5	6.3	6.0
25-29	7.6	6.3	6.1
30-34	7.5	6.1	5.7
35-39	7.5	6.8	5.7
40-44	7.5	6.8	6.0
45-49	5.1	7.0	6.0
50-54	5.1	6.7	5.8
55-59	5.3	6.5	6.2
60-64	5.1	6.2	6.1
65-69	4.7	4.1	6.0
70-74	2.6	3.8	5.5
75-79	3.0	3.5	4.9
80-84	2.3	2.8	4.0
85-89	1.2	1.9	2.1
90-94	0.4	0.5	1.2
95-99	0.1	0.2	0.5
100+	0.01	0.03	0.1

Source: Population Division of the Department of Economic and Social Affairs of the United Nations Secretariat, *World Population Prospects: The 2008 Revision*, 2009.

Figure 8.38 French population by age band (%)

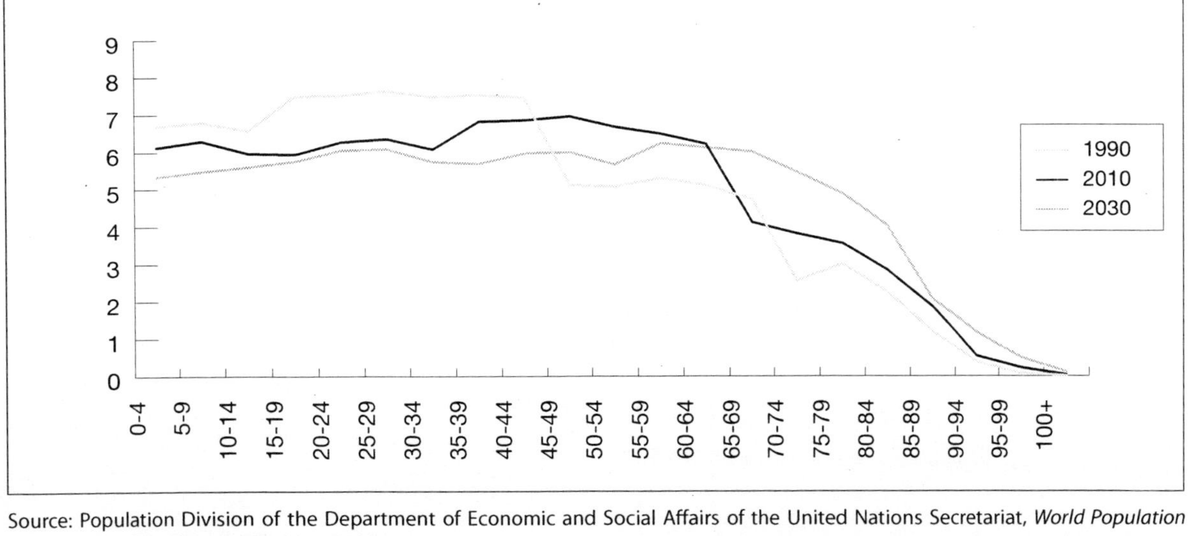

Source: Population Division of the Department of Economic and Social Affairs of the United Nations Secretariat, *World Population Prospects: The 2008 Revision*, 2009.

Figure 8.39 French population by gender (males per hundred females)

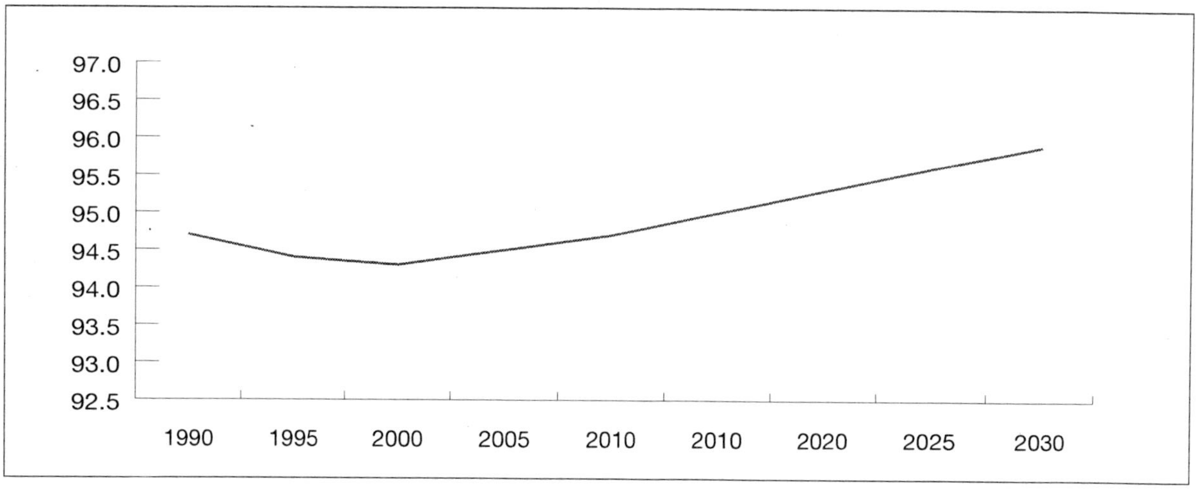

Source: Population Division of the Department of Economic and Social Affairs of the United Nations Secretariat, *World Population Prospects: The 2008 Revision*, 2009.

Figure 8.40 French urban population (%)

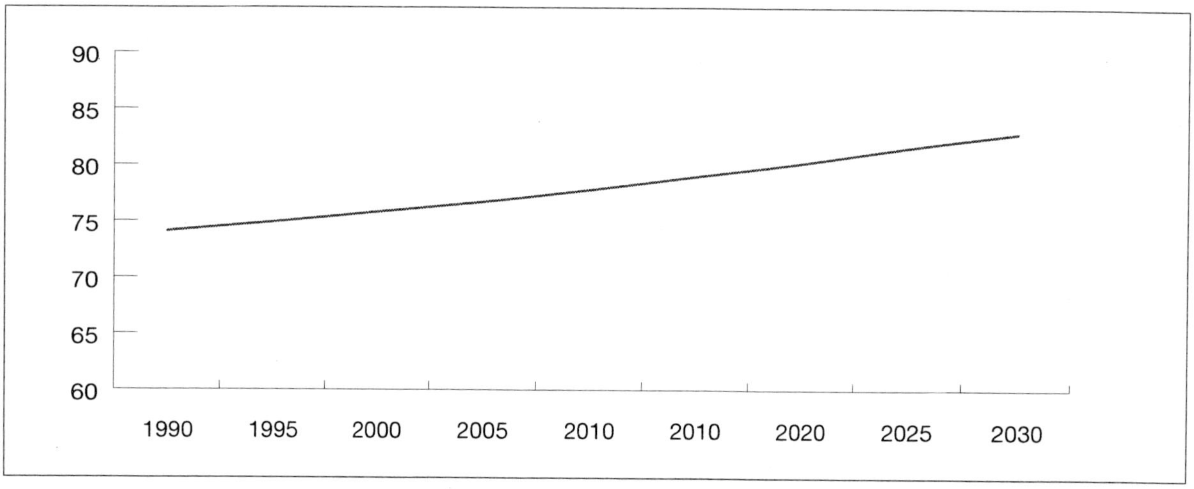

Source: Population Division of the Department of Economic and Social Affairs of the United Nations Secretariat, *World Population Prospects: The 2008 Revision*, 2009.

8.3.5 Germany

Figure 8.41 German fertility

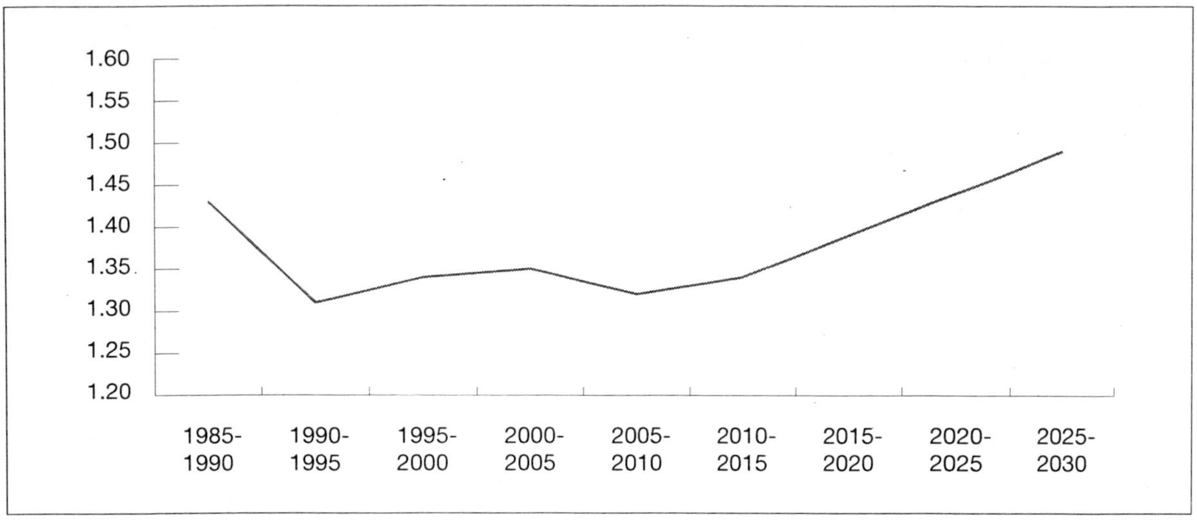

Source: Population Division of the Department of Economic and Social Affairs of the United Nations Secretariat, *World Population Prospects: The 2008 Revision*, 2009.

Table 8.20 German life expectancy (years)

Year	All	Male	Female
1985-1990	74.8	71.7	78.2
1990-1995	76.2	72.6	79.1
1995-2000	77.2	73.9	80.2
2000-2005	78.7	75.8	81.4
2005-2010	79.9	77.1	82.4
2010-2015	80.5	77.8	83.1
2015-2020	81.1	78.4	83.7
2020-2025	81.6	79.0	84.3
2025-2030	82.2	79.6	84.9

Source: Population Division of the Department of Economic and Social Affairs of the United Nations Secretariat, *World Population Prospects: The 2008 Revision*, 2009.

Table 8.21 German population by age band (%)

Age	1990	2010	2030
0-4	5.5	4.1	4.0
5-9	5.4	4.4	4.2
10-14	5.2	4.8	4.3
15-19	5.6	5.2	4.3
20-24	8.0	6.0	4.5
25-29	8.7	6.0	5.0
30-34	7.7	5.9	5.5
35-39	7.1	6.3	5.9
40-44	6.2	8.3	6.6
45-49	6.7	8.7	6.5
50-54	7.6	7.5	6.2
55-59	5.8	6.7	6.5
60-64	5.5	5.5	8.3
65-69	4.9	5.7	8.3
70-74	2.9	5.8	6.7
75-79	3.4	3.8	5.2
80-84	2.4	2.8	3.5
85-89	1.1	1.7	2.6
90-94	0.3	0.5	1.5
95-99	0.04	0.2	0.4
100+	0.00	0.02	0.1

Source: Population Division of the Department of Economic and Social Affairs of the United Nations Secretariat, *World Population Prospects: The 2008 Revision*, 2009.

Figure 8.42 German population by age band (%)

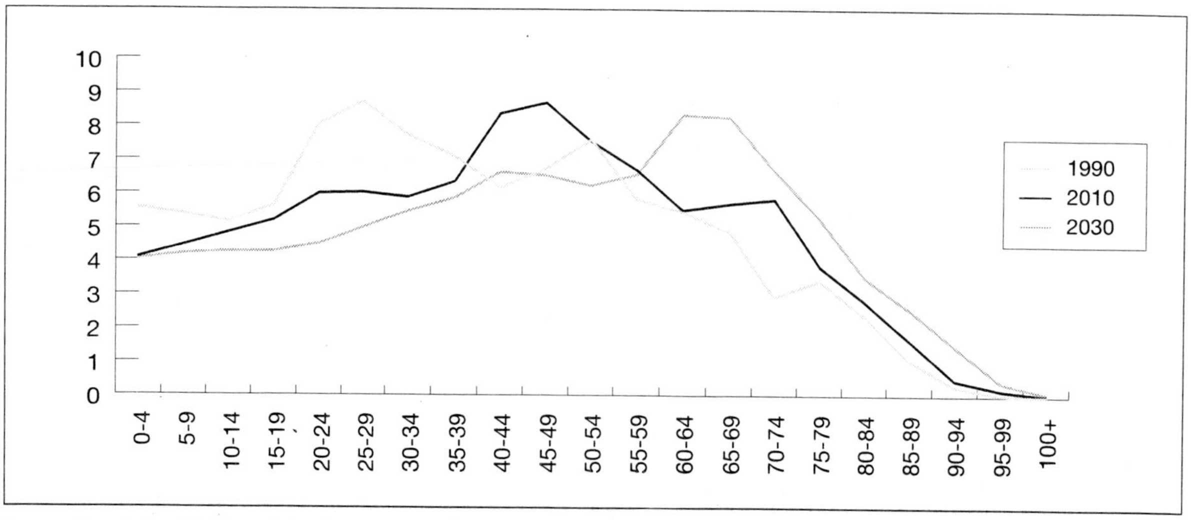

Source: Population Division of the Department of Economic and Social Affairs of the United Nations Secretariat, *World Population Prospects: The 2008 Revision*, 2009.

Figure 8.43 German population by gender (males per hundred females)

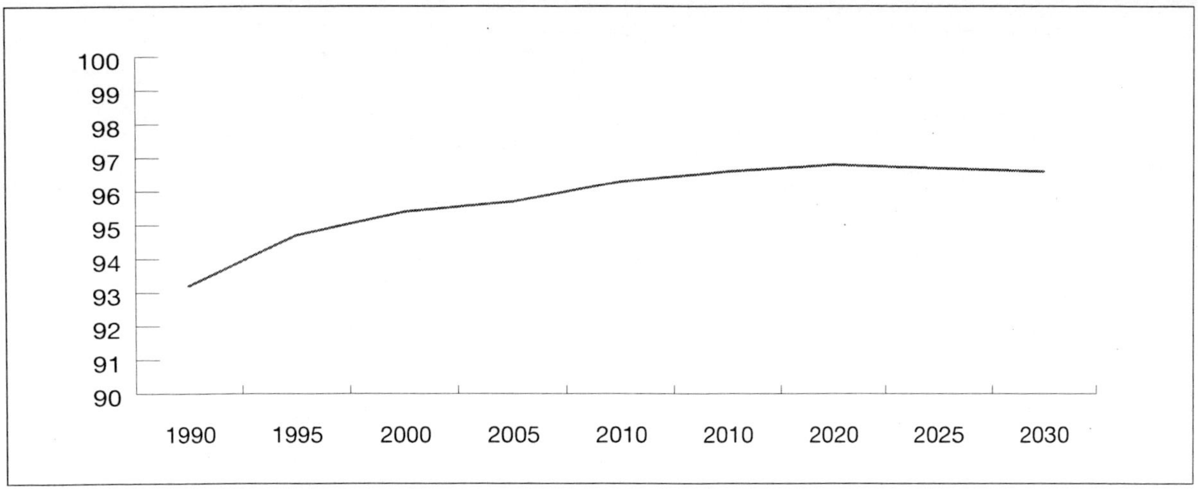

Source: Population Division of the Department of Economic and Social Affairs of the United Nations Secretariat, *World Population Prospects: The 2008 Revision,* 2009.

Figure 8.44 German urban population (%)

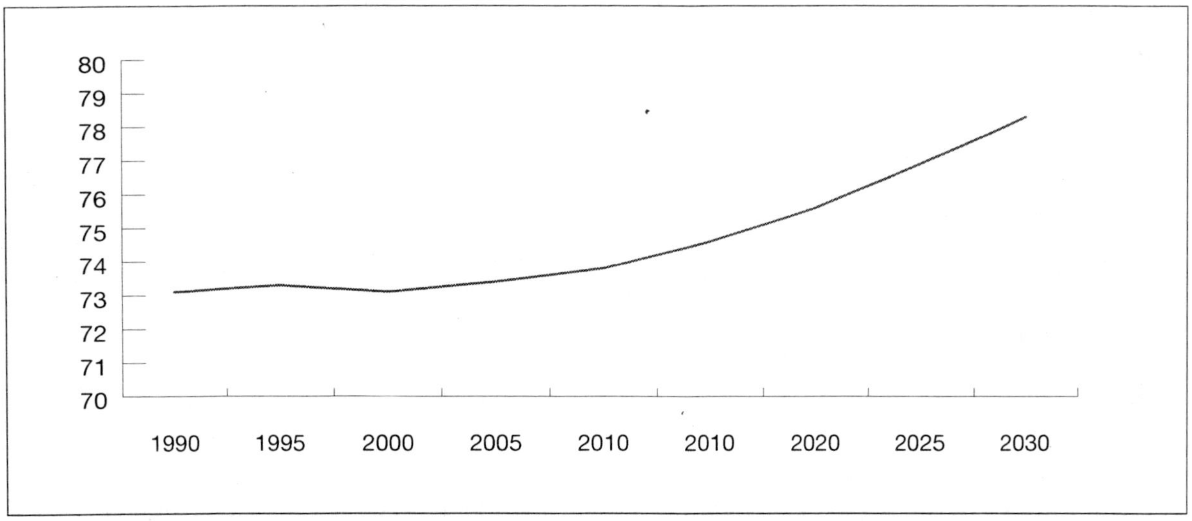

Source: Population Division of the Department of Economic and Social Affairs of the United Nations Secretariat, *World Population Prospects: The 2008 Revision,* 2009.

8.3.6 India

Figure 8.45 Indian fertility

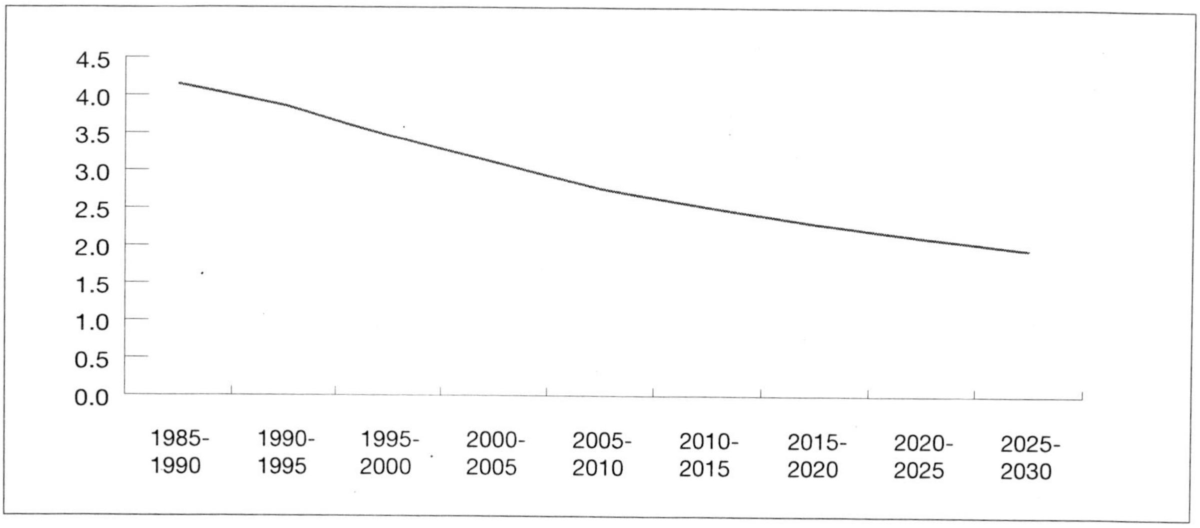

Source: Population Division of the Department of Economic and Social Affairs of the United Nations Secretariat, *World Population Prospects: The 2008 Revision*, 2009.

Table 8.22 Indian life expectancy (years)

Year	All	Male	Female
1985-1990	74.8	71.7	78.2
1990-1995	76.2	72.6	79.1
1995-2000	77.2	73.9	80.2
2000-2005	78.7	75.8	81.4
2005-2010	79.9	77.1	82.4
2010-2015	80.5	77.8	83.1
2015-2020	81.1	78.4	83.7
2020-2025	81.6	79.0	84.3
2025-2030	82.2	79.6	84.9

Source: Population Division of the Department of Economic and Social Affairs of the United Nations Secretariat, *World Population Prospects: The 2008 Revision*, 2009.

Table 8.23 Indian population by age band (%)

Age	1990	2010	2030
0-4	13.9	10.3	7.2
5-9	12.6	10.3	7.6
10-14	11.4	10.1	7.9
15-19	10.1	9.9	8.1
20-24	9.0	9.3	8.2
25-29	8.1	8.5	8.2
30-34	7.2	7.6	8.0
35-39	6.3	6.7	7.8
40-44	4.7	5.9	7.2
45-49	4.0	5.2	6.5
50-54	3.6	4.5	5.8
55-59	3.0	3.8	4.9
60-64	2.3	2.6	4.0
65-69	1.7	1.9	3.2
70-74	1.1	1.4	2.4
75-79	0.6	0.9	1.5
80-84	0.3	0.4	0.7
85-89	0.1	0.2	0.3
90-94	0.03	0.05	0.1
95-99	0.0	0.01	0.02
100+	0.0	0.00	0.00

Source: Population Division of the Department of Economic and Social Affairs of the United Nations Secretariat, *World Population Prospects: The 2008 Revision*, 2009.

Figure 8.46 Indian population by age band (%)

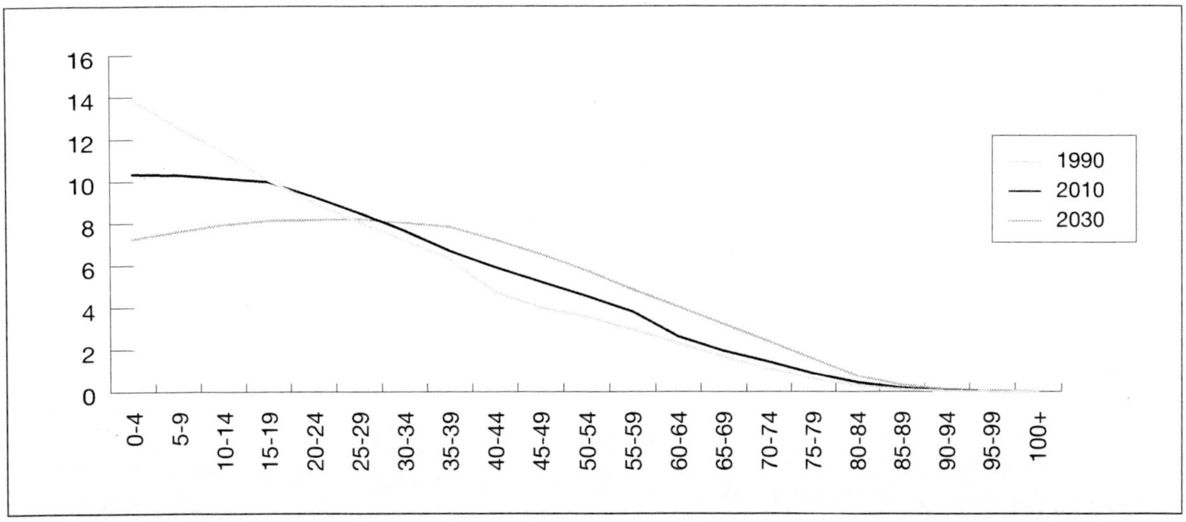

Source: Population Division of the Department of Economic and Social Affairs of the United Nations Secretariat, *World Population Prospects: The 2008 Revision*, 2009.

Figure 8.47 Indian population by gender (males per hundred females)

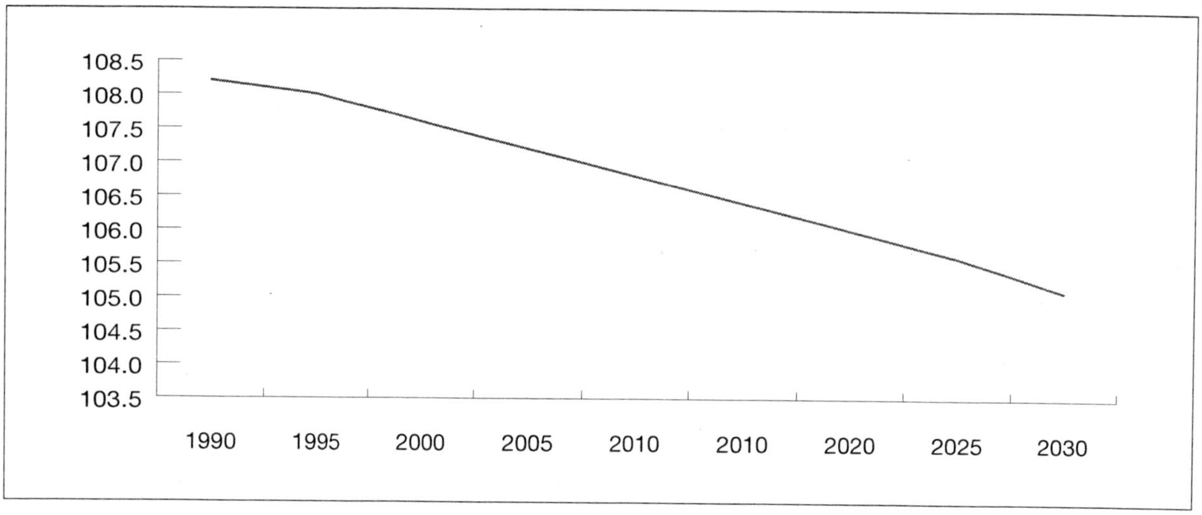

Source: Population Division of the Department of Economic and Social Affairs of the United Nations Secretariat, *World Population Prospects: The 2008 Revision*, 2009.

Figure 8.48 Indian urban population (%)

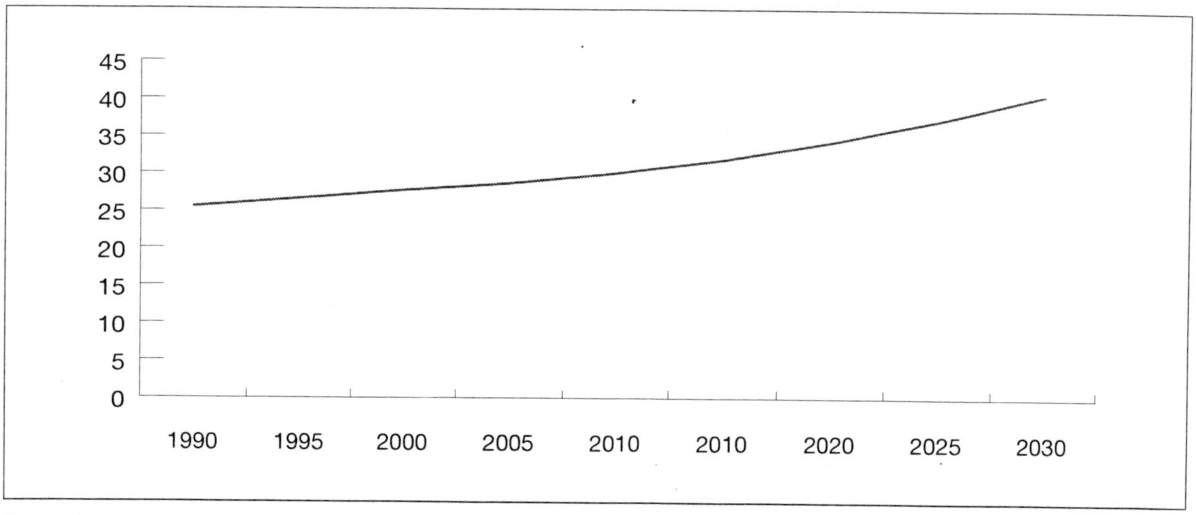

Source: Population Division of the Department of Economic and Social Affairs of the United Nations Secretariat, *World Population Prospects: The 2008 Revision*, 2009.

8.3.7 Italy

Figure 8.49 Italian fertility

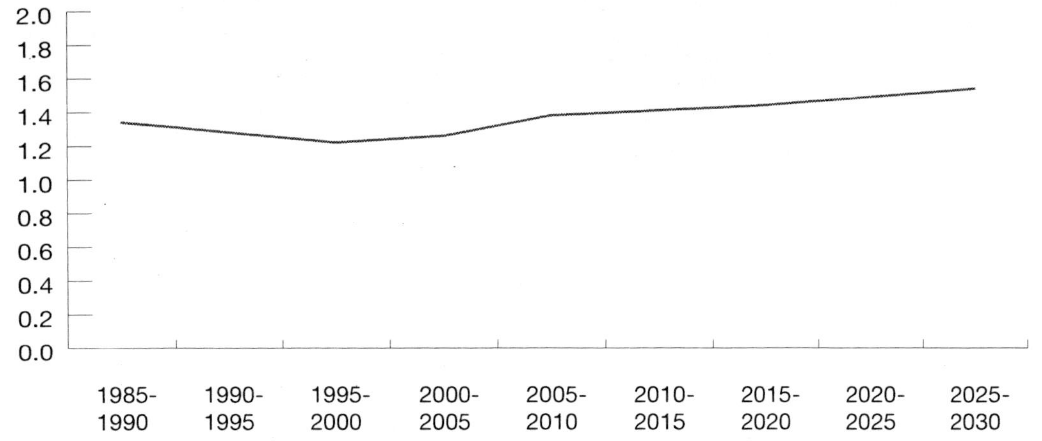

Source: Population Division of the Department of Economic and Social Affairs of the United Nations Secretariat, *World Population Prospects: The 2008 Revision*, 2009.

Table 8.24 Italian life expectancy (years)

Year	All	Male	Female
1985-1990	76.3	72.9	79.5
1990-1995	77.4	74.0	80.7
1995-2000	78.7	75.4	81.8
2000-2005	80.2	77.2	83.1
2005-2010	81.2	78.1	84.1
2010-2015	81.6	78.6	84.6
2015-2020	82.2	79.2	85.2
2020-2025	82.8	79.8	85.7
2025-2030	83.3	80.3	86.3

Source: Population Division of the Department of Economic and Social Affairs of the United Nations Secretariat, *World Population Prospects: The 2008 Revision*, 2009.

Table 8.25 Italian population by age band (%)

Age	1990	2010	2030
0-4	4.9	4.8	4.0
5-9	5.2	4.7	4.0
10-14	6.3	4.6	4.2
15-19	7.7	4.8	4.6
20-24	8.1	5.0	5.1
25-29	7.9	5.7	5.2
30-34	7.0	6.8	5.2
35-39	6.6	8.1	5.5
40-44	6.9	8.2	5.7
45-49	6.0	7.8	6.2
50-54	6.3	6.7	7.2
55-59	6.0	6.1	8.1
60-64	5.7	6.2	8.0
65-69	5.2	5.2	7.3
70-74	3.1	5.1	5.9
75-79	3.3	4.2	4.8
80-84	2.2	3.1	4.1
85-89	1.0	2.0	2.5
90-94	0.3	0.6	1.4
95-99	0.05	0.3	0.5
100+	0.01	0.05	0.1

Source: Population Division of the Department of Economic and Social Affairs of the United Nations Secretariat, *World Population Prospects: The 2008 Revision*, 2009.

Figure 8.50 Italian population by age band (%)

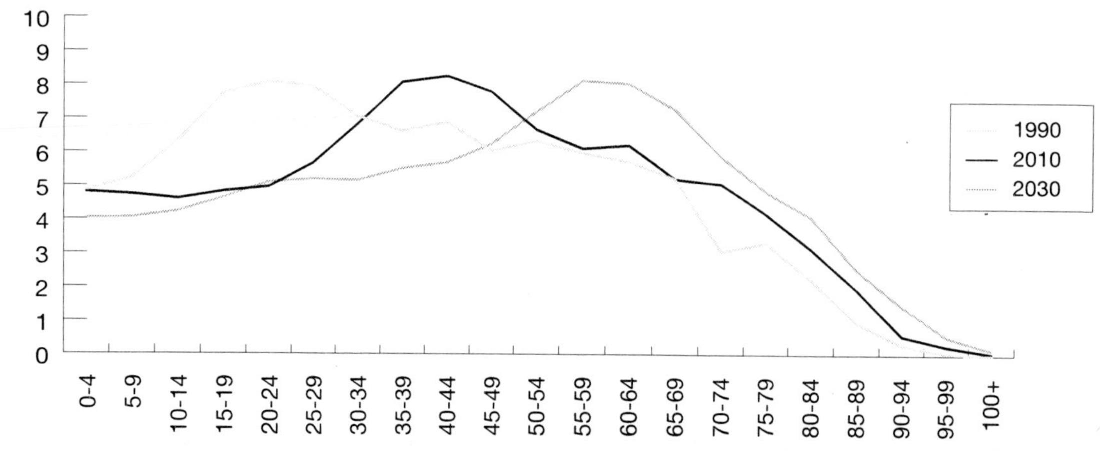

Source: Population Division of the Department of Economic and Social Affairs of the United Nations Secretariat, *World Population Prospects: The 2008 Revision*, 2009.

Figure 8.51 Italian population by gender (males per hundred females)

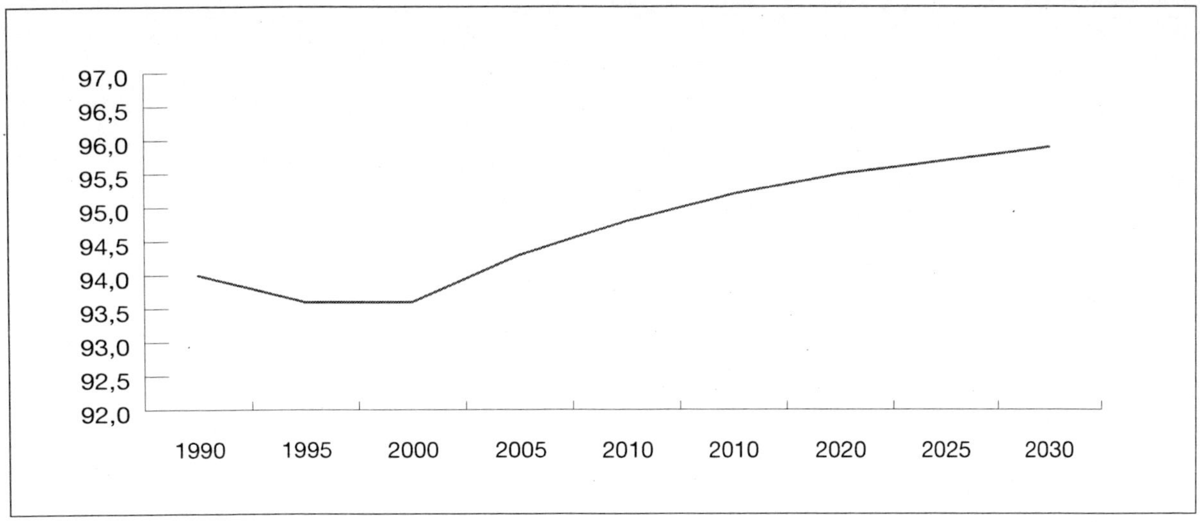

Source: Population Division of the Department of Economic and Social Affairs of the United Nations Secretariat, *World Population Prospects: The 2008 Revision*, 2009.

Figure 8.52 Italian urban population (%)

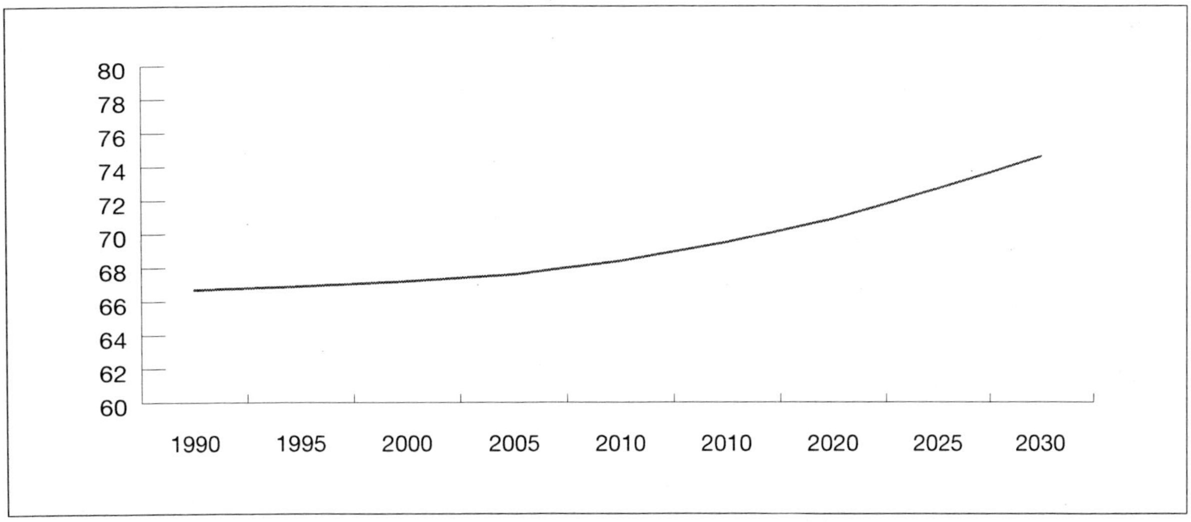

Source: Population Division of the Department of Economic and Social Affairs of the United Nations Secretariat, *World Population Prospects: The 2008 Revision*, 2009.

8.3.8 Japan

Figure 8.53 Japanese fertility

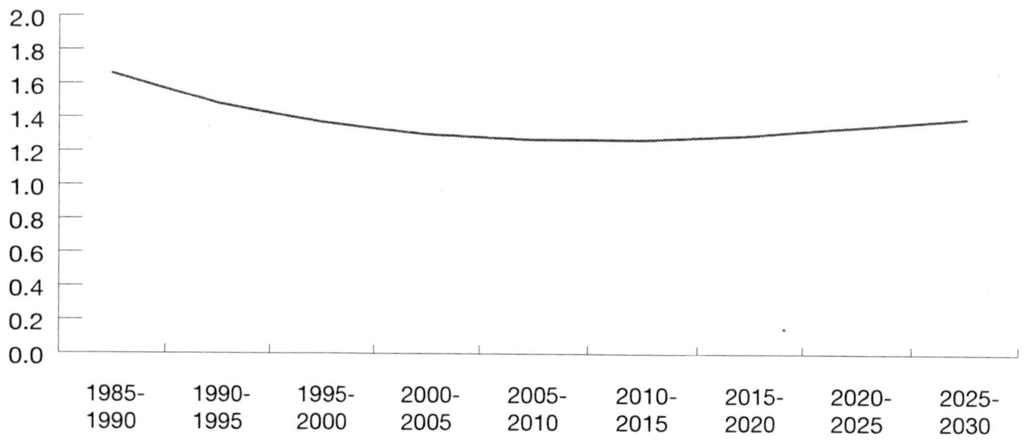

Source: Population Division of the Department of Economic and Social Affairs of the United Nations Secretariat, *World Population Prospects: The 2008 Revision*, 2009.

Table 8.26 Japanese life expectancy (years)

Year	All	Male	Female
1985-1990	78.5	75.5	81.3
1990-1995	79.5	76.3	82.5
1995-2000	80.6	77.1	83.9
2000-2005	82.1	78.3	85.7
2005-2010	82.7	79.0	86.2
2010-2015	83.7	80.1	87.2
2015-2020	84.4	80.7	87.9
2020-2025	84.9	81.2	88.4
2025-2030	85.3	81.7	88.9

Source: Population Division of the Department of Economic and Social Affairs of the United Nations Secretariat, *World Population Prospects: The 2008 Revision*, 2009.

Table 8.27 Japanese population by age band (%)

Age	1990	2010	2030
0-4	5.2	4.1	3.5
5-9	6.1	4.4	3.6
10-14	7.0	4.6	3.7
15-19	8.2	4.7	4.1
20-24	7.1	5.2	4.5
25-29	6.5	5.9	4.9
30-34	6.3	6.7	5.1
35-39	7.4	7.7	5.2
40-44	8.7	6.8	5.7
45-49	7.3	6.3	6.4
50-54	6.5	6.0	7.1
55-59	6.3	6.9	8.2
60-64	5.4	7.9	7.1
65-69	4.1	6.3	6.3
70-74	3.1	5.4	5.7
75-79	2.4	4.5	5.9
80-84	1.4	3.3	5.9
85-89	0.7	1.9	3.7
90-94	0.2	0.8	2.1
95-99	0.03	0.3	1.0
100+	0.00	0.1	0.3

Source: Population Division of the Department of Economic and Social Affairs of the United Nations Secretariat, *World Population Prospects: The 2008 Revision*, 2009.

Figure 8.54 Japanese population by age band (%)

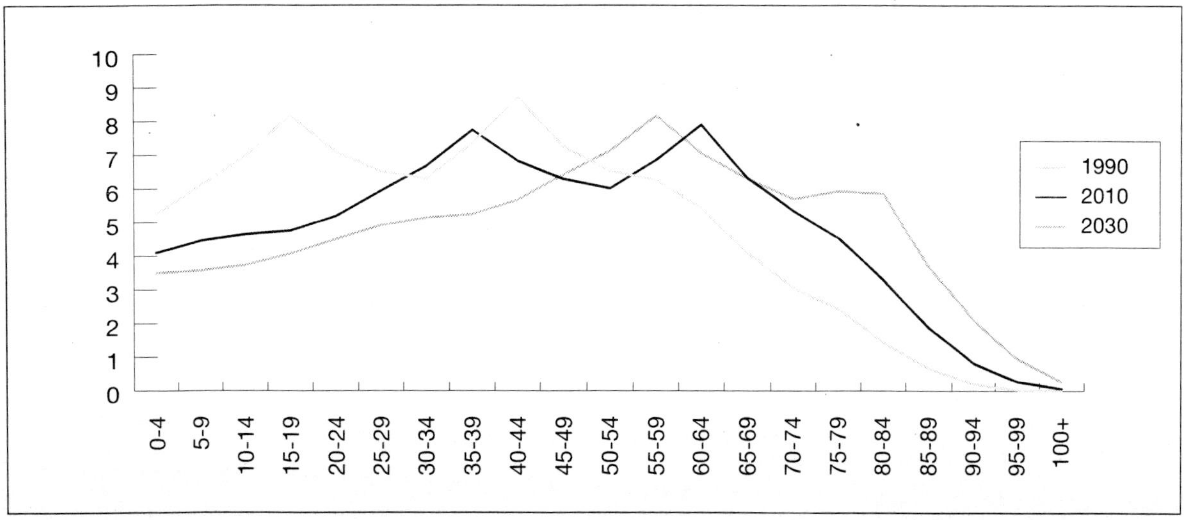

Source: Population Division of the Department of Economic and Social Affairs of the United Nations Secretariat, *World Population Prospects: The 2008 Revision*, 2009.

Figure 8.55 Japanese population by gender (males per hundred females)

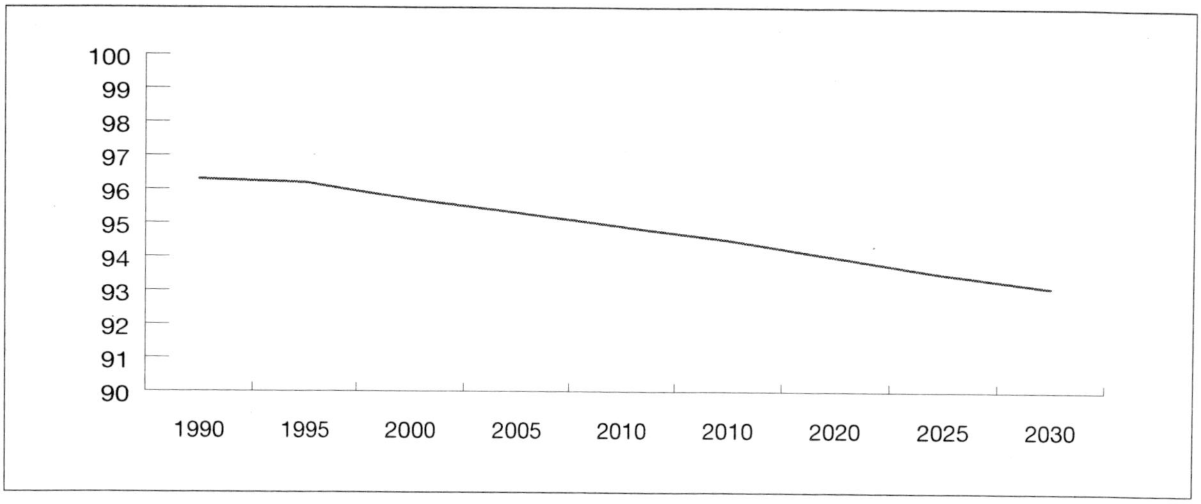

Source: Population Division of the Department of Economic and Social Affairs of the United Nations Secretariat, *World Population Prospects: The 2008 Revision*, 2009.

Figure 8.56 Japanese urban population (%)

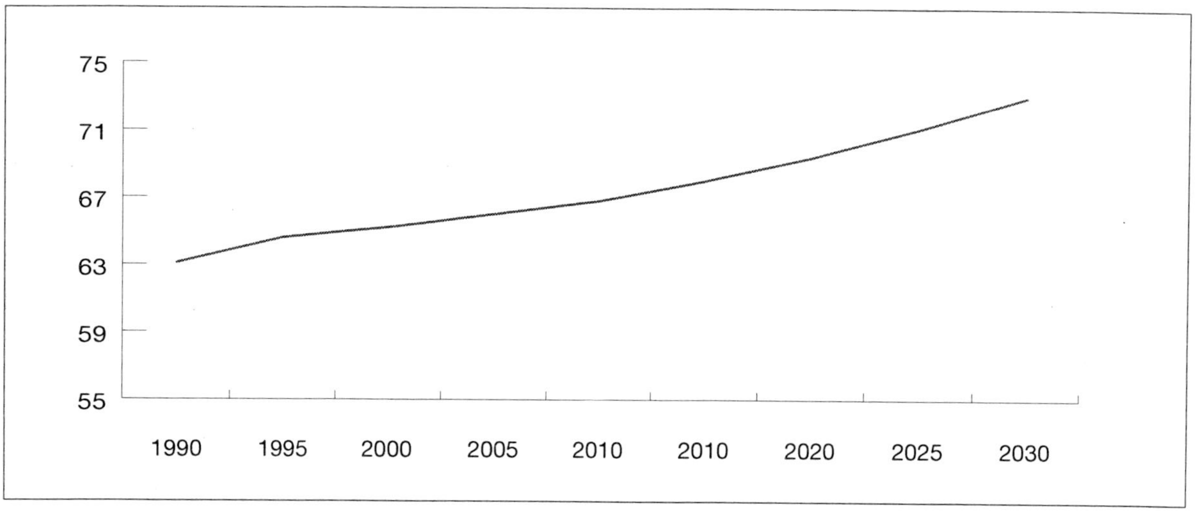

Source: Population Division of the Department of Economic and Social Affairs of the United Nations Secretariat, *World Population Prospects: The 2008 Revision*, 2009.

8.3.9 The Netherlands

Figure 8.57 Netherlands fertility

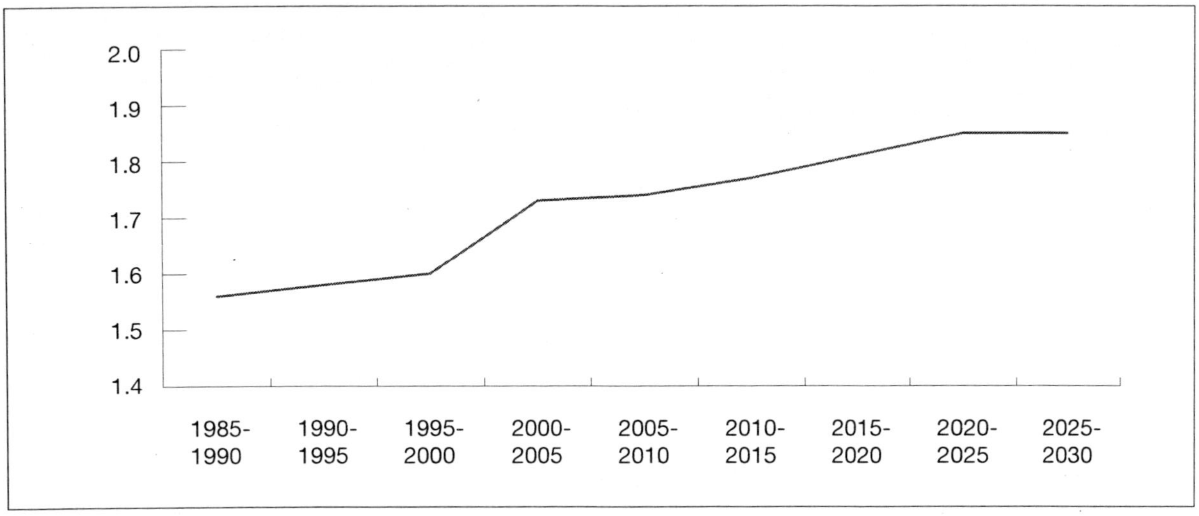

Source: Population Division of the Department of Economic and Social Affairs of the United Nations Secretariat, *World Population Prospects: The 2008 Revision*, 2009.

Table 8.28 Netherlands life expectancy (years)

Year	All	Male	Female
1985-1990	76.7	73.5	79.9
1990-1995	77.3	74.2	80.2
1995-2000	77.8	75.1	80.5
2000-2005	78.7	76.3	81.0
2005-2010	80.0	77.8	82.0
2010-2015	80.6	78.5	82.6
2015-2020	81.1	79.1	83.2
2020-2025	81.7	79.6	83.7
2025-2030	82.2	80.2	84.2

Source: Population Division of the Department of Economic and Social Affairs of the United Nations Secretariat, *World Population Prospects: The 2008 Revision*, 2009.

Table 8.29 Netherlands population by age (%)

Age	1990	2010	2030
0-4	6.3	5.6	5.5
5-9	5.9	6.0	5.5
10-14	6.0	6.0	5.3
15-19	7.2	6.1	5.3
20-24	8.5	6.1	5.6
25-29	8.7	5.9	6.1
30-34	8.2	6.0	6.1
35-39	7.7	7.0	6.1
40-44	8.0	7.9	6.0
45-49	6.1	7.8	5.6
50-54	5.3	7.2	5.6
55-59	4.9	6.5	6.4
60-64	4.5	6.6	7.0
65-69	4.2	4.7	6.7
70-74	3.2	3.7	5.7
75-79	2.5	3.0	4.6
80-84	1.7	2.1	3.8
85-89	0.9	1.3	1.9
90-94	0.3	0.4	0.8
95-99	0.1	0.1	0.2
100+	0.01	0.01	0.04

Source: Population Division of the Department of Economic and Social Affairs of the United Nations Secretariat, *World Population Prospects: The 2008 Revision*, 2009.

Figure 8.58 Netherlands population by age (%)

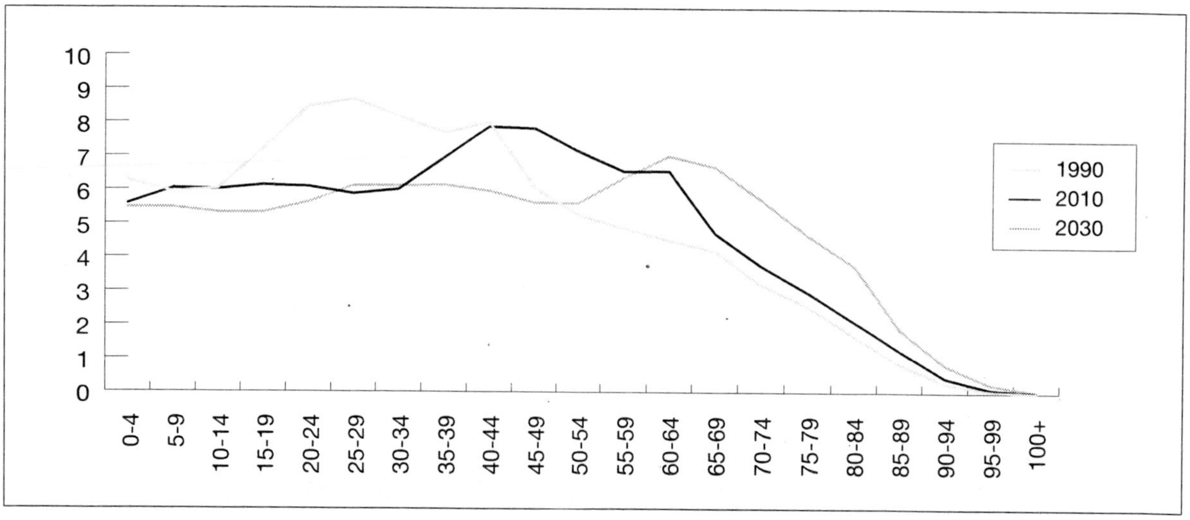

Source: Population Division of the Department of Economic and Social Affairs of the United Nations Secretariat, *World Population Prospects: The 2008 Revision*, 2009.

Figure 8.59 Netherlands population by gender (males per hundred females)

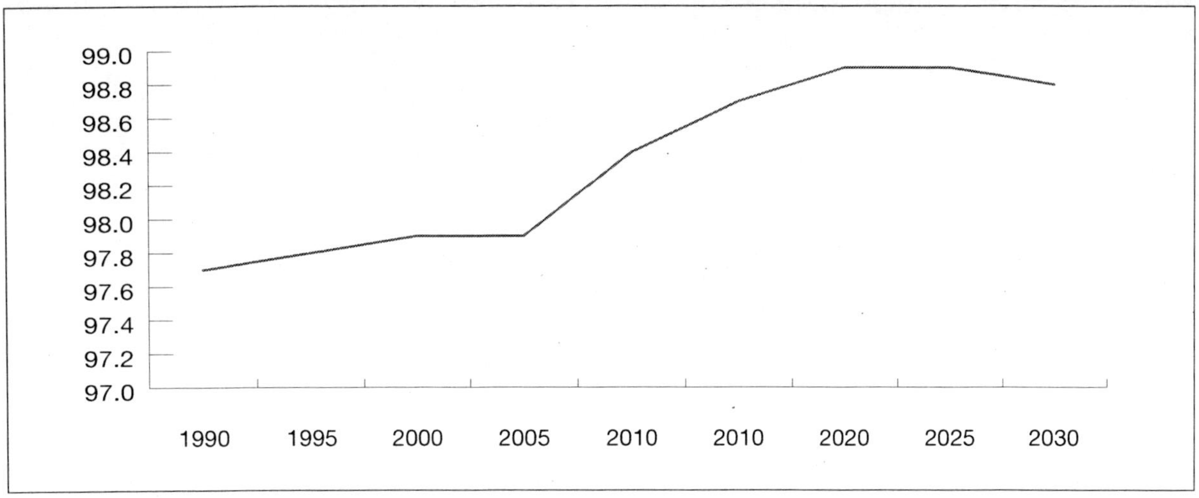

Source: Population Division of the Department of Economic and Social Affairs of the United Nations Secretariat, *World Population Prospects: The 2008 Revision*, 2009.

Figure 8.60 Netherlands urban population (%)

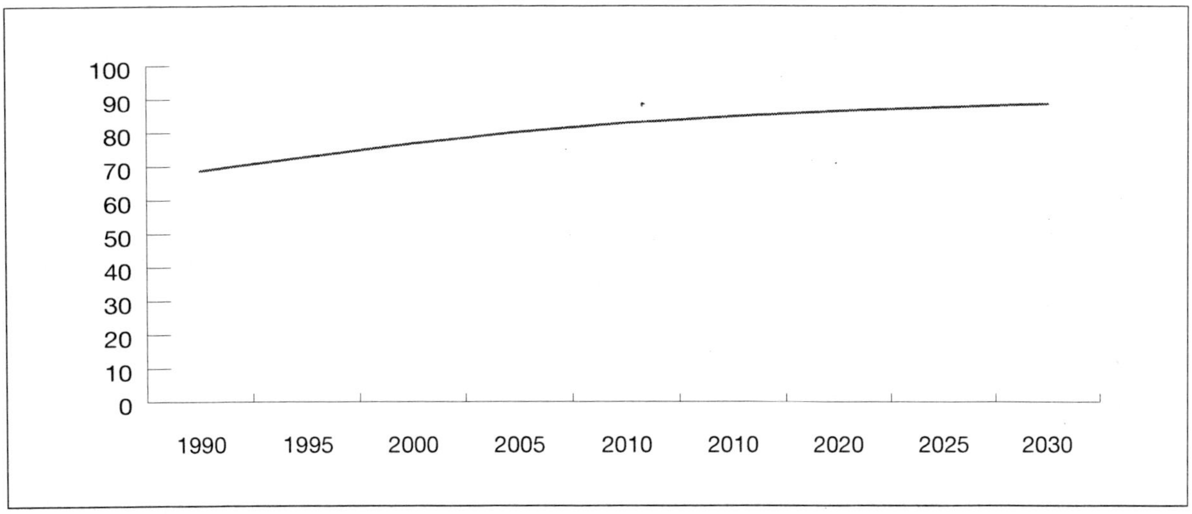

Source: Population Division of the Department of Economic and Social Affairs of the United Nations Secretariat, *World Population Prospects: The 2008 Revision*, 2009.

8.3.10 Russian Federation

Figure 8.61 Russian fertility

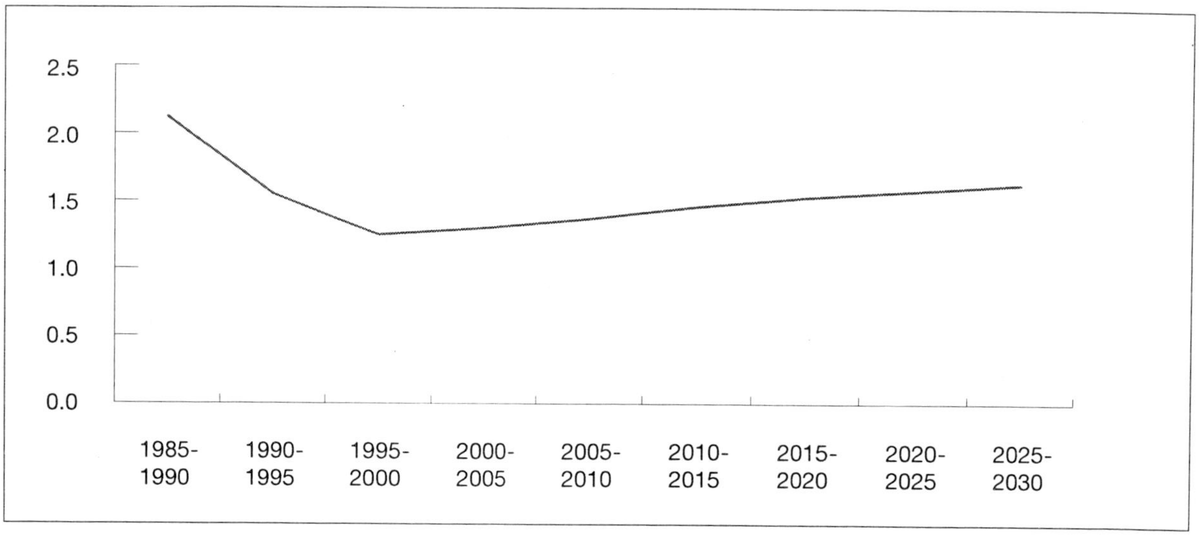

Source: Population Division of the Department of Economic and Social Affairs of the United Nations Secretariat, *World Population Prospects: The 2008 Revision*, 2009.

Table 8.30 Russian life expectancy (years)

Year	All	Male	Female
1985-1990	69.0	63.8	73.6
1990-1995	66.4	60.5	72.5
1995-2000	65.7	59.6	72.2
2000-2005	64.8	58.5	71.8
2005-2010	66.5	60.3	73.1
2010-2015	67.9	61.9	74.1
2015-2020	69.3	63.6	75.0
2020-2025	70.6	65.2	75.8
2025-2030	71.6	66.5	76.5

Source: Population Division of the Department of Economic and Social Affairs of the United Nations Secretariat, *World Population Prospects: The 2008 Revision*, 2009.

Table 8.31 Russian population by age band (%)

Age	1990	2010	2030
0-4	8.0	5.4	4.6
5-9	7.9	5.0	5.0
10-14	7.3	4.6	5.6
15-19	6.9	5.8	6.0
20-24	6.4	8.6	5.9
25-29	7.9	8.6	5.4
30-34	8.8	7.6	5.0
35-39	8.1	7.1	6.1
40-44	6.5	6.5	8.9
45-49	4.1	7.7	8.6
50-54	7.1	8.0	7.3
55-59	5.2	7.0	6.5
60-64	5.9	5.2	5.6
65-69	3.6	3.0	6.0
70-74	2.2	4.4	5.6
75-79	2.3	2.5	4.0
80-84	1.3	2.0	2.2
85-89	0.5	0.7	0.8
90-94	0.1	0.2	0.5
95-99	0.02	0.05	0.1
100+	0.00	0.00	0.02

Source: Population Division of the Department of Economic and Social Affairs of the United Nations Secretariat, *World Population Prospects: The 2008 Revision*, 2009.

Figure 8.62 Russian population by age band (%)

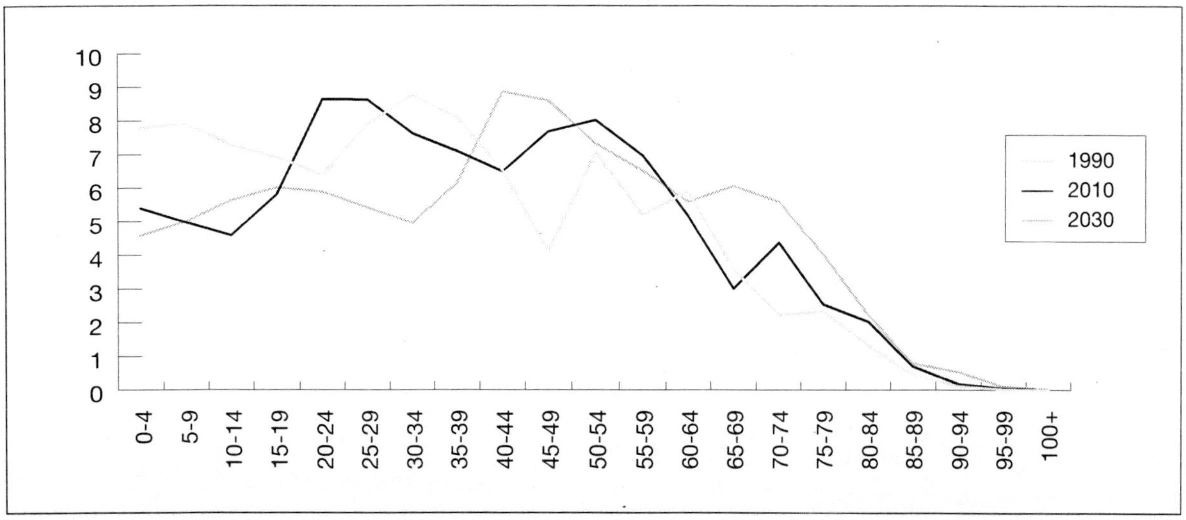

Source: Population Division of the Department of Economic and Social Affairs of the United Nations Secretariat, *World Population Prospects: The 2008 Revision*, 2009.

Figure 8.63 Russian population by gender (males per hundred females)

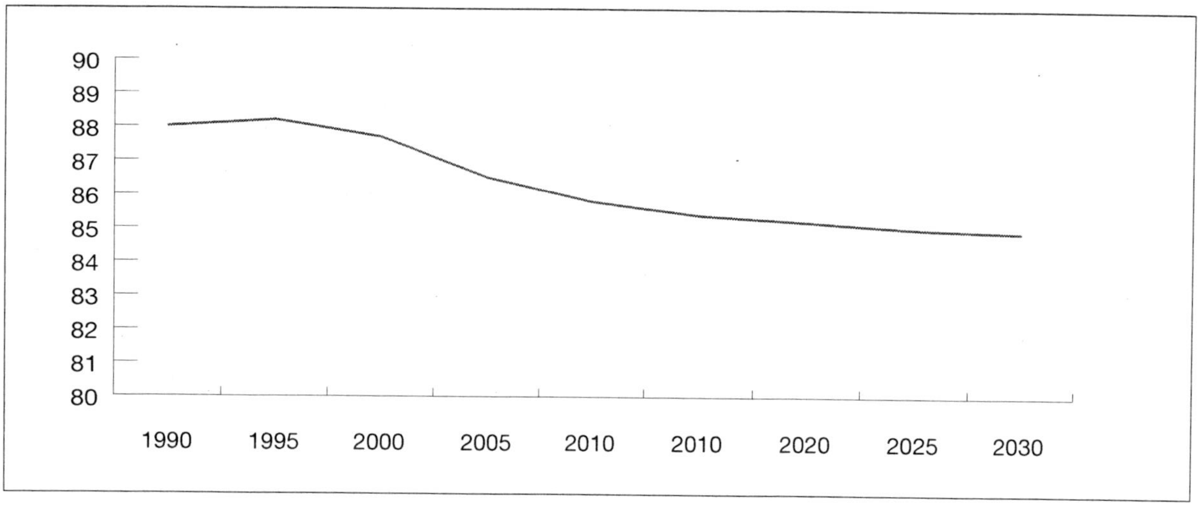

Source: Population Division of the Department of Economic and Social Affairs of the United Nations Secretariat, *World Population Prospects: The 2008 Revision*, 2009.

Figure 8.64 Russian urban population (%)

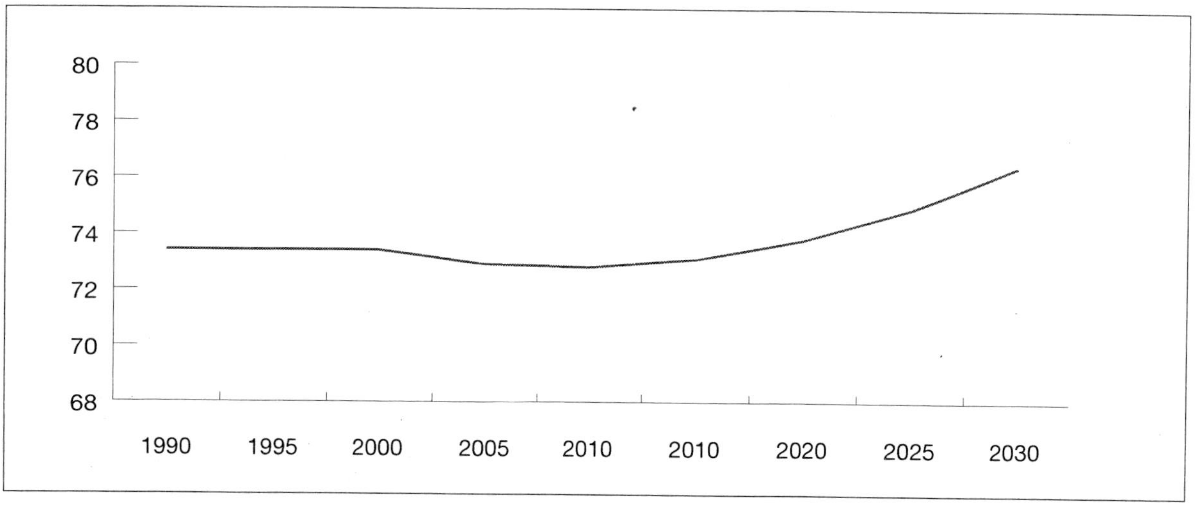

Source: Population Division of the Department of Economic and Social Affairs of the United Nations Secretariat, *World Population Prospects: The 2008 Revision*, 2009.

Figure 8.65 Proportion of World populace in the Russian Federation, 1990-2030

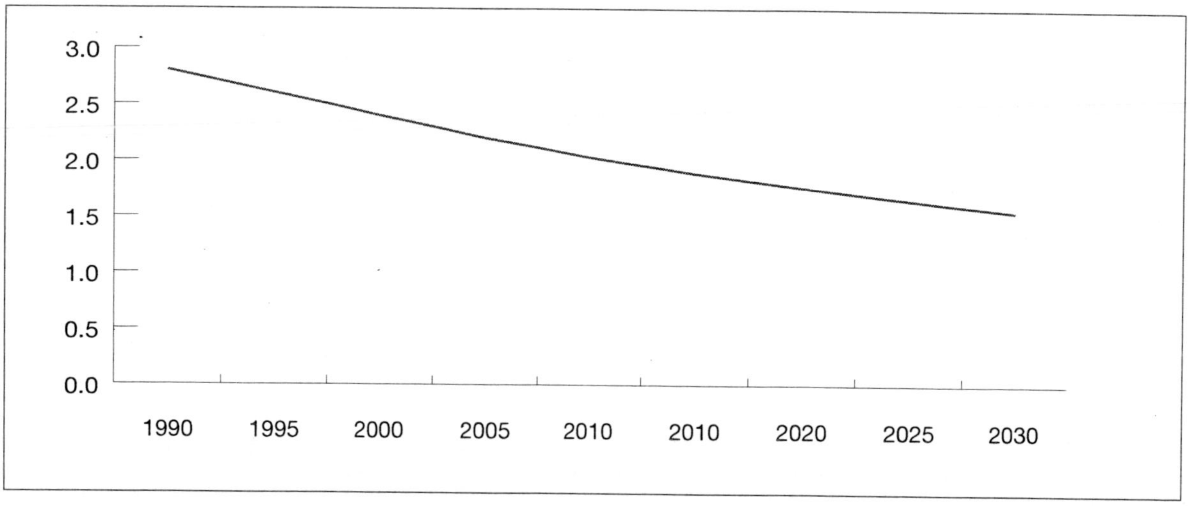

Source: Population Division of the Department of Economic and Social Affairs of the United Nations Secretariat, *World Population Prospects: The 2008 Revision*, 2009.

8.3.11 Spain

Figure 8.66 Spanish fertility

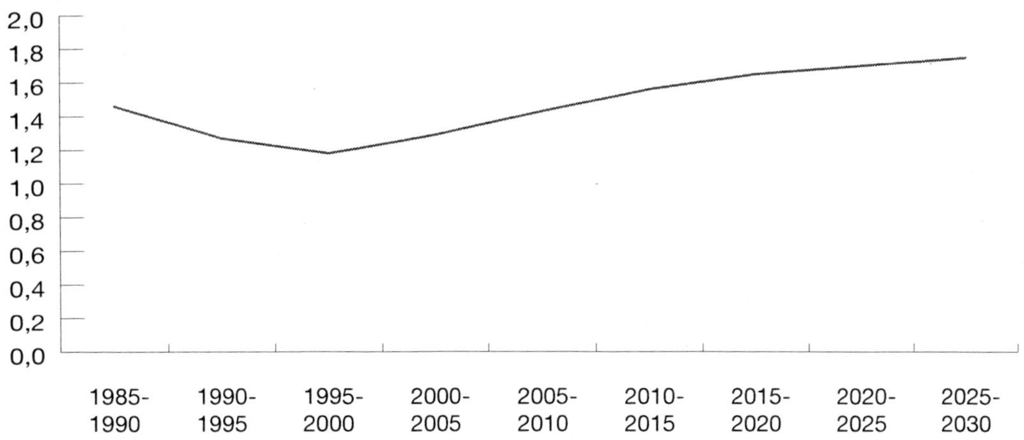

Source: Population Division of the Department of Economic and Social Affairs of the United Nations Secretariat, *World Population Prospects: The 2008 Revision*, 2009.

Table 8.32 Spanish life expectancy (years)

Year	All	Male	Female
1985-1990	76.6	73.3	80.2
1990-1995	77.4	73.9	81.2
1995-2000	78.6	75.1	82.2
2000-2005	79.8	76.4	83.1
2005-2010	80.9	77.6	84.1
2010-2015	81.6	78.6	84.7
2015-2020	82.4	79.5	85.2
2020-2025	83.0	80.3	85.8
2025-2030	83.6	81.0	86.3

Source: Population Division of the Department of Economic and Social Affairs of the United Nations Secretariat, *World Population Prospects: The 2008 Revision*, 2009.

Table 8.33 Spanish population by age band (%)

Age	1990	2010	2030
0-4	5.3	5.4	4.4
5-9	6.4	5.0	4.6
10-14	8.1	4.5	5.0
15-19	8.5	4.9	5.4
20-24	8.3	5.5	5.4
25-29	8.0	7.1	5.2
30-34	7.2	8.6	4.9
35-39	6.4	8.6	5.4
40-44	6.2	8.1	5.9
45-49	5.5	7.5	7.2
50-54	5.2	6.6	8.4
55-59	5.8	5.7	8.1
60-64	5.3	5.2	7.3
65-69	4.6	4.5	6.5
70-74	3.4	3.9	5.3
75-79	2.7	3.8	4.1
80-84	1.8	2.7	3.2
85-89	0.8	1.5	2.0
90-94	0.2	0.6	1.0
95-99	0.04	0.1	0.4
100+	0.01	0.02	0.1

Source: Population Division of the Department of Economic and Social Affairs of the United Nations Secretariat, *World Population Prospects: The 2008 Revision*, 2009.

Figure 8.67 Spanish population by age band (%)

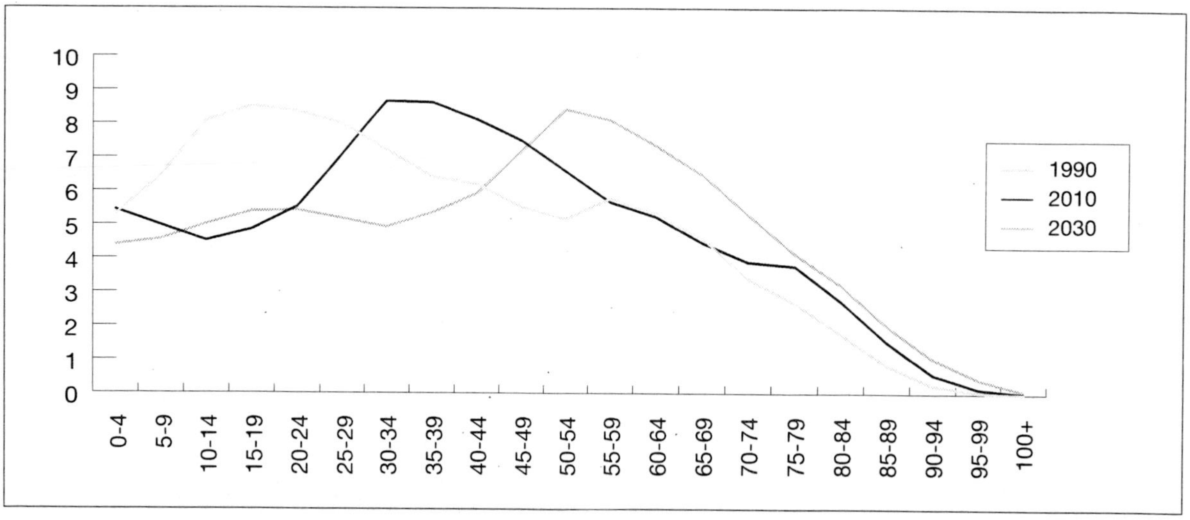

Source: Population Division of the Department of Economic and Social Affairs of the United Nations Secretariat, *World Population Prospects: The 2008 Revision*, 2009.

Figure 8.68 Spanish population by gender (males per hundred females)

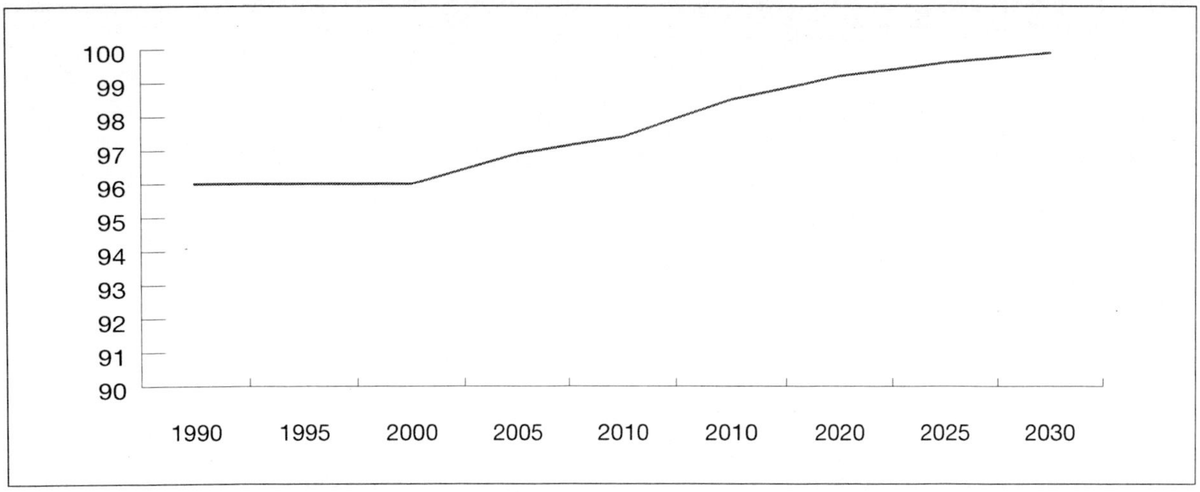

Source: Population Division of the Department of Economic and Social Affairs of the United Nations Secretariat, *World Population Prospects: The 2008 Revision*, 2009.

Figure 8.69 Spain urban population (%)

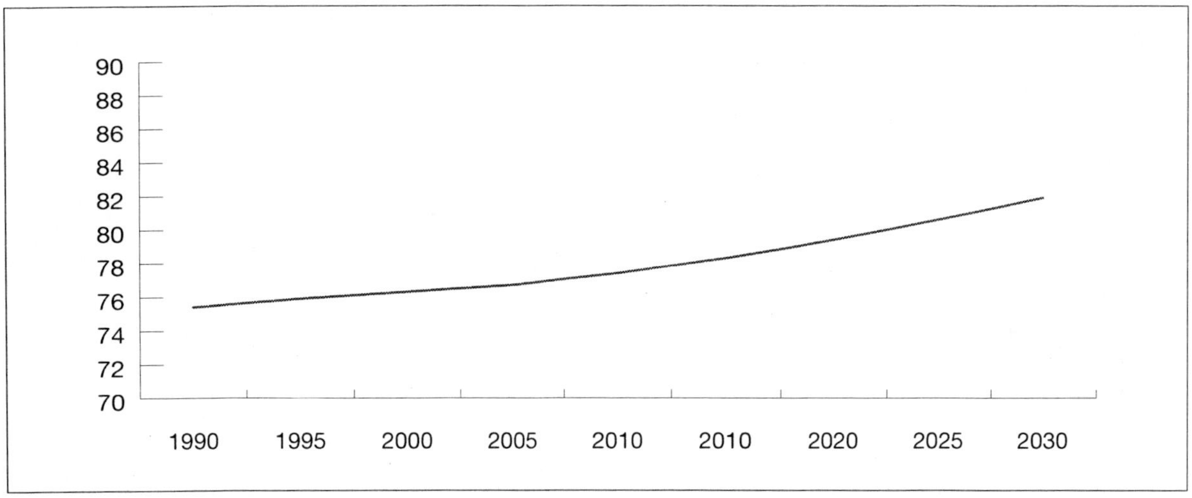

Source: Population Division of the Department of Economic and Social Affairs of the United Nations Secretariat, *World Population Prospects: The 2008 Revision*, 2009.

8.3.12 United Kingdom

Figure 8.70 United Kingdom fertility

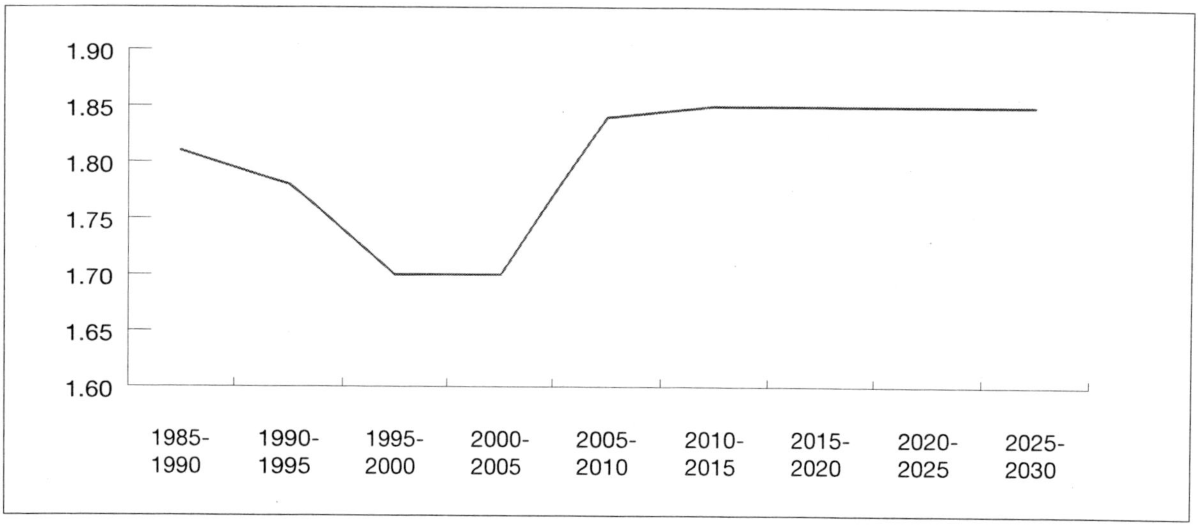

Source: Population Division of the Department of Economic and Social Affairs of the United Nations Secretariat, *World Population Prospects: The 2008 Revision*, 2009.

Table 8.34 United Kingdom life expectancy (years)

Year	All	Male	Female
1985-1990	75.0	72.3	78.0
1990-1995	76.4	73.6	79.0
1995-2000	77.2	74.7	79.7
2000-2005	78.5	76.1	80.7
2005-2010	79.4	77.2	81.6
2010-2015	80.1	77.8	82.3
2015-2020	80.7	78.5	82.9
2020-2025	81.3	79.1	83.5
2025-2030	81.9	79.6	84.1

Source: Population Division of the Department of Economic and Social Affairs of the United Nations Secretariat, *World Population Prospects: The 2008 Revision*, 2009.

Table 8.35 United Kingdom population by age band (%)

Age	1990	2010	2030
0-4	6.7	6.0	5.7
5-9	6.3	5.6	5.7
10-14	6.0	5.8	5.7
15-19	6.8	6.4	5.8
20-24	7.9	6.8	6.1
25-29	8.1	6.6	6.0
30-34	7.1	6.2	6.3
35-39	6.6	6.8	6.8
40-44	7.2	7.5	6.8
45-49	5.9	7.4	6.3
50-54	5.4	6.4	5.7
55-59	5.1	5.8	6.0
60-64	5.1	6.1	6.3
65-69	5.0	4.7	6.0
70-74	3.8	4.0	4.8
75-79	3.3	3.2	3.8
80-84	2.2	2.4	3.2
85-89	1.0	1.5	1.8
90-94	0.3	0.6	0.8
95-99	0.1	0.2	0.3
100+	0.01	0.03	0.06

Source: Population Division of the Department of Economic and Social Affairs of the United Nations Secretariat, *World Population Prospects: The 2008 Revision*, 2009.

Figure 8.71 United Kingdom population by age band (%)

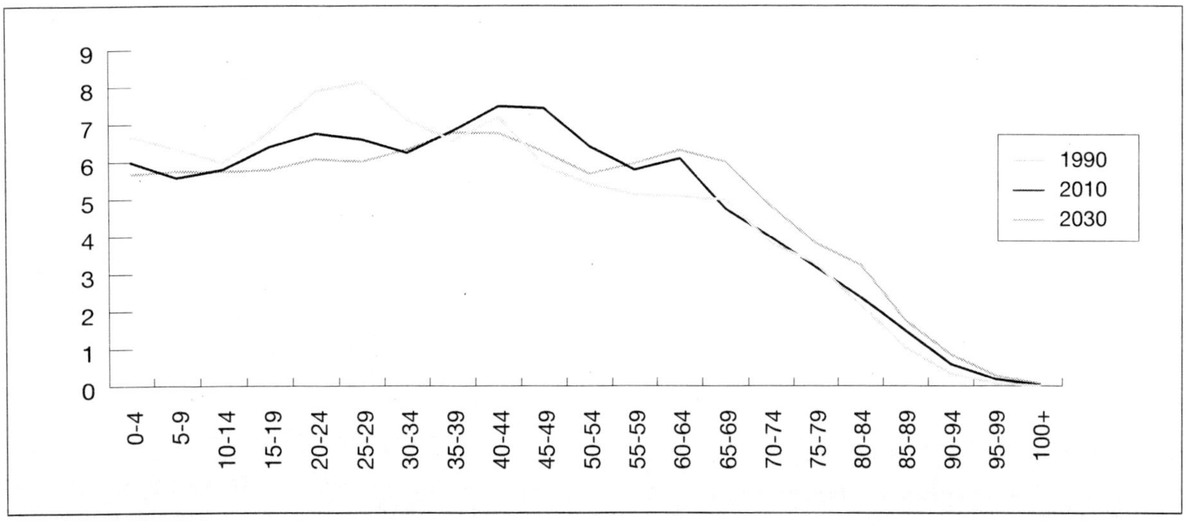

Source: Population Division of the Department of Economic and Social Affairs of the United Nations Secretariat, *World Population Prospects: The 2008 Revision*, 2009.

Figure 8.72 United Kingdom population by gender (males per hundred females)

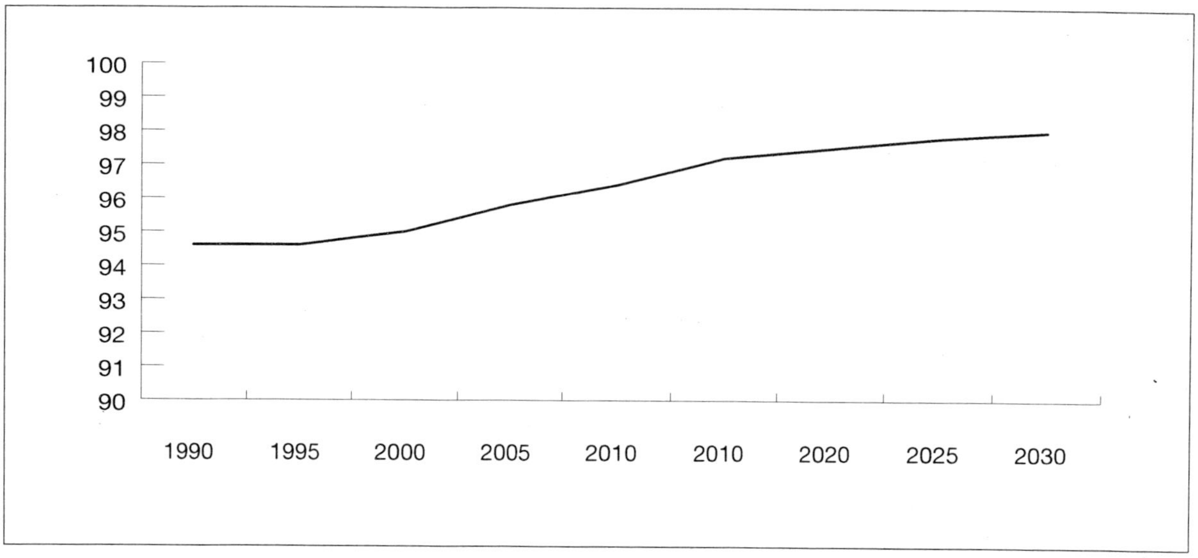

Source: Population Division of the Department of Economic and Social Affairs of the United Nations Secretariat, *World Population Prospects: The 2008 Revision*, 2009.

Figure 8.73 United Kingdom urban population (%)

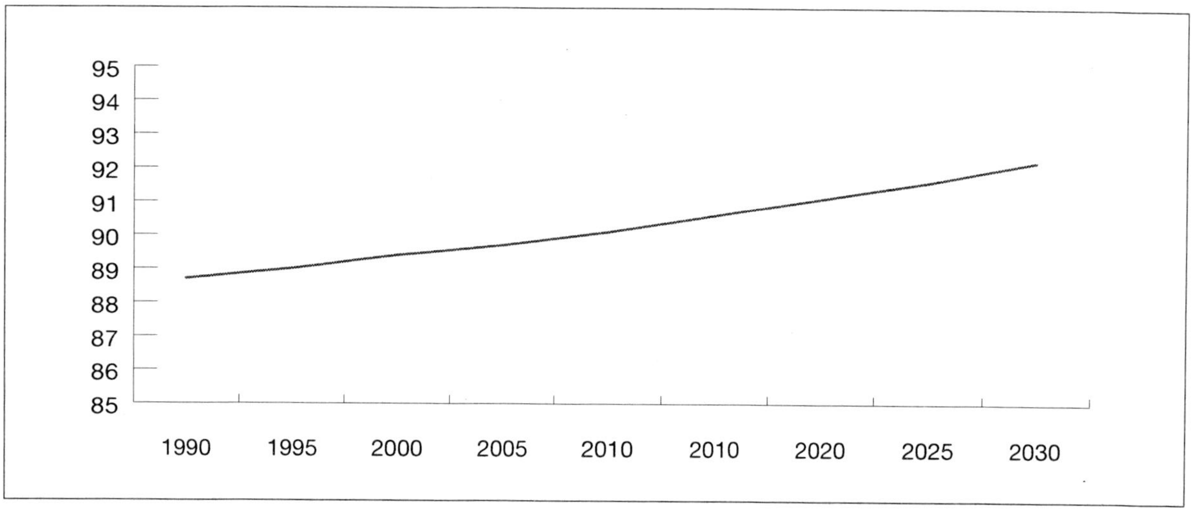

Source: Population Division of the Department of Economic and Social Affairs of the United Nations Secretariat, *World Population Prospects: The 2008 Revision*, 2009.

8.3.13 United States of America

Figure 8.74 Fertility of the United States of America

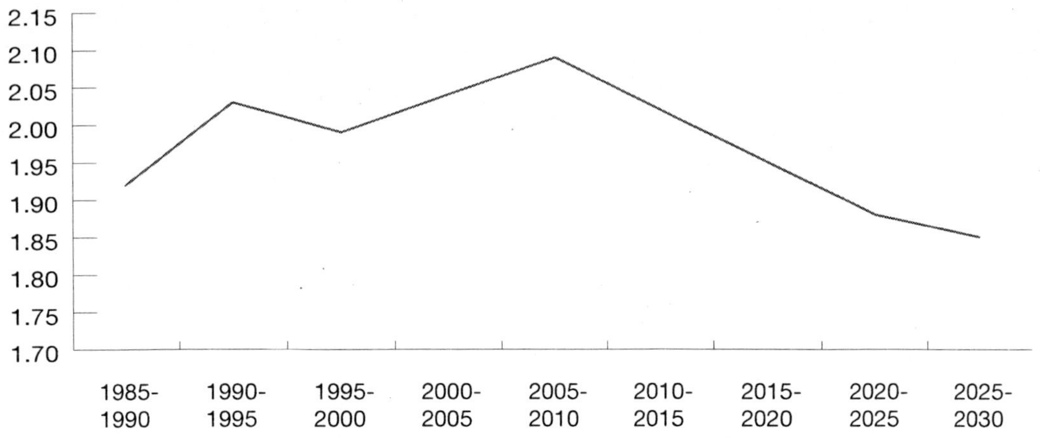

Source: Population Division of the Department of Economic and Social Affairs of the United Nations Secretariat, *World Population Prospects: The 2008 Revision*, 2009.

Table 8.36 Life expectancy of the United States of America (years)

Year	All	Male	Female
1985-1990	75.0	71.5	78.4
1990-1995	75.7	72.4	78.9
1995-2000	77.6	75.2	79.8
2000-2005	78.3	75.8	80.6
2005-2010	79.2	76.9	81.4
2010-2015	79.9	77.7	82.1
2015-2020	80.5	78.3	82.7
2020-2025	81.0	78.7	83.2
2025-2030	81.4	79.1	83.7

Source: Population Division of the Department of Economic and Social Affairs of the United Nations Secretariat, *World Population Prospects: The 2008 Revision*, 2009.

Table 8.37 Population of the United States of America by age band (%)

Age	1990	2010	2030
0-4	7.7	6.9	5.9
5-9	7.2	6.7	6.0
10-14	6.8	6.6	6.1
15-19	7.0	7.1	6.3
20-24	7.6	7.1	6.6
25-29	8.7	6.9	6.5
30-34	8.9	6.6	6.5
35-39	8.1	6.6	6.7
40-44	7.0	6.8	6.6
45-49	5.6	7.2	6.2
50-54	4.6	7.1	5.8
55-59	4.2	6.2	5.6
60-64	4.2	5.2	5.5
65-69	4.0	3.9	5.6
70-74	3.2	2.9	5.1
75-79	2.4	2.3	3.9
80-84	1.5	1.8	2.7
85-89	0.8	1.2	1.5
90-94	0.3	0.5	0.7
95-99	0.1	0.2	0.2
100+	0.02	0.04	0.1

Source: Population Division of the Department of Economic and Social Affairs of the United Nations Secretariat, *World Population Prospects: The 2008 Revision*, 2009.

Figure 8.75 United States of America population by age band (%)

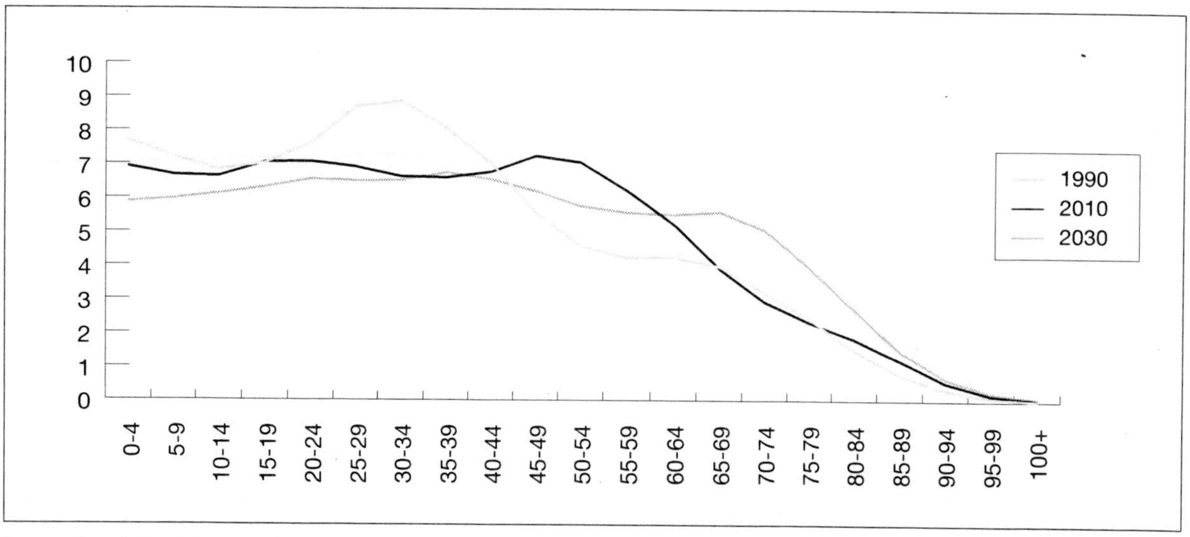

Source: Population Division of the Department of Economic and Social Affairs of the United Nations Secretariat, *World Population Prospects: The 2008 Revision*, 2009.

Figure 8.76 Population of the United States of America by gender (males per hundred females)

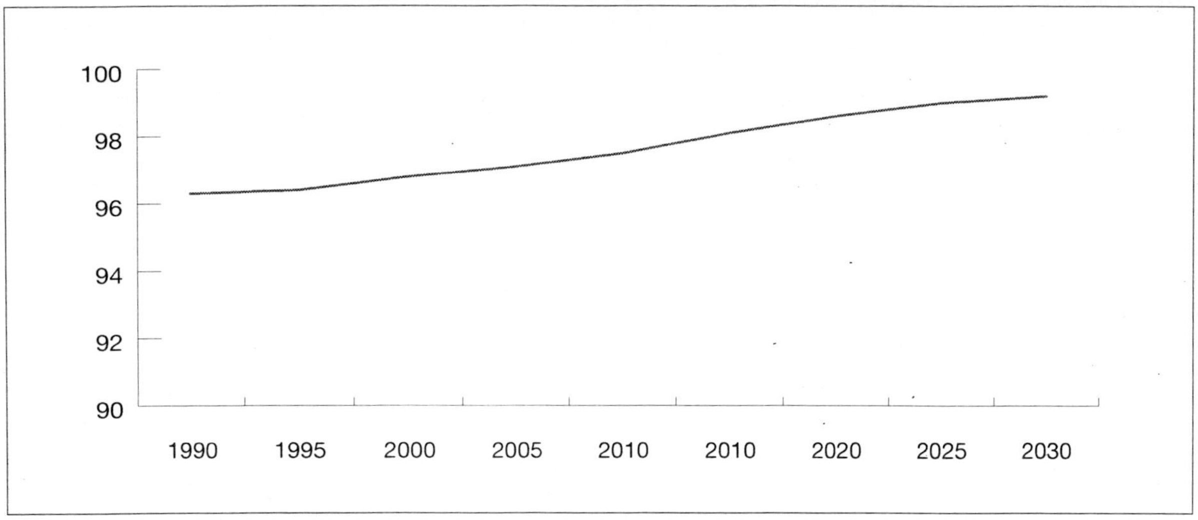

Source: Population Division of the Department of Economic and Social Affairs of the United Nations Secretariat, *World Population Prospects: The 2008 Revision,* 2009.

Figure 8.77 Urban Population of the United States of America (%)

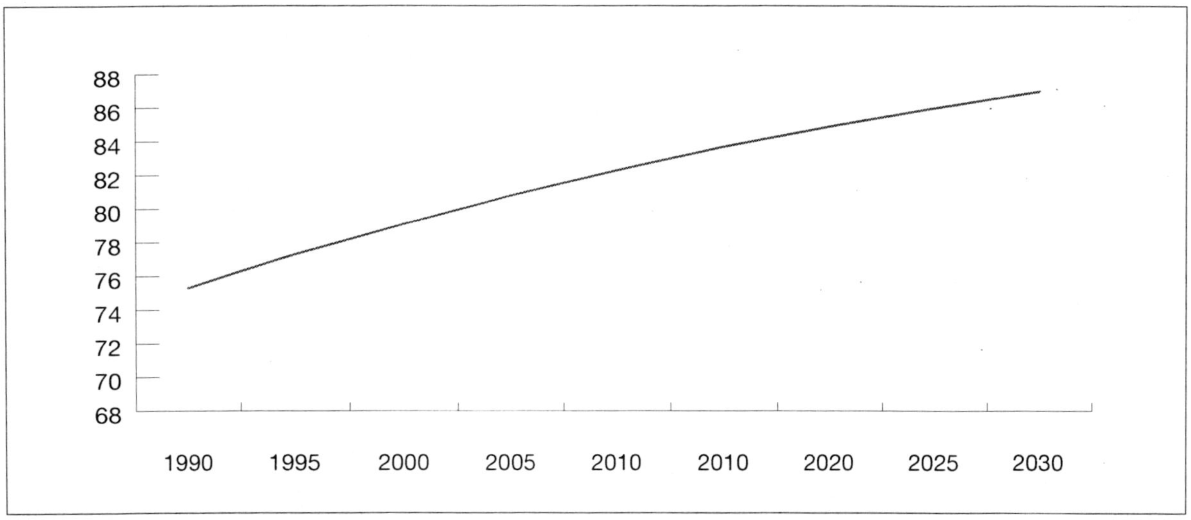

Source: Population Division of the Department of Economic and Social Affairs of the United Nations Secretariat, *World Population Prospects: The 2008 Revision,* 2009.

Bibliography

Branigan, T. (2009), 'China's lonely Hearts find Freedom to Choose is not the Answer', *The Guardian* (19-05-09).

Calvert, G. (1977), *Pensions and Survival – The Coming Crisis of Money and Retirement,* Maclean-Hunter, London.

Carr, P. (2007), *The Unofficial Tourist's Guide to Second Life,* Pan Macmillan, London.

Castles, F. G. (2003), 'The World Turned Upside Down: Below Replacement Fertility, Changing Preferences and Family-Friendly Policy in 21 OECD Countries', *Journal of European Social Policy* (Online), vol. 13 (3), pp. 209-227. DOI: 10.1177/09589287030133001 (08-08-08).

Diversity Best Practices (2009), *BRIC Countries and South Africa, a Snapshot of Demographic, Social and Economic Data* (Online), available: http://global.diversitybestpractices.com/resources/articles/dbp-primer.pdf (2009).

Ehrman, R. (2009), *The Power of Number's – Why Europe Needs to Get Younger,* Policy Exchange, London.

Experts Committee EURAG, European Federation of the Elderly, and Association of Retired and Persons over 50 (1998), *Europe: A Changing Society – The Effects of Demographic Change in the Next Millennium,* EURAG.

Glover, P. and Prideaux, B. (2009), 'Populations Aging for the Development of Tourism Products and Destinations', *Journal of Vacation Marketing* (Online), vol. 15 (1), pp. 25-37. DOI: 10.1177/1356766708098169 (15-08-09).

Gretzel, U. (2007), *Online Travel Review Study: Role & Impact of Online Travel Reviews,* Laboratory for Intelligent Systems in Tourism, Texas A&M University.

Grimm, B. et al. (2009), *The Impact of Demographic Change on Tourism and Conclusions for Tourism Policy* (abridged), Federal Ministry of Economics and Technology, Berlin.

HSBC (2009), *The Future of Retirement – It's Time to Prepare* (Online), http://www.hsbc.com/1/PA_1_1_S5/content/assets/retirement/2009_for_report_en.pdf (28-06-09).

Institut National D'Etudes Démographiques (2008), 'Population and Societies', *Population Trends in the United States and Europe: Similarities and Differences,* no. 440.

Institut National D'Etudes Démographiques (2006), *Demographic Factors in Europe and the US* (Online), http://www.ined.fr/fichier/t_publication/1364/publi_pdf2_pesa446.pdf.

Institut National D'Etudes Démographiques (2006), *Stabilising India's Population: Easier Said than Done* (Online), http://www.ined.fr/en/publications/pop_soc/bdd/publication/1172/ (17-05-09).

International Longevity Centre (2003), *Unjust Deserts, Financial Realities for Older Women* (Online), http://www.ilcusa.org/media/pdfs/unjustdesserts.pdf.

Nazareth, L. (2007), *The Leisure Economy: How Changing Demographics, Economics and Generational Attitudes will Reshape our Lives and our Industries,* John Wiley and Sons, New Jersey.

Netherlands Interdisciplinary Demographic Institute (2004), *Family Solidarity Alive and Well in Europe* (Online), http://www.nidi.knaw.nl/en/demos/ (17-05-09).

Patterson, I. (2006), *Growing Older: Tourism and Leisure Behaviour of Older Adults,* CABI, Oxfordshire.

Scholefield, A. J. (2000), *The Death of Europe – How Demographic Decline Will Destroy the European Union.*

The Tour Operators Initiative (2003), *Sustainable Tourism: The Tour Operators' Contribution,* TOI, Paris.

United Nations Population Division (2009), *World Population Prospects: The 2008 Revision* (Online), Population Database, Department of Economic and Social Affairs of the United Nations Secretariat, http://esa.un.org/unpp/index.asp?panel=2 (15-05-09).

United Nations Population Division (2008), *World Urbanization Prospects: The 2007 Revision* (Online), Population Database, Department of Economic and Social Affairs of the united Nations Secretariat, http://esa.un.org/unup/ (15-05-09).

Willmott, P. and Young, M. (1975), *The Symmetrical Family: Study of Work and Leisure in the London Region,* Pelican, London.

World Bank (2007), *Diffusion of the Internet, a Cross-Country Analysis* (Online), http://econ.worldbank.org/external/default/main?pagePK=64165259&theSitePK=469372&piPK=64165421&menuPK=64166093&entityID=000158349_20071203114216 (27-08-09).

World Tourism Organization (2009), *The Indian Outbound Travel Market with Special Insight into the Image of Europe as a Destination,* UNWTO, Madrid.

World Tourism Organization (2009), *Tourism and Migration – Exploring the Relationship between Two Global Phenomena,* UNWTO, Madrid.

World Tourism Organization (2009), *Tourism Highlight 2009 Edition,* UNWTO, Madrid.

World Tourism Organization (2001), *Tourism 2020 Vision,* UNWTO, Madrid.

World Values Survey (2008), *Fourth Wave Survey* (Online), available: http://www.worldvaluessurvey.org/ (14-06-09).